NurtureShock

ALSO BY PO BRONSON

Why Do I Love These People?
What Should I Do With My Life?
The Nudist on the Late Shift
The First $20 Million Is Always the Hardest
Bombardiers

NEW THINKING ABOUT CHILDREN

NurtureShock

PO BRONSON
&
ASHLEY MERRYMAN

TWELVE

NEW YORK   BOSTON

Copyright © 2009 by Po Bronson
All rights reserved. Except as permitted under the U.S. Copyright Act of 1976, no part of this publication may be reproduced, distributed, or transmitted in any form or by any means, or stored in a database or retrieval system, without the prior written permission of the publisher.

Twelve
Hachette Book Group
237 Park Avenue
New York, NY 10017

Visit our website at www.HachetteBookGroup.com.

Twelve is an imprint of Grand Central Publishing.
The Twelve name and logo are trademarks of Hachette Book Group, Inc.

Chapters 1, 2, and 4 originally appeared in *New York* magazine in abridged form. Grateful acknowledgment is made to *New York* magazine for permission to include these chapters in edited and expanded form.

Printed in the United States of America

First Edition: September 2009

10 9 8 7 6 5 4 3 2 1

Library of Congress Cataloging-in-Publication Data

Bronson, Po
  Nurtureshock : new thinking about children / Po Bronson and Ashley Merryman.
    p. cm.
  Includes index.
  ISBN 978-0-446-50412-6
  1. Child development. 2. Child psychology. 3. Child rearing.
4. Parenting. I. Merryman, Ashley. II. Title.
  HQ772.B8455 2009
  305.231—dc22

2009006290

CONTENTS

Preface
    Cary Grant is at the door.   vii

Introduction
    Why our instincts about children can be so off the mark.   1

1. THE INVERSE POWER OF PRAISE
    Sure, he's special. But new research suggests if you tell him that, you'll ruin him. It's a neurobiological fact.   9

2. THE LOST HOUR
    Around the world, children get an hour less sleep than they did thirty years ago. The cost: IQ points, emotional well-being, ADHD, and obesity.   27

3. WHY WHITE PARENTS DON'T TALK ABOUT RACE
    Does teaching children about race and skin color make them better off or worse?   45

4. WHY KIDS LIE
    We may treasure honesty, but the research is clear. Most classic strategies to promote truthfulness just encourage kids to be better liars.   71

5. THE SEARCH FOR INTELLIGENT LIFE IN KINDERGARTEN
    Millions of kids are competing for seats in gifted programs and private schools. Admissions officers say it's an art: new science says they're wrong, 73% of the time.   93

Contents

6. THE SIBLING EFFECT
Freud was wrong. Shakespeare was right. Why siblings really fight. 115

7. THE SCIENCE OF TEEN REBELLION
Why, for adolescents, arguing with adults is a sign of respect, not disrespect—and arguing is constructive to the relationship, not destructive. 131

8. CAN SELF-CONTROL BE TAUGHT?
Developers of a new kind of preschool keep losing their grant money—the students are so successful they're no longer "at-risk enough" to warrant further study. What's their secret? 155

9. PLAYS WELL WITH OTHERS
Why modern involved parenting has failed to produce a generation of angels. 177

10. WHY HANNAH TALKS AND ALYSSA DOESN'T
Despite scientists' admonitions, parents still spend billions every year on gimmicks and videos, hoping to jump-start infants' language skills. What's the right way to accomplish this goal? 197

CONCLUSION
The Myth of the Supertrait. 225

Acknowledgments 241

Notes 245

Selected Sources and References 265

About the Authors 329

Index 331

PREFACE

Cary Grant is at the door.

During the late 1960s, visitors to the Magic Castle—a private nightclub in Hollywood, California, run by professional magicians—were often delighted to see that the club had hired a Cary Grant look-alike as its doorman. As they'd step up to the portico, the door would be swung open by a dashing man in an impeccably tailored suit. "Welcome to the Castle," he charmed, seeming to enjoy his doppelgänger status. Once the guests were through the lobby, they would titter over just how much the doorman resembled the iconic actor. The nightclub is mere yards from the Chinese Theatre and the Walk of Fame. To have the best Cary Grant impersonator in the world holding the door for you was the perfect embodiment of the magic of Hollywood in all its forms.

However, the doorman pretending to be Cary Grant wasn't an impostor after all. It was, in fact, the real Cary Grant.

Grant, a charter member of the Castle, had been intrigued by magic since he was a kid. Part of the Castle's appeal to Grant and many other celebrities, though, was that the club has an ironclad rule—no cameras, no photographs, and no reporters. It gave stars the ability to have a quiet night out without gossip columns knowing.

Grant hung out in the lobby to be with the receptionist, Joan Lawton. They spent the hours talking about a more profound kind of Magic—something Grant cared more deeply about than the stage.

Children.

Lawton's work at the Castle was her night job. By day, she was pursuing a certificate in the science of child development. Grant, then the father of a toddler, was fascinated by her study. He plied her for every scrap of research she was learning. "He wanted to know everything about kids," she recalled. Whenever he heard a car arrive outside, he'd jump to the door. He wasn't intentionally trying to fool the guests, but that was often the result. The normally autograph-seeking patrons left him alone.

So why didn't guests recognize he was the real thing?

The context threw them off. Nobody expected the real Cary Grant would appear in the humdrum position of a doorman. Magicians who performed at the Magic Castle were the best anywhere, so the guests came prepared to witness illusions. They assumed the handsome doorman was just the first illusion of the evening.

Here's the thing. When everything is all dressed up as entertainment—when it's all supposed to be magical and surprising and fascinating—the Real Thing may be perceived as just another tidbit for our amusement.

That is certainly the case in the realm of science.

In the immediacy of today's 24-7 news cycle, with television news, constant blogging, press releases, and e-mail, it feels as if no scientific breakthrough escapes notice. But these scientific findings are used like B-list celebrities—they're filler for when the real newsmakers aren't generating headlines. Each one gets its ten minutes of fame, more for our entertainment than our serious consideration. The next day, they are tossed aside, lipstick asmear, as the press wire churns out the science *du jour*. When they're presented as quick sound bites, it's impossible to know which findings really merit our attention.

Most scientific investigations can't live up to the demands of media packaging. At least for the science of child development, there have been no "Eureka!" moments that fit the classic characterization of a major scientific breakthrough. Rather than being the work of a single scholar, the new ideas have been hashed out by many scholars, sometimes dozens, who have been conducting research at universities the world over. Rather than new truths arriving on the wings of a single experiment, they have come at a crawl, over a decade, from various studies replicating and refining prior ones.

The result is that many important ideas have been right under our noses, building up over the last decade. As a society, collectively, we never recognized they were the real thing.

NurtureShock

Introduction

Why our instincts about children can be so off the mark.

My wife has great taste in art, with one exception. In the guest bedroom of our house hangs an acrylic still life—a pot of red geraniums beside an ocher-toned watering can, with a brown picket fence in the background. It's ugly, but that's not its worst sin. My real problem is that it's from a paint-by-numbers kit.

Every time I look at it, I want to sneak it out of the house and dump it in the corner trash can.

My wife won't let me, though, because it was painted way back in 1961 by her great-grandmother. I am all for hanging on to things for sentimental reasons, and our house is full of her family's artifacts, but I just don't think this painting contains or conveys any genuine sentiment. There was probably a hint of it the day her great-grandmother bought the paint-by-numbers kit at the crafts store—a glimmer of a more creative, inspired life—but the finished product, in my opinion, kind of insults that hope. Rather than commemorating her memory, it diminishes it.

Painting by numbers skyrocketed to success in the early 1950s. It was *hugely* popular—the iPod of its time. It was marketed on the premise that homemakers were going to have a vast surplus of free time thanks to dishwashers, vacuum cleaners, and washing machines. In three years, the Palmer Paint Company sold over twelve million kits. As popular as the phenomenon was, it was also always surrounded by controversy. Critics were torn between the democratic ideal of letting everyone express themselves and the robotic, conformist way that expression was actually being manifested.

The other day, I was trying to remember how I felt about the science of child development before Ashley Merryman and I began this book, several years ago—when all of a sudden that painting of potted geraniums popped into my head. I had to go home and stare at that ugly painting for an evening before I could figure out why. Which I ultimately realized was this:

The mix of feelings engendered by paint-by-numbers is similar to the mix of feelings engendered by books about the science of children. This is because the science has always carried with it the connotation that parenting should be "by the book." If the science says X, you're supposed to do X, just like paint-by-numbers instructed hobbyists to use Cornsilk and Burnt Umber for the handle of the watering can.

So if a few years ago, someone had told me, "You really ought to read this book about the new science of kids," I would have politely thanked him and then completely ignored his recommendation.

Like most parents, my wife and I bought a few baby books when our son was born. After the first year, we put them away, until three years later, when our daughter was born and the books once again graced our shelves. Until our daughter turned one—after that, we no longer had any interest in the books.

Most of our friends felt the same way. We agreed that we didn't parent "by the book," nor did we want to. We parented on instinct. We were madly in love with our children, and we were careful observers of their needs and development. That seemed enough.

At that same time, Ashley and I had been co-writing columns for *Time Magazine*. Living in Los Angeles, Ashley had spent years running a small tutoring program for inner-city children. She has been something like a fairy godmother to about 40 kids, a constant presence in their lives from kindergarten through high school. Guided

Introduction

by her instincts, Ashley has had no shortage of ideas about how to steer the kids in her program. She has never lacked inspiration. All she felt she needed was more tutors and some school supplies.

In that sense, neither Ashley nor I were aware of what we were missing. We did not say to ourselves, "Wow, I really need to brush up on the science of child development, because I'm messing up." Instead, we were going fairly merrily along, until we sort of stumbled into writing this book.

We had been researching the science of motivation in grown-ups, and one day we wondered where kids get their self-confidence from. We began to investigate this new angle. (The story we ultimately wrote ran on the cover of *New York Magazine* in February of 2007, and it's expanded here as Chapter 1 of this book.) What we learned surprised us and was simultaneously disorienting. Prior to that story, our instincts led us to believe, quite firmly, that it was important to tell young children they were smart, in order to buoy their confidence. However, we uncovered a body of science that argued, extremely convincingly, that this habit of telling kids they're smart was backfiring. It was in fact undermining children's confidence.

We changed our behavior after researching that story, but we were left with a lingering question: how could our instincts have been so off-base?

According to lore, the maternal instinct is innate. Women are assured it doesn't matter if they spent their twenties avoiding babies, or if they don't consider themselves very maternal. The moment after birth, when the baby's first handed to his mother, maternal instincts magically kick in, right along with the hormones. As a mother, you will *know* what to do, and you will continue to know for the next eighteen years. This fountain of knowledge is supposed to come as part of a matched set of ovaries and a desire to wear expensive high heels.

Thanks to this mythos, we use the word "instinct" to convey the collective wisdom gleaned intuitively from our experiences raising kids. But this is an overgeneralization of the term. Really, the actual instinct—the biological drive that kicks in—is the fierce impulse to nurture and protect one's child. Neuroscientists have even located the exact neural network in the brain where this impulse fires. Expecting parents can rely on this impulse kicking in—but as for how *best* to nurture, they have to figure it out.

In other words, our "instincts" can be so off-base because they are not actually instincts.

Today, with three years of investigation behind us, Ashley and I now see that what we imagined were our "instincts" were instead just intelligent, informed reactions. Things we had figured out. Along the way, we also discovered that those reactions were polluted by a hodgepodge of wishful thinking, moralistic biases, contagious fads, personal history, and old (disproven) psychology—all at the expense of common sense.

"Nurture shock," as the term is generally used, refers to the panic—common among new parents—that the mythical fountain of knowledge is not magically kicking in at all.

This book will deliver a similar shock—it will use the fascinating new science of children to reveal just how many of our bedrock assumptions about kids can no longer be counted on.

The central premise of this book is that many of modern society's strategies for nurturing children are in fact backfiring—because key twists in the science have been overlooked.

The resulting errant assumptions about child development have distorted parenting habits, school programs, and social policies. They affect how we think about kids, and thus how we interpret child behavior and communicate with the young. The intent of this book is not to be alarmist, but to teach us to think differently—more deeply and clearly—about children. Small corrections in our thinking today could alter the character of society long-term, one future-citizen at a time.

The topics covered in this book are wide-ranging, devoted to equal parts brain fiber and moral fiber. They relate to children of every age from tots to teens. It could not be further from a paint-by-numbers approach. Specifically, we have chapters devoted to confidence, sleep, lying, racial attitudes, intelligence, sibling conflict, teen rebellion, self-control, aggression, gratitude, and the acquisition of language. The prose throughout is our mutual collaboration.

Along the way, we will push you to rethink many sacred cows—too many to fully list here, but some highlights include the following: self-esteem, Noam Chomsky, Driver's Ed, the idea that children are naturally blind to racial constructs, emotional intelligence, warning kids not to tattle, educational cartoons, the early identification of the gifted, the notion that television is making kids fat, and the presumption that it's necessarily a good sign if a child can say "no" to peer pressure.

We chose these topics because the research surprised us—it directly challenged the conventional point of view on how kids grow up.

However, once we parsed through the science and reviewed the evidence, the new thinking about children felt self-evident and logical, even obvious. It did not feel like we had to raise children "by the book." It felt entirely natural, a restoration of common sense. The old assumptions we once had seemed to be nothing but a projection of wishful thinking. Once we overcame the initial shock, we found ourselves plugged into children in a whole new way.

ONE

The Inverse Power of Praise

Sure, he's special. But new research suggests if you tell him that, you'll ruin him. It's a neurobiological fact.

What do we make of a boy like Thomas?

Thomas (his middle name) is a fifth-grader at the highly competitive P.S. 334, the Anderson School on West 84th in New York City. Slim as they get, Thomas recently had his long sandy-blond hair cut short to look like the new James Bond (he took a photo of Daniel Craig to the barber). Unlike Bond, he prefers a uniform of cargo pants and a T-shirt emblazoned with a photo of one of his heroes: Frank Zappa. Thomas hangs out with five friends from the Anderson School. They are "the smart kids." Thomas is one of them, and he likes belonging.

Since Thomas could walk, he has constantly heard that he's smart. Not just from his parents but from any adult who has come in contact with this precocious child. When he applied to Anderson for kindergarten, his intelligence was statistically confirmed. The school is reserved for the top 1 percent of all applicants, and an IQ test is required. Thomas didn't just score in the top 1 percent. He scored in the top 1 percent of the top 1 percent.

But as Thomas has progressed through school, this self-awareness that he's smart hasn't always translated into fearless confidence when attacking his schoolwork. In fact, Thomas's father noticed just the opposite. "Thomas didn't want to try things he wouldn't be successful at," his father says. "Some things came very quickly to him, but when they didn't, he gave up almost immediately, concluding, 'I'm not good at this.'" With no more than a glance, Thomas was dividing the world into two—things he was naturally good at and things he wasn't.

For instance, in the early grades, Thomas wasn't very good at spelling, so he simply demurred from spelling out loud. When Thomas took his first look at fractions, he balked. The biggest hurdle came in third grade. He was supposed to learn cursive penmanship, but he wouldn't even try for weeks. By then, his teacher was demanding homework be completed in cursive. Rather than play catch-up on his penmanship, Thomas refused outright. Thomas's father tried to reason with him. "Look, just because you're smart doesn't mean you don't have to put out some effort." (Eventually, Thomas mastered cursive, but not without a lot of cajoling from his father.)

Why does this child, who is measurably at the very top of the charts, lack confidence about his ability to tackle routine school challenges?

Thomas is not alone. For a few decades, it's been noted that a large percentage of all gifted students (those who score in the top 10 percent on aptitude tests) severely underestimate their own abilities. Those afflicted with this lack of perceived competence adopt lower standards for success and expect less of themselves. They underrate the importance of effort, and they overrate how much help they need from a parent.

When parents praise their children's intelligence, they believe they are providing the solution to this problem. According to a survey conducted by Columbia University, 85 percent of American parents think it's important to tell their kids that they're smart. In and around the New York area, according to my own (admittedly nonscientific) poll, the number is more like 100 percent. *Everyone* does it, habitually. "You're so smart, Kiddo," just seems to roll off the tongue.

"Early and often," bragged one mom, of how often she praised. Another dad throws praise around "every chance I get." I heard that kids are going to school with affirming handwritten notes in their lunchboxes and—when they come home—there are star charts on the refrigerator. Boys are earning baseball cards for clearing their plates after dinner, and girls are winning manicures for doing their homework. These kids are saturated with messages that they're doing great—that they *are* great, innately so. They have what it takes.

The presumption is that if a child believes he's smart (having been told so, repeatedly), he won't be intimidated by new academic challenges. The constant praise is meant to be an angel on the shoulder, ensuring that children do not sell their talents short.

But a growing body of research—and a new study from the trenches of the New York City public school system—strongly suggests it might be the other way around. Giving kids the label of "smart" does not prevent them from underperforming. It might actually be causing it.

Though Dr. Carol Dweck recently joined the faculty at Stanford, most of her life has been spent in New York; she was raised in Brooklyn, went to college at Barnard, and taught at Columbia for decades. This reluctant new Californian just got her first driver's license—at age sixty. Other Stanford faculty have joked that she'll soon be sporting bright colors in her couture, but so far Dweck sticks to New York black—black suede boots, black skirt, trim black jacket. All of which matches her hair and her big black eyebrows—one of which is raised up, perpetually, as if in disbelief. Tiny as a bird, she uses her hands in elaborate gestures, almost as if she's holding her idea in front of her, physically rotating it in three-dimensional space. Her speech pattern, though, is not at the impatient pace of most New Yorkers. She talks as if she's reading a children's lullaby, with gently punched-up moments of drama.

For the last ten years, Dweck and her team at Columbia have studied the effect of praise on students in twenty New York schools. Her seminal work—a series of experiments on 400 fifth-graders—paints the picture most clearly. Prior to these experiments, praise for intelligence had been shown to boost children's confidence. But Dweck suspected this would backfire the first moment kids experienced failure or difficulty.

Dweck sent four female research assistants into New York fifth-grade classrooms. The researchers would take a single child out of the classroom for a nonverbal IQ test consisting of a series of puzzles—puzzles easy enough that all the children would do fairly well. Once the child finished the test, the researchers told each student his score, then gave him a single line of praise. Randomly divided into groups, some were praised for their *intelligence*. They were told, "You must be smart at this." Other students were praised for their *effort*: "You must have worked really hard."

Why just a single line of praise? "We wanted to see how sensitive children were," Dweck explained. "We had a hunch that one line might be enough to see an effect."

Then the students were given a choice of test for the second round. One choice was a test that would be more difficult than the first, but the researchers told the kids that they'd learn a lot from attempting the puzzles. The other choice, Dweck's team explained, was an easy test, just like the first. Of those praised for their effort, 90 percent chose the *harder* set of puzzles. Of those praised for their intelligence, a majority chose the *easy* test. The "smart" kids took the cop-out.

Why did this happen? "When we praise children for their intelligence," Dweck wrote in her study summary, "we tell them that this is the name of the game: look smart, don't risk making mistakes." And that's what the fifth-graders had done. They'd chosen to look smart and avoid the risk of being embarrassed.

In a subsequent round, none of the fifth-graders had a choice. The test was difficult, designed for kids two years ahead of their grade level. Predictably, everyone failed. But again, the two groups of children, divided at random at the study's start, responded differently. Those praised for their effort on the first test assumed they simply hadn't focused hard enough on this test. "They got very involved, willing to try every solution to the puzzles," Dweck recalled. "Many of them remarked, unprovoked, 'This is my favorite test.'" Not so for those praised for their smarts. They assumed their failure was evidence that they weren't really smart at all. "Just watching them, you could see the strain. They were sweating and miserable."

Having artificially induced a round of failure, Dweck's researchers then gave all the fifth-graders a final round of tests that were engineered to be as easy as the first round. Those who had been praised for their effort significantly improved on their first score—by about 30 percent. Those who'd been told they were smart did worse than they had at the very beginning—by about 20 percent.

Dweck had suspected that praise could backfire, but even she was surprised by the magnitude of the effect. "Emphasizing effort gives a child a variable that they can control," she explains. "They come to see themselves as in control of their success. Emphasizing natural intelligence takes it out of the child's control, and it provides no good recipe for responding to a failure."

In follow-up interviews, Dweck discovered that those who think that innate intelligence is the key to success begin to discount the importance of effort. *I am smart*, the kids' reasoning goes; *I don't need to put out effort*. Expending effort becomes stigmatized—it's public proof that you can't cut it on your natural gifts.

Repeating her experiments, Dweck found this effect of praise on performance held true for students of every socioeconomic class. It hit both boys and girls—the very brightest girls especially (they collapsed the most following failure). Even preschoolers weren't immune to the inverse power of praise.

Jill Abraham is a mother of three in Scarsdale, and her view is typical of those in my straw poll. I told her about Dweck's research on praise, and she flatly wasn't interested in brief tests without long-term follow-up. Abraham is one of the 85 percent who think praising her children's intelligence is important.

Jill explains that her family lives in a very competitive community—a competition well under way by the time babies are a year and a half old and being interviewed for day care. "Children who don't have a firm belief in themselves get pushed around—not just in the playground, but the classroom as well." So Jill wants to arm her children with a strong belief in their innate abilities. She praises them liberally. "I don't care what the experts say," Jill says defiantly. "I'm living it."

Jill wasn't the only one to express such scorn of these so-called "experts." The consensus was that brief experiments in a controlled setting don't compare to the wisdom of parents raising their kids day in and day out.

Even those who've accepted the new research on praise have trouble putting it into practice. Sue Needleman is both a mother of two and an elementary school teacher with eleven years' experience. Last year, she was a fourth-grade teacher at Ridge Ranch Elementary in Paramus, New Jersey. She has never heard of Carol Dweck, but the gist of Dweck's research has trickled down to her school, and Needleman has learned to say, "I like how you keep trying." She tries to keep her praise specific, rather than general, so that a child knows exactly what she did to earn the praise (and thus can get more). She will occasionally tell a child, "You're good at math," but she'll never tell a child he's bad at math.

But that's at school, as a teacher. At home, old habits die hard. Her eight-year-old daughter and her five-year-old son are indeed smart, and sometimes she hears herself saying, "You're great. You did it. You're smart." When I press her on this, Needleman says that what comes out of academia often feels artificial. "When I read the mock dialogues, my first thought is, *Oh, please. How corny.*"

No such qualms exist for teachers at the Life Sciences Secondary School in East Harlem, because they've seen Dweck's theories applied to their junior high students. Dweck and her protégée, Dr. Lisa Blackwell, published a report in the academic journal *Child Development* about the effect of a semester-long intervention conducted to improve students' math scores.

Life Sciences is a health-science magnet school with high aspirations but 700 students whose main attributes are being predominantly minority and low achieving. Blackwell split her kids into two groups for an eight-session workshop. The control group was taught study skills, and the others got study skills and a special module on how intelligence is not innate. These students took turns reading aloud an essay on how the brain grows new neurons when challenged. They saw slides of the brain and acted out skits. "Even as I was teaching these ideas," Blackwell noted, "I would hear the students joking, calling one another 'dummy' or 'stupid.'" After the module was concluded, Blackwell tracked her students' grades to see if it had any effect.

It didn't take long. The teachers—who hadn't known which students had been assigned to which workshop—could pick out the students who had been taught that intelligence can be developed. They improved their study habits and grades. In a single semester, Blackwell reversed the students' longtime trend of decreasing math grades.

The only difference between the control group and the test group were two lessons, a total of 50 minutes spent teaching not math but a single idea: that the brain is a muscle. Giving it a harder workout makes you smarter. That alone improved their math scores.

"These are very persuasive findings," says Columbia's Dr. Geraldine Downey, a specialist in children's sensitivity to rejection. "They show how you can take a specific theory and develop a curriculum that works." Downey's comment is typical of what other scholars in the field are saying. Dr. Mahzarin Banaji, a Harvard social psychologist who is an expert in stereotyping, told me, "Carol Dweck is a flat-out genius. I hope the work is taken seriously. It scares people when they see these results."

Since the 1969 publication of *The Psychology of Self-Esteem*, in which Nathaniel Branden opined that self-esteem was the single most important facet of a person, the belief that one must do whatever he can to achieve positive self-esteem has become a movement with broad societal effects.

By 1984, the California legislature had created an official self-esteem task force, believing that improving citizens' self-esteem would do everything from lower dependence on welfare to decrease teen pregnancy. Such arguments turned self-esteem into an unstoppable train, particularly when it came to children. Anything potentially damaging to kids' self-esteem was axed. Competitions were frowned upon. Soccer coaches stopped counting goals and handed out trophies to everyone. Teachers threw out their red pencils. Criticism was replaced with ubiquitous, even undeserved, praise. (There's even a school district in Massachusetts that has kids in gym class "jumping rope" without a rope—lest they suffer the embarrassment of tripping.)

Dweck and Blackwell's work is part of a larger academic challenge to one of the self-esteem movement's key tenets: that praise, self-esteem, and performance rise and fall together. From 1970 to 2000, there were over 15,000 scholarly articles written on self-esteem and its relationship to everything—from sex to career advancement. But the results were often contradictory or inconclusive. So in 2003 the Association for Psychological Science asked Dr. Roy Baumeister, then a leading proponent of self-esteem, to review this literature. His team concluded that self-esteem research was polluted with flawed science. Most of those 15,000 studies asked people to rate their self-esteem and then asked them to rate their own intelligence, career success, relationship skills, etc. These self-reports were extremely unreliable, since people with high self-esteem have an inflated perception of their abilities. Only 200 of the studies employed a scientifically-sound way to measure self-esteem and its outcomes.

After reviewing those 200 studies, Baumeister concluded that having high self-esteem didn't improve grades or career achievement. It didn't even reduce alcohol usage. And it especially did not lower violence of any sort. (Highly aggressive, violent people happen to think very highly of themselves, debunking the theory that people are aggressive to make up for low self-esteem.)

At the time, Baumeister was quoted as saying that his findings were "the biggest disappointment of my career."

Now he's on Dweck's side of the argument, and his work is going in a similar direction. He recently published an article showing that for college students on the verge of failing in class, esteem-building praise causes their grades to sink further. Baumeister has come to believe the continued appeal of self-esteem is largely tied to parents' pride in their children's achievements: it's so strong that "when they praise their kids, it's not that far from praising themselves."

※

By and large, the literature on praise shows that it can be effective—a positive, motivating force. In one study, University of Notre Dame researchers tested praise's efficacy on a losing college hockey team. The experiment worked: the team got into the playoffs. But all praise is not equal—and, as Dweck demonstrated, the effects of praise can vary significantly, depending on the praise given. To be effective, researchers have found, praise needs to be specific. (The hockey players were specifically complimented on the number of times they checked an opponent.)

Sincerity of praise is also crucial. According to Dweck, the biggest mistake parents make is assuming students aren't sophisticated enough to see and feel our true intentions. Just as we can sniff out the true meaning of a backhanded compliment or a disingenuous apology, children, too, scrutinize praise for hidden agendas. Only young children—under the age of seven—take praise at face value: older children are just as suspicious of it as adults.

Psychologist Wulf-Uwe Meyer, a pioneer in the field, conducted a series of studies during which children watched other students receive praise. According to Meyer's findings, by the age of twelve, children believe that earning praise from a teacher is not a sign you did well—it's actually a sign you lack ability and the teacher thinks you need extra encouragement. They've picked up the pattern: kids who are falling behind get drowned in praise. Teens, Meyer found, discounted praise to such an extent that they believed it's a teacher's criticism—not praise at all—that really conveys a positive belief in a student's aptitude.

In the opinion of cognitive scientist Daniel T. Willingham, a teacher who praises a child may be unwittingly sending the message that the student reached the limit of his innate ability, while a teacher who criticizes a pupil conveys the message that he can improve his performance even further.

New York University professor of psychiatry Judith Brook explains that the issue is one of credibility. "Praise is important, but not vacuous praise," she says. "It has to be based on a real thing—some skill or talent they have." Once children hear praise they interpret as meritless, they discount not just the insincere praise, but sincere praise as well.

Excessive praise also distorts children's motivation; they begin doing things merely to hear the praise, losing sight of intrinsic enjoyment. Scholars from Reed College and Stanford reviewed over 150 praise studies. Their meta-analysis determined that praised students become risk-averse and lack perceived autonomy. The scholars found consistent correlations between a liberal use of praise and students' "shorter task persistence, more eye-checking with the teacher, and inflected speech such that answers have the intonation of questions." When they get to college, heavily-praised students commonly drop out of classes rather than suffer a mediocre grade, and they have a hard time picking a major—they're afraid to commit to something because they're afraid of not succeeding.

One suburban New Jersey high school English teacher told me she can spot the kids who get overpraised at home. Their parents *think* they're just being supportive, but the students sense their parents' high expectations, and feel so much pressure they can't concentrate on the subject, only the grade they will receive. "I had a mother say, 'You are destroying my child's self-esteem,' because I'd given her son a C. I told her, 'Your child is capable of better work.' I'm not there to make them *feel* better. I'm there to make them *do* better."

While we might imagine that overpraised kids grow up to be unmotivated softies, the researchers are reporting the opposite consequence. Dweck and others have found that frequently-praised children get more competitive and more interested in tearing others down. Image-maintenance becomes their primary concern. A raft of very alarming studies—again by Dweck—illustrates this.

In one study, students are given two puzzle tests. Between the first and the second, they are offered a choice between learning a new puzzle strategy for the second test or finding out how they did compared with other students on the first test: they have only enough time to do one or the other. Students praised for intelligence choose to find out their class rank, rather than use the time to prepare.

In another study, students get a do-it-yourself report card and are told these forms will be mailed to students at another school—they'll never meet these students and won't know their names. Of the kids praised for their intelligence, 40 percent lie, inflating their scores. Of the kids praised for effort, few lie.

When students transition into junior high, some who'd done well in elementary school inevitably struggle in the larger and more demanding environment. Those who equated their earlier success with their innate ability surmise they've been dumb all along. Their grades never recover because the likely key to their recovery—increasing effort—they view as just further proof of their failure. In interviews many confess they would "seriously consider cheating."

Students turn to cheating because they haven't developed a strategy for handling failure. The problem is compounded when a parent ignores a child's failures and insists he'll do better next time. Michigan scholar Jennifer Crocker studies this exact scenario and explains that the child may come to believe failure is something so terrible, the family can't acknowledge its existence. A child deprived of the opportunity to discuss mistakes can't learn from them.

Brushing aside failure, and just focusing on the positive, isn't the norm all over the world. A young scholar at the University of Illinois, Dr. Florrie Ng, reproduced Dweck's paradigm with fifth-graders both in Illinois and in Hong Kong. Ng added an interesting dimension to the experiment. Rather than having the kids take the short IQ tests at their school, the children's mothers brought them to the scholars' offices on campus (both in Urbana-Champaign and at the University of Hong Kong). While the moms sat in the waiting room, half the kids were randomly given the really hard test, where they could get only about half right—inducing a sense of failure. At that point, the kids were given a five-minute break before the second test, and the moms were allowed into the testing room to talk with their child. On the way in, the moms were told their child's actual raw score and were told a lie—that this score represented a below-average result. Hidden cameras recorded the five-minute interaction between mother and child.

The American mothers carefully avoided making negative comments. They remained fairly upbeat and positive with their child. The majority of the minutes were spent talking about something other than the testing at hand, such as what they might have for dinner. But the Chinese children were likely to hear, "You didn't concentrate when doing it," and "Let's look over your test." The majority of the break was spent discussing the test and its importance.

After the break, the Chinese kids' scores on the second test jumped 33 percent, more than twice the gain of the Americans.

The trade-off here would seem to be that the Chinese mothers acted harsh or cruel—but that stereotype may not reflect modern parenting in Hong Kong. Nor was it quite what Ng saw on the videotapes. While their words were firm, the Chinese mothers actually smiled and hugged their children every bit as much as the American mothers (and were no more likely to frown or raise their voices).

※

My son, Luke, is in kindergarten. He seems supersensitive to the potential judgment of his peers. Luke justifies it by saying, "I'm shy," but he's not really shy. He has no fear of strange cities or talking to strangers, and at his school, he has sung in front of large audiences. Rather, I'd say he's proud and self-conscious. His school has simple uniforms (navy T-shirt, navy pants), and he loves that his choice of clothes can't be ridiculed, "because then they'd be teasing themselves too."

After reading Carol Dweck's research, I began to alter how I praised him, but not completely. I suppose my hesitation was that the mindset Dweck wants students to have—a firm belief that the way to bounce back from failure is to work harder—sounds awfully clichéd: try, try again.

But it turns out that the ability to repeatedly respond to failure by exerting more effort—instead of simply giving up—is a trait well studied in psychology. People with this trait, persistence, rebound well and can sustain their motivation through long periods of delayed gratification. Delving into this research, I learned that persistence turns out to be more than a conscious act of will; it's also an unconscious response, governed by a circuit in the brain. Dr. Robert Cloninger at Washington University in St. Louis located this neural network running through the prefrontal cortex and ventral striatum. This circuit monitors the reward center of the brain, and like a switch, it intervenes when there's a lack of immediate reward. When it switches on, it's telling the rest of the brain, "Don't stop trying. There's dopa [the brain's chemical reward for success] on the horizon." While putting people through MRI scans, Cloninger could see this switch lighting up regularly in some. In others, barely at all.

What makes some people wired to have an active circuit?

Cloninger has trained rats and mice in mazes to have persistence by carefully *not* rewarding them when they get to the finish. "The key is intermittent reinforcement," says Cloninger. The brain has to learn that frustrating spells can be worked through. "A person who grows up getting too frequent rewards will not have persistence, because they'll quit when the rewards disappear."

That sold me. I'd thought "praise junkie" was just an expression—but suddenly, it seemed as if I could be setting up my son's brain for an actual chemical need for constant reward.

What would it mean, to give up praising our children so often? Well, if I am one example, there are stages of withdrawal, each of them subtle. In the first stage, I fell off the wagon around other parents when they were busy praising their kids. I didn't want Luke to feel left out. I felt like a former alcoholic who continues to drink socially. I became a Social Praiser.

Then I tried to use the specific-type praise that Dweck recommends. I praised Luke, but I attempted to praise his "process." This was easier said than done. What are the processes that go on in a five-year-old's mind? In my impression, 80 percent of his brain processes lengthy scenarios for his action figures.

But every night he has math homework and is supposed to read a phonics book aloud. Each takes about five minutes if he concentrates, but he's easily distracted. So I praised him for concentrating without asking to take a break. If he listened to instructions carefully, I praised him for that. After soccer games, I praised him for looking to pass, rather than just saying, "You played great." And if he worked hard to get to the ball, I praised the effort he applied.

Just as the research promised, this focused praise helped him see strategies he could apply the next day. It was remarkable how noticeably effective this new form of praise was.

Truth be told, while my son was getting along fine under the new praise regime, it was I who was suffering. It turns out that I was the real praise junkie in the family. Praising him for just a particular skill or task felt like I left other parts of him ignored and unappreciated. I recognized that praising him with the universal "You're great—I'm proud of you" was a way I expressed unconditional love.

Offering praise has become a sort of panacea for the anxieties of modern parenting. Out of our children's lives from breakfast to dinner, we turn it up a notch when we get home. In those few hours together, we want them to hear the things we can't say during the day—*We are in your corner, we are here for you, we believe in you.*

In a similar way, we put our children in high-pressure environments, seeking out the best schools we can find, then we use the constant praise to soften the intensity of those environments. We expect so much of them, but we hide our expectations behind constant glowing praise. For me, the duplicity became glaring.

Eventually, in my final stage of praise withdrawal, I realized that not telling my son he was smart meant I was leaving it up to him to make his own conclusion about his intelligence. Jumping in with praise is like jumping in too soon with the answer to a homework problem—it robs him of the chance to make the deduction himself.

But what if he makes the wrong conclusion?

Can I really leave this up to him, at his age?

I'm still an anxious parent. This morning, I tested him on the way to school: "What happens to your brain, again, when it gets to think about something hard?"

"It gets bigger, like a muscle," he responded, having aced this one before.

TWO

The Lost Hour

Around the world, children get an hour less sleep than they did thirty years ago. The cost: IQ points, emotional well-being, ADHD, and obesity.

Morgan Fichter is a ten-year-old fifth-grader in Roxbury, New Jersey. She's fair-skinned and petite, with freckles across her nose and wavy, light brown hair. Her father, Bill, is a police sergeant on duty until three a.m. Her mother, Heather, works part-time, devoting herself to shuffling Morgan and her brother to their many activities. Morgan plays soccer (Heather's the team coach), but Morgan's first love is competitive swimming, with year-round workouts that have broadened her shoulders. She's also a violinist in the school orchestra, with two practices and a private lesson each week, on top of the five nights she practices alone. Every night, Heather and Morgan sit down to her homework, then watch *Flip This House* or another design show on TLC. Morgan has always appeared to be an enthusiastic, well-balanced child.

But once Morgan spent a year in the classroom of a hypercritical teacher, she could no longer unwind at night. Despite a reasonable bedtime of 9:30 p.m., she would lay awake in frustration until 11:30, sometimes midnight, clutching her leopard-fur pillow. On her fairy-dust purple bedroom walls were taped index cards, each a vocabulary word Morgan had trouble with. Unable to sleep, she turned back to her studies, determined not to let her grades suffer. Instead, she saw herself fall apart emotionally. During the day, she was crabby and prone to crying easily. Occasionally Morgan fell asleep in class.

Morgan moved on from that teacher's classroom the next year, but the lack of sleep persisted. Heather began to worry why her daughter couldn't sleep. Was it stress, or hormones? Heather forbade caffeinated soda, especially after noon, having noticed that one cola in the afternoon could keep her daughter awake until two a.m. Morgan held herself together as best she could, but twice a month she suffered an emotional meltdown, a kind of overreacting crying tantrum usually seen only in three-year-olds who missed their nap. "I feel very sad for her," Heather agonized. "I wouldn't wish it on anyone—I was worried it was going to be a problem forever."

Concerned about her daughter's well-being, Heather asked the pediatrician about her daughter's sleep. "He kind of blew me off, and didn't seem interested in it," she recalled. "He said, 'So, she gets tired once in a while. She'll outgrow it.'"

The opinion of Heather's pediatrician is typical. According to surveys by the National Sleep Foundation, 90% of American parents think their child is getting enough sleep.

The kids themselves say otherwise: 60% of high schoolers report extreme daytime sleepiness. A quarter admit their grades have dropped because of it. Depending on what study you look at, anywhere from 20% to 33% are falling asleep in class at least once a week.

The raw numbers more than back them up. Half of all adolescents get less than seven hours of sleep on weeknights. By the time they are seniors in high school, according to studies by Dr. Frederick Danner at the University of Kentucky, they're averaging only slightly more than 6.5 hours of sleep a night. Only 5% of high school seniors average eight hours. Sure, we remember being tired when we went to school. But not like today's kids.

It is an overlooked fact that children—from elementary school through high school—get an hour less sleep each night than they did thirty years ago. While modern parents obsess about our babies' sleep, this concern falls off the priority list after preschool. Even kindergartners get thirty minutes less a night than they used to.

There are as many causes for this lost hour of sleep as there are types of family. Overscheduling of activities, burdensome homework, lax bedtimes, televisions and cell phones in the bedroom—they all contribute. So does guilt; home from work after dark, parents want time with their children and are reluctant to play the hardass who orders them to bed. (One study from Rhode Island found that 94% of high schoolers set their own bedtimes.) All these reasons converge on one simple twist of convenient ignorance—until now, we could ignore the lost hour because we never really knew its true cost to children.

Using newly developed technological and statistical tools, sleep scientists have recently been able to isolate and measure the impact of this single lost hour. Because children's brains are a work in progress until the age of 21, and because much of that work is done while a child is asleep, this lost hour appears to have an exponential impact on children that it simply doesn't have on adults.

The surprise is not merely that sleep *matters*—but how much it matters, demonstrably, not just to academic performance and emotional stability, but to phenomena that we assumed to be entirely unrelated, such as the international obesity epidemic and the rise of ADHD. A few scientists theorize that sleep problems during formative years can cause permanent changes in a child's brain structure—damage that one can't sleep off like a hangover. It's even possible that many of the hallmark characteristics of being a tweener and teen—moodiness, depression, and even binge eating—are actually just symptoms of chronic sleep deprivation.

✻

Dr. Avi Sadeh at Tel Aviv University is one of the dozen or so bigwigs in the field, frequently collaborating on papers with the sleep scholars at Brown University. A couple years ago, Sadeh sent 77 fourth-graders and sixth-graders home with randomly-drawn instructions to either go to bed earlier or stay up later, for three nights. Each child was given an actigraph—a wristwatch-like device that's equivalent to a seismograph for sleep activity—which allows the researchers to see how much sleep a child is really getting when she's in bed. Using the actigraphy, Sadeh's team learned that the first group managed to get 30 minutes more of true sleep per night. The latter got 31 minutes less of true sleep.

After the third night's sleep, a researcher went to the school in the morning to give the children a test of neurobiological functioning. The test, a computerized version of parts of the Wechsler Intelligence Scale for Children, is highly predictive of current achievement test scores and how teachers rate a child's ability to maintain attention in class.

Sadeh knew that his experiment was a big risk. "The last situation I wanted to be in was reporting to my grantors, 'Well, I deprived the subjects of only an hour, and there was no measurable effect at all, sorry—but can I have some more money for my other experiments?'"

Sadeh needn't have worried. The effect was indeed measurable—and sizeable. The performance gap caused by an hour's difference in sleep was bigger than the gap between a normal fourth-grader and a normal sixth-grader. Which is another way of saying that a slightly-sleepy sixth-grader will perform in class like a mere fourth-grader. "A loss of one hour of sleep is equivalent to [the loss of] two years of cognitive maturation and development," Sadeh explained.

"Sadeh's work is an outstanding contribution," says Penn State's Dr. Douglas Teti, Professor of Human Development and Family Studies. His opinion is echoed by Brown's Dr. Mary Carskadon, a specialist on the biological systems that regulate sleep. "Sadeh's research is an important reminder of how fragile children are."

Sadeh's findings are consistent with a number of other researchers' work—all of which points to the large academic consequences of small sleep differences. Dr. Monique LeBourgeois, also at Brown, studies how sleep affects prekindergartners. Virtually all young children are allowed to stay up later on weekends. They don't get less sleep, and they're not sleep deprived—they merely shift their sleep to later at night on Fridays and Saturdays. Yet she's discovered that the sleep shift factor alone is correlated with performance on a standardized IQ test. Every hour of weekend shift costs a child seven points on the test. Dr. Paul Suratt at the University of Virginia studied the impact of sleep problems on vocabulary test scores taken by elementary school students. He also found a seven-point reduction in scores. Seven points, Suratt notes, is significant: "Sleep disorders can impair children's IQ as much as lead exposure."

If these findings are accurate, then it should add up over the long term: we should expect to see a correlation between sleep and school grades. Every study done shows this connection—from a study of second- and third-graders in Chappaqua, New York, up to a study of eighth-graders in Chicago.

These correlations really spike in high school, because that's when there's a steep drop-off in kids' sleep. University of Minnesota's Dr. Kyla Wahlstrom surveyed over 7,000 high schoolers in Minnesota about their sleep habits and grades. Teens who received A's averaged about fifteen more minutes sleep than the B students, who in turn averaged fifteen more minutes than the C's, and so on. Wahlstrom's data was an almost perfect replication of results from an earlier study of over 3,000 Rhode Island high schoolers by Brown's Carskadon. Certainly, these are averages, but the consistency of the two studies stands out. Every fifteen minutes counts.

※

With the benefit of functional MRI scans, researchers are now starting to understand exactly how sleep loss impairs a child's brain.

Tired children can't remember what they just learned, for instance, because neurons lose their plasticity, becoming incapable of forming the new synaptic connections necessary to encode a memory.

A different mechanism causes children to be inattentive in class. Sleep loss debilitates the body's ability to extract glucose from the bloodstream. Without this stream of basic energy, one part of the brain suffers more than the rest—the prefrontal cortex, which is responsible for what's called "Executive Function." Among these executive functions are the orchestration of thoughts to fulfill a goal, prediction of outcomes, and perceiving consequences of actions. So tired people have difficulty with impulse control, and their abstract goals like studying take a back seat to more entertaining diversions. A tired brain perseverates—it gets stuck on a wrong answer and can't come up with a more creative solution, repeatedly returning to the same answer it already knows is erroneous.

Both those mechanisms weaken a child's capacity to learn during the day. But the most exciting science concerns what the brain is up to, when a child is asleep at night. UC Berkeley's Dr. Matthew Walker explains that during sleep, the brain shifts what it learned that day to more efficient storage regions of the brain. Each stage of sleep plays its own unique role in capturing memories. For example, studying a foreign language requires learning vocabulary, auditory memory of new sounds, and motor skills to correctly enunciate the new word. The vocabulary is synthesized by the hippocampus early in the night during "slow-wave sleep," a deep slumber without dreams. The motor skills of enunciation are processed during stage 2 non-REM sleep, and the auditory memories are encoded across all stages. Memories that are emotionally laden get processed during REM sleep. The more you learned during the day, the more you need to sleep that night.

To reconsolidate these memories, certain genes appear to upregulate during sleep—they literally turn on, or get activated. One of these genes is essential for synaptic plasticity, the strengthening of neural connections. The brain does synthesize some memories during the day, but they're enhanced and concretized during the night—new inferences and associations are drawn, leading to insights the next day.

Kids' sleep is qualitatively different than grownups' sleep because children spend more than 40% of their asleep time in the slow-wave stage (which is ten times the proportion that older adults spend). This is why a good night's sleep is so important for long-term learning of vocabulary words, times tables, historical dates, and all other factual minutiae.

Perhaps most fascinating, the emotional context of a memory affects *where* it gets processed. Negative stimuli get processed by the amygdala; positive or neutral memories gets processed by the hippocampus. Sleep deprivation hits the hippocampus harder than the amygdala. The result is that sleep-deprived people fail to recall pleasant memories, yet recall gloomy memories just fine.

In one experiment by Walker, sleep-deprived college students tried to memorize a list of words. They could remember 81% of the words with a negative connotation, like "cancer." But they could remember only 31% of the words with a positive or neutral connotation, like "sunshine" or "basket."

"We have an incendiary situation today," Walker remarked, "where the intensity of learning that kids are going through is so much greater, yet the amount of sleep they get to process that learning is so much less. If these linear trends continue, the rubber band will soon snap."

※

While all kids are impacted by sleep loss, for teenagers, sleep is a special challenge.

Brown's Mary Carskadon has demonstrated that during puberty, the circadian system—the biological clock—does a "phase shift" that keeps adolescents up later. In prepubescents and grownups, when it gets dark outside, the brain produces melatonin, which makes us sleepy. But adolescent brains don't release melatonin for another 90 minutes. So even if teenagers are in bed at ten p.m. (which they aren't), they lie awake, staring at the ceiling.

Awakened at dawn by alarm clocks, teen brains are still releasing melatonin. This pressures them to fall back asleep—either in first period at school or, more dangerously, during the drive to school. Which is one of the reasons young adults are responsible for more than half of the 100,000 "fall asleep" crashes annually.

Persuaded by this research, a few school districts around the nation decided to push back the time school starts in the morning.

The best known of these is Edina, Minnesota, an affluent suburb of Minneapolis, which changed its high school start times from 7:25 to 8:30. The results were startling, and it affected the brightest kids the most. In the year preceding the time change, math/verbal SAT scores for the top 10% of Edina's 1,600 students averaged 683/605. A year later, the top 10% averaged 739/761. In case you're too drowsy to do that math, getting another hour of sleep boosted math SAT scores of Edina's Best and Brightest up 56 points, and their verbal SAT score a whopping 156 points. ("Truly flabbergasting," gasped a stunned and disbelieving Brian O'Reilly, the College Board's Executive Director for SAT Program Relations, when he heard the results.) And the students reported higher levels of motivation and lower levels of depression. In short, an hour more of sleep improved students' quality of life.

That's particularly remarkable since most kids get less sleep during high school, and their quality of life goes down: University of Kentucky's Danner has studied how, on a national level, sleep decreases each year during high school. In their first year, 60% of kids got at least eight hours on average. By the second year, that was down to 30%. Right alongside this decline went their moods; dropping below eight hours doubled the rate of *clinical-level* depression. Over one-eighth of the students reached this classification, which makes one only wonder how many more suffer from melancholy of a lesser degree.

Another trailblazing school district is Lexington, Kentucky, which also moved its start time an hour later. Danner has been studying the before/after equation. The finding that most jumps out from his data is that after the time change, teenage car accidents in Lexington were down 25%, compared to the rest of the state.

While the evidence is compelling, few districts have followed this lead. Conversely, 85% of America's public high schools start before 8:15 a.m., and 35% start at or before 7:30 a.m.

Obstacles against later start times are numerous. Having high schools start earlier often allows buses to first deliver the older students, then do a second run with the younger children. So starting later could mean doubling the size of the bus fleet. Teachers prefer driving to school before other commuters clog the roads. Coaches worry their student-athletes will miss games because they're still in their class at kickoff time. Many simply aren't persuaded by the science. When Westchester schools declined an initiative to start high schools later, then-superintendent Dr. Karen McCarthy opined, "There's still something that doesn't click for me."

Dr. Mark Mahowald has heard all those arguments. As Director of the Minnesota Regional Sleep Disorders Center, he's been at the center of many school start time debates. But of all the arguments he's heard, no one's argument is that children *learn more* at 7:15 a.m. than at 8:30. Instead, he forcefully reasons, schools are scheduled for adult convenience: there's no educational reason we start schools as early as we do. "If schools are for education, then we should promote learning instead of interfere with it," he challenges.

"We thought the evidence was staggering," Carole Young-Kleinfeld recalled.

Kleinfeld is a mother in Wilton, Connecticut, thirty miles up I-95 from New York City. Wilton, too, had saved money by running buses in two shifts, starting the high school at 7:35. Then a few years ago, Kleinfeld was at a meeting for the local League of Women Voters. Then-state senator Kevin Sullivan spoke about Carskadon and others' research, and how starting high school at a more reasonable hour was the answer.

Kleinfeld had a sullen teenager of her own, and when she went to local high schools to register kids to vote, she regularly saw students sleeping in the halls during class. So the idea hit home. She and others formed a committee to learn about the issue. Eventually, they convinced the district to move the high school's start time to 8:20.

For Kleinfeld, the change "was a godsend."

Her son Zach had once been a perfectly happy kid, but when he hit high school he became the prototypical disengaged, unenthralled-by-everything teen. He was so negative, so withdrawn that "I really thought we'd lost him," Kleinfeld sighed. "We'd lost that sense of connection."

After the high school start time shifted, Kleinfeld couldn't believe it. "We got our kid back." Zack would bound downstairs in the morning with a smile, wanting to share a funny story he'd read in *The Onion*. His SAT scores went up, too.

Several scholars have noted that many hallmark traits of modern adolescence—moodiness, impulsiveness, disengagement—are also symptoms of chronic sleep deprivation. Might our culture-wide perception of what it means to be a teenager be unwittingly skewed by the fact they don't get enough sleep?

University of Pittsburgh's Dr. Ronald Dahl agrees, observing: "Is it adding one percent or sixty percent, we don't know. But clearly a lack of sleep makes it much worse."

Let's consider the hidden role sleep has played in the obesity epidemic.

It's often noted that in the last three decades childhood obesity has tripled. Half of all kids are at least "at risk of being overweight"—a BMI score two clicks down from obesity.

The federal government spends over $1 billion a year on nutrition education programs in our schools. A recent review by McMaster University of 57 such programs showed that 53 had no impact at all—and the results of the four good ones were so meager it was barely worth mentioning.

For a long time, there's been one culprit to blame for our failed efforts: television. Rather than running around the neighborhood like when we were young, today's kids sit in front of the boob tube an average of 3.3 hours a day. The connection to obesity seemed so obvious, and was so often repeated, that few people thought it even needed to be supported scientifically.

Dr. Elizabeth Vandewater at the University of Texas at Austin got fed up with hearing fellow scholars blame it all on television with only weak data to support their claim. "It's treated as gospel without any evidence," she grumbled. "It's just bad science." Vandewater analyzed the best large dataset available—the Panel Study of Income Dynamics, which has extensively surveyed 8,000 families since 1968. She found that obese kids watch no more television than kids who aren't obese. All the thin kids watch massive amounts of television, too. There was no statistical correlation between obesity and media use, period. "It's just not the smoking gun we assumed it to be."

Vandewater examined the children's time diaries, and she realized why the earlier research had got it wrong. Kids don't trade television time for physical activity. "Children trade functionally-equivalent things. If the television's off, they don't go play soccer," she said. "They do some other sedentary behavior."

In fact, while obesity has spiked exponentially since the 1970s, kids watch only seven minutes more of TV a day. While they do average a half-hour of video games and internet surfing on top of television viewing, the leap in obesity began in 1980, well before home video games and the invention of the web browser. This obviously doesn't mean it's good for the waistline to watch television. But it does mean that something—other than television—is making kids even heavier.

"We've just done diet and exercise studies for a hundred years and they don't work well, and it's time to look for different causes," proclaimed Dr. Richard Atkinson, co-editor-in-chief of the *International Journal of Obesity*.

Five years ago, already aware of an association between sleep apnea and diabetes, Dr. Eve Van Cauter discovered a "neuroendocrine cascade" which links sleep to obesity. Sleep loss increases the hormone ghrelin, which signals hunger, and decreases its metabolic opposite, leptin, which suppresses appetite. Sleep loss also elevates the stress hormone cortisol. Cortisol is lipogenic, meaning it stimulates your body to make fat. Human growth hormone is also disrupted. Normally secreted as a single big pulse at the beginning of sleep, growth hormone is essential for the breakdown of fat.

It's drilled into us that we need to be more active to lose weight. So it spins the mind to hear that a key to staying thin is to spend more time doing the most sedentary inactivity humanly possible. Yet this is exactly what scientists are finding. In light of Van Cauter's discoveries, sleep scientists have performed a flurry of analyses on large datasets of children. All the studies point in the same direction: on average, children who sleep less are fatter than children who sleep more. This isn't just here, in America—scholars all around the world are considering it, because children everywhere are both getting fatter and getting less sleep.

Three of those studies showed strikingly similar results. One analyzed Japanese first graders, one Canadian kindergarten boys, and Australian young boys the third. They showed that those kids who get less than eight hours sleep have about a 300% higher rate of obesity than those who get a full ten hours of sleep. Within that two-hour window, it was a "dose-response" relationship, according to the Japanese scholars.

Research in the Houston public schools proved this isn't just fattening up young kids. Among the middle schoolers and high schoolers studied, the odds of obesity went up 80% for each hour of lost sleep.

Van Cauter has gone on to discover that the stage of slow-wave sleep is especially critical to proper insulin sensitivity and glucose tolerance. When she lets subjects sleep, but interrupts them with gentle door knocks just loud enough to keep them from passing into the slow-wave stage (without actually waking the subjects), their hormone levels respond in a way that's akin to a weight gain of twenty to thirty pounds. As previously noted, children spend over 40% of their asleep time in this slow-wave stage, while older adults are in this stage only about 4% of the night. This could explain why the relationship between poor sleep and obesity is much stronger in children than in adults.

How sleep impacts hormones is an entirely different way of explaining what makes people fat or thin—we normally just think of weight gain as a straightforward calories-consumed/calories-burned equation. But even by that familiar equation, the relation of sleep to weight makes sense. While very few calories are being burned while blacked out on the sheets, at least a kid is not eating when he's asleep. In addition, kids who don't sleep well are often too tired to exercise—it's been shown that the less sleep kids get, the less active they are during the day. So the net calorie burn, after a good night's rest, is higher.

In a 2005 paper in *Archives of Internal Medicine*, Dr. Fred Turek called out traditional obesity researchers for ignoring sleep's effect on metabolism. Turek is Director of Northwestern University's Center for Circadian Biology and Medicine. He noted that a standard reference guide for physicians on childhood obesity never discusses the effect of sleep loss on weight—not once in 269 pages.

Dr. Atkinson believes the research he's seen on children's sleep loss and obesity is positively "alarming." Yet he regrets that it is just off the radar screens of most obesity researchers.

In 2007, the United States Department of Agriculture and the Centers for Disease Control reported to us that they'd done no independent research on the issue. They weren't even willing to offer an opinion on the work already done—despite the fact they annually spend hundreds of millions on obesity research and prevention programs. However, within a year, the data had become too powerful to ignore. The CDC now recommends that high schools consider later starts: its representatives are now opining that a change in school start times can change lives.

※

Despite how convincing all this science is, somehow it still feels like a huge leap of faith to consider giving back an hour of our children's lives to slumber. Statistical correlations are fine evidence for scientists, but for parents, we want more—we want control.

Dr. Judith Owens runs a sleep clinic in Providence, affiliated with Brown. Recently, a father came in with his fifteen-year-old daughter, who was complaining of severe headaches. Interviewing the patient, Owens quickly learned that her daily routine was a brutal grind; after flute lessons, bassoon lessons, dance classes, and the homework from honors classes, she was able to get only five hours sleep a night before waking every morning at 4:30 to tromp off to the gym. The father wanted to know if a lack of sleep could be causing her headaches. Owens told him that was probably the case. She recommended his daughter cut back on her schedule.

The word "probably" made this father hesitant. He would let her cut back, but only if Owens could *prove*, in advance, that sacrificing an activity would stop the headaches. Sure, he knew that sleep was important, but was it more important than Honors French? Was it more important than getting into a great college?

Owens tried her standard argument. "Would you let your daughter ride in a car without a seat belt? You have to think of sleep the same way."

But Owens' pleadings didn't persuade. In this dad's mind, the transaction went the other way around: cutting back was putting his daughter at risk. What if the headaches didn't stop, and she gave up one of her great passions, like dance, for no reason?

Long before children become overscheduled high schoolers gunning for college, parents—guardians of their children's slumber—start making trade-offs between their sleep and their other needs. This is especially true in the last hour of our child's day—a time zone let's call the Slush Hour. The slush hour is both a rush to sleep and a slush fund of potential time, sort of a petty cash drawer from which we withdraw ten minute increments. During the slush hour, children *should* be in bed, but there are so many priorities lobbying for another stroke of attention. As a result, sleep is treated much like the national debt—what's another half-hour on the bill? We're surviving; kids can too.

Sleep is a biological imperative for every species on earth. But humans alone try to resist its pull. Instead, we see sleep not as a physical need but a statement of character. It's considered a sign of weakness to admit fatigue—and it's a sign of strength to refuse to succomb to slumber. Sleep is for Wusses.

But perhaps we are blind to the toll it is taking on us. University of Pennsylvania's Dr. David Dinges did an experiment shortening adults' sleep to six hours a night. After two weeks, they reported that they were doing okay. Yet on a battery of tests, they proved to be just as impaired as someone who has stayed awake for 24 hours straight.

Dinges did the experiment to demonstrate how sleep loss is cumulative, and how our judgment can be fooled by sleep deprivation. Nevertheless, it's tempting to read of his experiment and think, "I would suffer, but not *that* bad. I would be the exception." We've coped on too-little sleep for years, and managed to get by. We have some familiarity with this.

But when it comes to a child's developing brain, are we willing to keep taking the same brazen dare?

THREE

Why White Parents Don't Talk About Race

Does teaching children about race and skin color make them better off or worse?

At the Children's Research Lab at the University of Texas, a database is kept of thousands of families in the Austin area who have volunteered to be available for scholarly research. In 2006, doctoral student Birgitte Vittrup recruited from the database about a hundred of these families, all of whom were Caucasian with a child five to seven years old. This project was her Ph.D. dissertation. The goal of Vittrup's study was to learn if typical children's videos with multicultural story lines actually have any beneficial effect on children's racial attitudes.

Her first step was to test the children, and their parents, with a Racial Attitude Measure designed by one of her mentors at the university, Dr. Rebecca Bigler. Using this measure, Vittrup asked the child a series of questions, such as:

"How many White people are nice?"
(Almost all) (A lot) (Some) (Not many) (None)

"How many Black people are nice?"
(Almost all) (A lot) (Some) (Not many) (None)

Over the test, the descriptive adjective "nice" was replaced with over twenty other adjectives like "Dishonest," "Pretty," "Curious," and "Snobby." If the kid was too shy to answer, he could point to a picture that corresponded to each of the possible answers.

Of the families, Vittrup sent a third of them home with typical multiculturally-themed videos for a week, such as an episode of *Sesame Street* where the characters visit an African American family's home, and an episode of *Little Bill*, where the entire neighborhood comes together to clean the local park.

In truth, Vittrup didn't expect that children's racial attitudes would change very much from just watching these videos. Prior research by Bigler had shown that multicultural curriculum in schools has far less impact than we intend it to—largely because the implicit message "We're all friends" is too vague for children to understand it refers to skin color.

Yet Vittrup figured that if the educational videos were supplemented with explicit conversations from parents, there would be a significant impact. So a second group of families got the videos, and Vittrup told these parents to use the videos as the jumping-off point for a conversation about interracial friendship. She gave these sets of parents a checklist of points to make, echoing the theme of the shows. "I really believed it was going to work," Vittrup recalled. Her Ph.D. depended upon it.

The last third were also given the checklist of topics, but no videos. These parents were supposed to bring up racial equality on their own, every night for five nights. This was a bit tricky, especially if the parents had never put names to kids' races before. The parents were to say things like:

> Some people on TV or at school have different skin color than us. White children and Black children and Mexican children often like the same things even though they come from different backgrounds. They are still good people and you can be their friend. If a child of a different skin color lived in our neighborhood, would you like to be his friend?

At this point, something interesting happened. Five of the families in the last group abruptly quit the study. Two directly told Vittrup, "We don't want to have these conversations with our child. We don't want to point out skin color."

Vittrup was taken aback—these families had volunteered knowing full-well it was a study of children's racial attitudes. Yet once told this required talking openly about race, they started dropping out. Three others refused to say why they were quitting, but their silence made Vittrup suspect they were withdrawing for the same reason.

This avoidance of talking about race was something Vittrup also picked up in her initial test of parents' racial attitudes. It was no surprise that in a liberal city like Austin, every parent was a welcoming multiculturalist, embracing diversity. But Vittrup had also noticed, in the original surveys, that hardly any of these white parents had ever talked to their children directly about race. They might have asserted vague principles in the home—like "Everybody's equal" or "God made all of us" or "Under the skin, we're all the same"—but they had almost never called attention to racial differences.

They wanted their children to grow up color-blind. But Vittrup could also see from her first test of the kids that they weren't color-blind at all. Asked how many white people are mean, these children commonly answered "Almost none." Asked how many blacks are mean, many answered "Some" or "A lot." Even kids who attended diverse schools answered some of the questions this way.

More disturbingly, Vittrup had also asked all the kids a very blunt question: "Do your parents like black people?" If the white parents never talked about race explicitly, did the kids know that their parents liked black people?

Apparently not: 14% said, outright, "No, my parents don't like black people"; 38% of the kids answered, "I don't know." In this supposed race-free vacuum being created by parents, kids were left to improvise their own conclusions—many of which would be abhorrent to their parents.

Vittrup hoped the families she'd instructed to talk about race would follow through.

After watching the videos, the families returned to the Children's Research Lab for retesting. As Vittrup expected, for the families who had watched the videos without any parental reinforcement and conversation, there was no improvement over their scores from a week before. The message of multicultural harmony—seemingly so apparent in the episodes—wasn't affecting the kids at all.

But to her surprise, after she crunched the numbers, Vittrup learned that neither of the other two groups of children (whose parents talked to them about interracial friendship) had improved their racial attitudes. At first look, the study was a failure. She felt like she was watching her promising career vanish before her own eyes. She'd had visions of her findings published in a major journal—but now she was just wondering if she'd even make it through her dissertation defense and get her Ph.D.

Scrambling, Vittrup consulted her dissertation advisors until she eventually sought out Bigler.

"Whether the study worked or not," Bigler replied, "it's still telling you something." Maybe there was something interesting in why it had no effect?

Combing through the parents' study diaries, Vittrup noticed an aberration. When she'd given the parents the checklist of race topics to discuss with their kindergartners, she had also asked them to record whether this had been a meaningful interaction. Did the parents merely mention the item on the checklist? Did they expand on the checklist item? Did it lead to a true discussion?

Almost all the parents reported merely mentioning the checklist items, briefly, in passing. Many just couldn't talk about race, and they quickly reverted to the vague "Everybody's equal" phrasing.

Of all the parents who were told to talk openly about interracial friendship, only six managed to do so. All of those six kids greatly improved their racial attitudes.

Vittrup sailed through her dissertation and is now an assistant professor at Texas Women's University in Dallas. Reflecting later about the study, Vittrup realized how challenging it had been for the families: "A lot of parents came to me afterwards and admitted they just didn't know what to say to their kids, and they didn't want the wrong thing coming out of the mouth of their kids."

We all want our children to be unintimidated by differences and have the social skills to integrate in a diverse world. The question is, do we make it worse, or do we make it better, by calling attention to race?

Of course, the election of President Barack Obama has marked the beginning of a new era in race relations in the United States—but it hasn't resolved the question as to what we should tell children about race. If anything, it's pushed that issue to the forefront. Many parents have explicitly pointed out Obama's brown skin to their young children, to reinforce the message that anyone can rise to become a leader, and anyone—regardless of skin color—can be a friend, be loved, and be admired.

But still others are thinking it's better to say nothing at all about the president's race or ethnicity—because saying something about it unavoidably teaches a child a racial construct. They worry that even a positive statement ("It's wonderful that a black person can be president") will still encourage the child to see divisions within society. For them, the better course is just to let a young child learn by the example; what kids see is what they'll think is normal. For their early formative years, at least, let the children know a time when skin color does not matter.

A 2007 study in the *Journal of Marriage and Family* found that out of 17,000 families with kindergartners, 45% said they'd never, or almost never, discussed race issues with their children. But that was for all ethnicities. Nonwhite parents are about three times more likely to discuss race than white parents; 75% of the latter never, or almost never, talk about race.

For decades, we assumed that children will only see race when society points it out to them. That approach was shared by much of the scientific community—the view was that race was a societal issue best left to sociologists and demographers to figure out. However, child development researchers have increasingly begun to question that presumption. They argue that children see racial differences as much as they see the difference between pink and blue—but we tell kids that "pink" means for girls and "blue" is for boys. "White" and "black" are mysteries we leave them to figure out on their own.

It takes remarkably little for children to develop in-group preferences once a difference has been recognized. Bigler ran an experiment in three preschool classrooms, where four- and five-year-olds were lined up and given T-shirts. Half the kids were given blue T-shirts, half red. The children wore the shirts for three weeks. During that time, the teachers never mentioned their colors and never again grouped the kids by shirt color. The teachers never referred to the "Blues" or the "Reds." Bigler wanted to see what would happen to the children naturally, once color groupings had been established.

The kids didn't segregate in their behavior. They played with each other freely at recess. But when asked which color team was better to belong to, or which team might win a race, they chose their own color. They liked the kids in their own group more and believed they were smarter than the other color. "The Reds never showed hatred for Blues," Bigler observed. "It was more like, 'Blues are fine, but not as good as us.'" When Reds were asked how many Reds were nice, they'd answer "All of us." Asked how many Blues were nice, they'd answer "Some." Some of the Blues were mean, and some were dumb—but not the Reds.

Bigler's experiment seems to show how children will use whatever you give them to create divisions—seeming to confirm that race becomes an issue only if we make it an issue. So why does Bigler think it's important to talk to children about race, as early as age three?

Her reasoning is that kids are *developmentally* prone to in-group favoritism; they're going to form these preferences on their own. Children categorize everything from food to toys to people at a young age. However, it takes years before their cognitive abilities allow them to successfully use more than one attribute to categorize anything. In the meantime, the attribute they rely on is that which is the most clearly visible.

Bigler contends that once a child identifies someone as most closely resembling himself, the child likes that person the most. And the child extends their shared appearances much further—believing that everything else he likes, those who look similar to him like as well. Anything he doesn't like thus belongs to those who look the least similar to him. The spontaneous tendency to assume your group shares characteristics—such as niceness, or smarts—is called *essentialism.* Kids never think groups are random.

We might imagine we're creating color-blind environments for children, but differences in skin color or hair or weight are like differences in gender—they're plainly visible. We don't have to label them for them to become salient. Even if no teacher or parent mentions race, kids will use skin color on their own, the same way they use T-shirt colors.

Within the past decade or so, developmental psychologists have begun a handful of longitudinal studies to determine exactly when children develop bias—the general premise being that the earlier the bias manifests itself, the more likely it is driven by developmental processes.

Dr. Phyllis Katz, then a professor at the University of Colorado, led one such study—following 100 black children and 100 white children for their first six years. She tested these children and their parents nine times during those six years, with the first test at six months old.

How do researchers test a six-month-old? It's actually a common test in child development research. They show babies photographs of faces, measuring how long the child's attention remains on the photographs. Looking at a photograph longer does not indicate a preference for that photo, or for that face. Rather, looking longer means the child's brain finds the face to be out of the ordinary; she stares at it longer because her brain is trying to make sense of it. So faces that are familiar actually get shorter visual attention. Children will stare significantly longer at photographs of faces that are a different race from their parents. Race itself has no ethnic meaning, per se—but children's brains are noticing skin color differences and trying to understand their meaning.

When the kids turned three, Katz showed them photographs of other children and asked them to choose whom they'd like to have as friends. Of the white children 86% picked children of their own race. When the kids were five and and six, Katz gave these children a small deck of cards, with drawings of people on them. Katz told the children to sort the cards into two piles any way they wanted. Only 16% of the kids used gender to split the piles. Another 16% used a variety of other factors, like the age or the mood of the people depicted. But 68% of the kids used race to split the cards, without any prompting.

In reporting her findings, Katz concluded: "I think it is fair to say that at no point in the study did the children exhibit the Rousseau-type of color-blindness that many adults expect."

The point Katz emphasizes is that during this period of our children's lives when we imagine it's most important to *not* talk about race is the very developmental period when children's minds are forming their first conclusions about race.

Several studies point to the possibility of developmental windows—stages when children's attitudes might be most amenable to change. During one experiment, teachers divided their students into groups of six kids, making sure each child was in a racially diverse group. Twice a week, for eight weeks, the groups met. Each child in a group had to learn a piece of the lesson and then turn around and teach it to the other five. The groups received a grade collectively. Then, the scholars watched the kids on the playground, to see if it led to more interaction cross-race. Every time a child played with another child at recess, it was noted—as was the race of the other child.

The researchers found this worked wonders on the first-grade children. Having been in the cross-race study groups led to significantly more cross-race play. But it made no difference on the third-grade children. It's possible that by third grade, when parents usually recognize it's safe to start talking a little about race, the developmental window has already closed.

The other deeply held assumption modern parents have is what Ashley and I have come to call the Diverse Environment Theory. If you raise a child with a fair amount of exposure to people of other races and cultures, the environment becomes the message. You don't have to talk about race—in fact, it's better to *not* talk about race. Just expose the child to diverse environments and he'll think it's entirely normal.

I know this mindset, because it perfectly describes the approach my wife and I took when our son, Luke, was born. When he was four months old, we enrolled him in a preschool located in San Francisco's Fillmore/Western Addition neighborhood. One of the many benefits of the school was its great racial diversity. For years he never once mentioned the color of anyone's skin—not at school or while watching television. We never once mentioned skin color either. We thought it was working perfectly.

Then came Martin Luther King Jr. Day at school, two months before his fifth birthday. Luke walked out of class that Friday before the weekend and started pointing at everyone, proudly announcing, "That guy comes from Africa. And she comes from Africa, too!" It was embarrassing how loudly he did this. Clearly, he had been taught to categorize skin color, and he was enchanted with his skill at doing so. "People with brown skin are from Africa," he'd repeat. He had not been taught the names for races—he had not heard the term "black" and he called us "people with pinkish-whitish skin." He named every kid in his schoolroom with brown skin, which was about half his class.

I was uncomfortable that the school hadn't warned us about the race-themed lesson. But my son's eagerness was revealing. It was obvious this was something he'd been wondering about for a while. He was relieved to have been finally given the key. Skin color was a sign of ancestral roots.

Over the next year, we started to overhear one of his white friends talking about the color of their skin. They still didn't know what to call their skin, so they used the phrase "skin like ours." And this notion of *ours versus theirs* started to take on a meaning of its own. As these kids searched for their identities, skin color had become salient. Soon, I overheard this particular white boy telling my son, "Parents don't like us to talk about our skin, so don't let them hear you."

Yet our son did mention it. When he watched basketball with us, he would say, "That guy's my favorite," and put his finger up to the screen to point the player out. "The guy with skin like ours," he would add. I questioned him at length, and I came to understand what was really going on. My young son had become self-conscious about his curly blond-brown hair. His hair would never look like the black players' hairstyles. The one white, Latvian player on the Golden State Warriors had cool hair the same color as my son's. That was the guy to root for. My son was looking for his own identity, and looking for role models. Race and hairstyle had both become part of the identity formula. Making free throws and playing tough defense hadn't.

I kept being surprised. As a parent, I dealt with these moments explicitly, telling my son it was wrong to choose anyone as his friend, or his "favorite," on the basis of their skin color or even their hairstyle. We pointed out how certain friends wouldn't be in our lives if we picked friends for their color. He got the message, and over time he not only accepted but embraced this lesson. Now he talks openly about equality and the wrongfulness of discrimination.

Not knowing then what I do now, I had a hard time understanding my son's initial impulses. I'd always thought racism was taught. If a child grows up in a non-racist world, why was he spontaneously showing race-based preferences? When did the environment that we were so proud of no longer become the message he listened to?

The Diverse Environment Theory is the core principle behind school desegregation today. Like most people, I assumed that after thirty years of school desegregation, it would have a long track record of scientific research proving that the Diverse Environment Theory works. Then Ashley and I began talking to the scholars who've compiled that very research.

For instance, Dr. Gary Orfield runs the Civil Rights Project, a think tank that was long based at Harvard but has moved to UCLA. In the summer of 2007, Orfield and a dozen top scholars wrote an amicus brief to the United States Supreme Court supporting school desegregation in Louisville, Kentucky, and Seattle, Washington. After completing the 86-page document, Orfield e-mailed it to all the social scientists on his mailing list, and he received 553 signatures of support. No fancy law firms put their stamp on it. Orfield was very proud that the brief was the work of scientists, not lawyers, thereby preserving its integrity and impartiality. "It was the authentic voice of social science," he recalled.

Privately, though, Orfield felt some frustration—even anger. He admitted the science available to make their case "wasn't what we really wanted." Despite having at their disposal at least a thousand research studies on desegregation's effects, "I was surprised none were longitudinal. It really has a substantial effect, but it has to be done the right way." Just throwing kids of different races into a school together isn't the right way, because they can self-segregate within the school. Orfield lamented the lack of funding to train teachers. Looking at the science available to make their case, Orfield recalled, "It depressed me that we've invested so little in finding the benefits of integration."

This ambiguity is visible in the text of the amicus brief. Scientists don't like to overstate their case. So the benefits of desegregation are qualified with words like "may lead" and "can improve." "Mere school integration is not a panacea," the brief warns.

UT's Bigler was one of the scholars who contributed to the brief, and she was heavily involved in the process of its creation. Her estimation of what they found is more candid than Orfield's. "In the end, I was disappointed with the amount of evidence social psychology could muster," she said. "Going to integrated schools gives you just as many chances to learn stereotypes as to unlearn them."

Calling attention to this can feel taboo. Bigler is an adamant proponent of desegregation in schools, on moral grounds. "It's an enormous step backward to increase social segregation," she commented. But it's important for parents to know that merely sending your child to a diverse school is no guarantee they'll have better racial attitudes than children at homogenous schools.

Race appears to be especially complex, compared to other objects of bias and discrimination. Dr. Thomas Pettigrew of the University of California at Santa Cruz analyzed over 500 research studies, all of which were examples of how exposure to others can potentially reduce bias. The studies that were most successful weren't about racial bias—rather, they were about bias toward the disabled, the elderly, and gays. Studies in other countries show success—such as a reduction in bias among Jews and Palestinians, or whites and blacks in South Africa. When it comes to race in America, the studies show only consistent, modest benefit among college-aged students. In high schools and elementary schools, it's a different story.

Recently, the Civil Rights Project studied high school juniors in six school districts around the country. One of those was Louisville, which appears to be a place where desegregation has had the intended benefits. Surveys of high school juniors there show that over 80% of students (of all races) feel their school experience has helped them work with and get along with members of other races and ethnic groups. Over 85% feel their school's diversity has prepared them to work in a diverse job setting.

But other districts didn't look so great. Lynn, Massachusetts, which is ten miles northeast of Boston, is generally regarded as another model of diversity and successful school desegregation. When its students were polled if they'd like to live in a diverse neighborhood when they grow up, about 70% of the nonwhite high school juniors said they wanted to. But only 35% of whites wanted to.

Dr. Walter Stephan, a professor emeritus at New Mexico State University, made it his life's work to survey students' racial attitudes after their first year of desegregation. He found that in 16% of the desegregated schools examined, the attitudes of whites toward African Americans became more favorable. In 36% of the schools, there was no difference. In 48% of the schools, white students' attitudes toward blacks became *worse*. Stephan is no segregationist—he signed the amicus brief, and he is one of the most respected scholars in the field.

The unfortunate twist of diverse schools is that they don't necessarily lead to more cross-race friendships. Often it's the opposite.

Duke University's Dr. James Moody—an expert on how adolescents form and maintain social networks—analyzed data on over 90,000 teenagers at 112 different schools from every region of the country. The students had been asked to name their five best male friends and their five best female friends. Moody matched the ethnicity of the student with the race of each of her named friends, then Moody compared the number of each student's cross-racial friendships with the school's overall diversity.

Moody found that the more diverse the school, the more the kids self-segregate by race and ethnicity within the school, and thus the likelihood that any two kids of different races have a friendship goes *down*.

As a result, junior high and high school children in diverse schools experience two completely-contrasting social cues on a daily basis. The first cue is inspiring—that many students have a friend of another race. The second cue is tragic—that far *more* kids just like to hang with their own. It's this second dynamic that becomes more and more visible as overall school diversity goes up. As a child circulates through school, she sees more groups that her race disqualifies her from, more tables in the lunchroom she can't sit at, and more implicit lines that are taboo to cross. This is unmissable even if she, personally, has friends of other races.

It's true that, for every extracurricular one kid has in common with a child of another race, the likelihood that they will be friends increases. But what's stunning about Moody's analysis is that he's taken that into account: Moody included statistical controls for activities, sports, academic tracking, and other school-structural conditions that tend to desegregate (or segregate) students within the school. And the rule still holds true: more diversity translates into more division between students.

Having done its own analysis of teen friendships, a team from the University of North Carolina, Chapel Hill, confirmed Moody's assessment. "More diverse schools have, overall, more potential interracial contact and hence more interracial dyads of 'potential' friends," these researchers explained—but this opportunity was being squandered: "The probability of interracial dyads being friends decreases in more diverse schools."

Those increased opportunities to interact are *also*, effectively, increased opportunities to reject each other. And that is what's happening.

"There has been a new resegregation among youth in primary and secondary schools and on college campuses across the country," wrote Dr. Brendesha Tynes of the University of Illinois, Urbana-Champaign. Tynes concluded, "Even in multiracial schools, once young people leave the classroom very little interrracial discussion takes place because a desire to associate with one's own ethnic group often discourages interaction between groups."

All told, the odds of a white high-schooler in America having a best friend of another race is only 8%. Those odds barely improve for the second-best friend, or the third best, or the fifth. For blacks, the odds aren't much better: 85% of black kids' best friends are also black. Cross-race friends also tend to share a single activity, rather than multiple activities; as a result, these friendships are more likely to be lost over time, as children transition from middle school to high school.

It is tempting to believe that because their generation is so diverse, today's children grow up knowing how to get along with people of every race. But numerous studies suggest that this is more of a fantasy than a fact.

I can't help but wonder—would the track record of desegregation be so mixed if parents reinforced it, rather than remaining silent?

※

Is it really so difficult to talk with children about race when they're very young? What jumped out at Phyllis Katz, in her study of 200 black and white children, was that parents are very comfortable talking to their children about gender, and they work very hard to counterprogram against boy-girl stereotypes. That ought to be our model for talking about race. The same way we remind our daughters, "Mommies can be doctors just like daddies," we ought to be telling all children that doctors can be any skin color. It's not complicated *what to say*. It's only a matter of how often we reinforce it.

Shushing children when they make an improper remark is an instinctive reflex, but often the wrong move. Prone to categorization, children's brains can't help but attempt to generalize rules from the examples they see. It's the worst kind of embarrassment when a child blurts out, "Only brown people can have breakfast at school," or "You can't play basketball, you're white, so you have to play baseball." But shushing them only sends the message that this topic is unspeakable, which makes race more loaded, and more intimidating.

Young children draw conclusions that may make parents cringe, even if they've seen a few counterexamples. Children are not passive absorbers of knowledge; rather, they are active constructors of concepts. Bigler has seen many examples where children distort their recollections of facts to fit the categories they've already formed in their minds. The brain's need for categories to fit perfectly is even stronger at age seven than at age five, so a second grader might make more distortions than a kindergartner to defend his categories. To a parent, it can seem as if the child is getting worse at understanding a diverse world, not better.

To be effective, researchers have found, conversations about race have to be explicit, in unmistakeable terms that children understand. A friend of mine repeatedly told her five-year-old son, "Remember, everybody's equal." She thought she was getting the message across. Finally, after seven months of this, her boy asked, "Mommy, what's 'equal' mean?"

Bigler ran a study where children read brief historical biographies of famous African Americans. For instance, in a biography of Jackie Robinson, they read that he was the first African American in the major leagues. But only half heard about how he'd previously been relegated to the Negro leagues, and how he suffered taunts from white fans. Those facts—in five brief sentences—were omitted in the version given to the other half of the children.

After the two-week history class, the children were surveyed on their racial attitudes. White children who got the full story about historical discrimination had significantly better attitudes toward blacks than those who got the neutered version. Explicitness works.

"It also made them feel some guilt," Bigler added. "It knocked down their glorified view of white people." They couldn't justify in-group superiority.

Bigler is very cautious about taking the conclusion of her Jackie Robinson study too far. She notes the bios were explicit, but about *historical* discrimination. "If we'd had them read stories of contemporary discrimination from today's newspapers, it's quite possible it would have made the whites defensive, and only made the blacks angry at whites."

Another scholar has something close to an answer on that. Dr. April Harris-Britt, a clinical psychologist and professor at University of North Carolina at Chapel Hill, studies how minority parents help their children develop a racial identity from a young age. All minority parents at some point tell their children that discrimination is out there, but they shouldn't let it stop them. However, these conversations are not triggered by their children bringing it up. Rather, the parent often suffers a discriminatory incident, and it pushes him to decide, "It's time I prepared my child for this."

Is it good for them? Harris-Britt found that some preparation for bias was beneficial to children, and that it was necessary—94% of African American eighth graders reported to Harris-Britt that they'd felt discriminated against in the prior three months. But if children heard these preparation-for-bias warnings often (rather than just occasionally), they were significantly less likely to connect their successes to effort, and much more likely to blame their failures on their teachers—whom they saw as biased against them.

Harris-Britt warns that frequent predictions of future discrimination ironically become as destructive as experiences of actual discrimination: "If you overfocus on those types of events, you give the children the message that the world is going to be hostile—you're just not valued and that's just the way the world is."

Preparation-for-bias is not, however, the only way minorities talk to their children about race. The other broad category of conversation, in Harris-Britt's analysis, is ethnic pride. From a very young age, minority children are coached to be proud of their ethnic history. She found that this was exceedingly good for children's self-confidence; in one study, black children who'd heard messages of ethnic pride were more engaged in school and more likely to attribute their success to their effort and ability.

That leads to the question that everyone wonders but rarely dares to ask. If "black pride" is good for African American children, where does that leave white children? It's horrifying to imagine kids being "proud to be white." Yet many scholars argue that's exactly what children's brains are already computing. Just as minority children are aware that they belong to an ethnic group with less status and wealth, most white children naturally decipher that they belong to the race that has more power, wealth, and control in society; this provides security, if not confidence. So a pride message would not just be abhorrent—it'd be redundant.

When talking to teens, it's helpful to understand how their tendency to form groups and cliques is partly a consequence of American culture. In America, we encourage individuality. Children freely and openly develop strong preferences—defining their self-identity by the things they like and dislike. They learn to see differences. Though singular identity is the long-term goal, in high school this identity-quest is satisfied by forming and joining distinctive subgroups. So, in an ironic twist, the more a culture emphasizes individualism, the more the high school years will be marked by subgroupism. Japan, for instance, values social harmony over individualism, and children are discouraged from asserting personal preferences. Thus, less groupism is observed in their high schools.

The security that comes from belonging to a group, especially for teens, is palpable. Traits that mark this membership are—whether we like it or not—central to this developmental period. University of Michigan researchers did a study that shows just how powerful this need to belong is, and how much it can affect a teen.

The researchers brought 100 Detroit black high school students in for one-on-one interviews. They asked each teen to rate himself on how light or dark he considered his skin tone to be. Then the scholars asked about the teens' confidence levels in social circles and school. From the high schools, the researchers obtained the teens' grade point averages.

Particularly for the boys, those who rated themselves as dark-skinned blacks had the highest GPAs. They also had the highest ratings for social acceptance and academic confidence. The boys with lighter skin tones were less secure socially and academically.

The researchers subsequently replicated these results with students who "looked Latino."

The researchers concluded that doing well in school could get a minority teen labeled as "acting white." Teens who were visibly sure of membership within the minority community were protected from this insult and thus more willing to act outside the group norm. But the light-skinned blacks and the Anglo-appearing Hispanics—their status within the minority felt more precarious. So they acted more in keeping with their image of the minority identity—even if it was a negative stereotype—in order to solidify their status within the group.

Over the course of our research, we heard many stories of how people—from parents to teachers—were struggling to talk about race with their children. For some, the conversations came up after a child had made an embarrassing comment in public. A number had the issue thrust on them, because of an interracial marriage or an international adoption. Still others were just introducing children into a diverse environment, wondering when and if the timing was right.

But the story that most affected us came from a small town in rural Ohio. Two first-grade teachers, Joy Bowman and Angela Johnson, had agreed to let a professor from Ohio State University, Dr. Jeane Copenhaver-Johnson, observe their classrooms for the year. Of the 33 children, about two-thirds identified themselves as "white" or even "hillbilly," while the others were black or of mixed-race descent.

It being December—just one month after Copenhaver's project had begun—the teachers both decided to follow up a few other Santa stories they'd read to their classes with *Twas the Night B'fore Christmas*, Melodye Rosales' retelling of the Clement C. Moore classic.

The room already dotted with holiday paraphernalia, Johnson had all of her first graders gather around the carpet for story time. As she began reading, the kids were excited by the book's depiction of a family waiting for Santa to come. A couple children burst out with stories of planned Christmas decorations and expectations for Santa's arrival to their own houses. A few of the children, however, quietly fidgeted. They seemed puzzled that this storybook was different: in this one, it was a black family all snug in their beds.

Then, there was the famed clatter on the roof. The children leaned in to get their first view of Santa and the sleigh as Johnson turned the page—

And they saw that Santa was black.

"He's black!" gasped a white little girl.

Another white boy exclaimed, "I thought he was white!"

Immediately, the children began to chatter about the stunning development.

At the ripe old ages of six and seven, the children had no doubt that there was a Real Santa. Of that fact, they were absolutely sure. But suddenly—there was this huge question mark. Could Santa be black? And if so, what did that mean?

While some of the black children were delighted with the idea that Santa could be black, still others were unsure. Some of the white children initially rejected this idea out of hand: a black Santa couldn't be real. But even the little girl who was the most adamant that the Real Santa must be white considered the possibility that a black Santa could fill in for White Santa if he was hurt. And she still gleefully yelled along with the black Santa's final "Merry Christmas to All! Y'all Sleep Tight." Still another of the white girls progressed from initially rejecting a black Santa outright to conceding that maybe Black Santa was a "Helper Santa." By the end of the story, she was asking if this black Santa couldn't somehow be a cousin or brother to the white Santa they already knew about. Her strong need that it was a white Santa who came to her house was clearly still intact—but those concessions were quite a switch in about ten pages.

Later that week, Copenhaver returned to see this play out again in another teacher's class. Similar debates ensued. A couple of the children offered the idea that perhaps Santa's "mixed with black and white"—perhaps Santa was something in the middle, like an Indian. One boy went with a Two-Santa Hypothesis: White Santa and Black Santa must be friends who take turns visiting children, he concluded. When Bowman made the apparently huge mistake of saying that she'd never seen Santa, the children all quickly corrected her: they knew everyone had seen Santa at the mall. Not that that clarified the situation any.

In both classes, the debate raged off-and-on for a week, until a school party. Santa was coming. And they were all sure it was the Real Santa who was coming.

Then Santa arrived at the party—and he was black. Just like in the picture book.

The black children were exultant—since this proved that Santa was black. Some of the white children said that this black Santa was too thin, and that meant that the Real Santa was the fat white one at Kmart. But one of the white girls retorted that she had met the man and was convinced. Santa was brown.

Amy, one of the white children who'd come up with the mixed-race Santa theory, abandoned that idea upon meeting Black Santa. But she wondered if maybe Black Santa went to the black kids' houses while White Santa delivered the white kids' presents. A black child also wondered if this Santa would take care of the white kids himself, or if perhaps he would pass along their toy requests to a white Santa hidden somewhere else.

Another black child, Brent, still doubted. He really wanted a black Santa to be true, but he wasn't convinced. So he bravely confronted Santa. "There ain't no black Santas!" Brent insisted.

"Son, what color do you see?" Santa replied.

"Black—but under your socks you might not be!"

"Lookit here." Santa pulled up a pant leg, to let Brent see the skin underneath.

A thrilled Brent was sold. "This is a black Santa!" he yelled. "He's got black skin and his black boots are like the white Santa's boots."

A black Santa storybook wasn't enough to change the children's mindsets. It didn't crush every stereotype. Even the black kids who were excited about a black Santa—when Johnson asked them to draw Santa—they still depicted a Santa whose skin was as snowy-white as his beard.

But the shock of the Santa storybook did allow the children to start talking about race in a way that had never before occurred to them. And their questions started a year-long dialogue about race issues.

By the end of the year, the teachers were regularly incorporating books that dealt directly with issues of racism into their reading. Both black and white children were collaborating on book projects on Martin Luther King Jr. And when the kids read one book about the civil rights movement, both a black and a white child noticed that white people were nowhere to be found in the story, and, troubled, they decided to find out just where in history both peoples were.

FOUR

Why Kids Lie

We may treasure honesty, but the research is clear. Most classic strategies to promote truthfulness just encourage kids to be better liars.

Ashley and I went to Montreal to visit the lab and operations of Dr. Victoria Talwar, one of the world's leading experts on children's lying behavior. Talwar is raven-haired and youthful, with an unusual accent—the combined result of Irish and Indian family ancestry, a British upbringing, and stints in American, Scottish, and Quebeçois academia. Her lab is in a Gothic Revival limestone mansion, overlooking the main campus of McGill University.

Almost immediately, Talwar recruited us for one of her ongoing experiments. She threw us in a small room with two of her students, Simone Muir and Sarah-Jane Renaud, who showed Ashley and me eight videos of children telling a story about a time they were bullied. Our role was to determine which kids were telling the truth and which had made their story up, as well as to rate how confident we were that our determination was correct.

The children ranged in age from seven to eleven years old. Each video segment began with an offscreen adult asking the child a leading question to get the story started, such as, "So tell me what happened when you went to Burger King?" In response, the child told her story over the next two and a half minutes, with the occasional gentle prod for details by the adult who was interviewing her. Those two-plus minutes were an extensive length of time for the child, offering plenty of chances to include contradictory details or hints that might give away her lie.

This format was crafted to simulate the conditions of children testifying in court cases, which is where the modern science of kids' lies began. Over 100,000 children testify in American courts every year, usually in custody disputes and abuse cases.

In those cases, children are frequently coached by someone to shape their story, so the children in Talwar's experiment were also coached, briefly, by their parents the night before. To prepare the videotape, each child rehearsed a true story and a fabricated tale, and told both stories to the interviewer on camera. The interviewer herself did not know which story was true. Then, one of the child's stories was included in the videotapes of eight. The stories chosen for the tapes were not picked because the child did an especially great job of lying. They were merely picked at random.

The adorable little girl with the Burger King story told how she was teased by a boy for being Chinese, and how he threw some French fries in her hair. I froze—would a total stranger throw fries in a girl's hair? She looked so young, and yet the story came out in full, complete—rehearsed? Just guessing, I marked this as a fabrication, but noted my confidence was nil. My confidence didn't improve with the next two children's stories.

"This is *hard*," I murmured, surprised that I didn't have the answers immediately. I pushed myself closer to the video monitor and cranked the volume up as loud as it could go.

Another girl told of being teased and left out of her group of friends after she scored 100 on a math test. She told her story with scant details and needed a lot of prodding; to me, that seemed genuine, childlike.

After the test, Ashley and I were scored. To my dismay, I got only four right. Ashley got only three correct.

Our results were not unusual. Talwar has run hundreds of people through this test, and on the whole, their results are no better than

Why Kids Lie

chance. People simply cannot tell when kids are lying. Their scores also tend to reveal some biases. They believe girls are telling the truth more than boys, when in fact boys do not lie more often. They believe younger kids are more prone to lying, whereas the opposite is true. And they believe introverts are less trustworthy, when introverts actually lie less often, lacking the social skills to pull off a lie.

There are many lie-detection systems created from the patterns in verbal and nonverbal behavior in adult lies, but these provide only small statistical advantages. Voice pitch, pupil dilation, eye tracking, lack of sensory details, and chronological storytelling are some indication of lying in adults. However, when accounting for the wild standard deviation of these behaviors in kids, those higher-than-average indicators become not much more reliable than flipping a coin.

Thus, police officers score worse than chance—at about 45%. Customs officers are trained to interview children during immigration processing and instantly determine if a child has been taken from his parents. Yet they, too, only score at chance on Talwar's test.

Talwar's students Muir and Renaud have run several versions of the experiment with both parents and teachers. "The teachers will score above chance—60%—but they get really upset if they didn't get 100%," said Muir. "They insist they'd do better with their own students."

Similarly, the parent's first defense against his child's tendency to lie is, "Well, I can tell when they're lying." Talwar's proven that to be a myth.

One might object that these bullying videotapes aren't like real lies, invented under pressure. They were coached, and the kid wasn't trying to get away with anything.

But Talwar has a variety of experiments where she tempts children to cheat in a game, which puts them in a position to offer real lies about their cheating. She videotapes these, too, and when she shows those videotapes to the child's *own* parent—and asks, "Is your child telling the truth?"—the parents score only slightly better than chance.

They don't take it well, either. When Renaud's on the telephone with parents to schedule the experiments, "They all believe that their kids aren't going to lie." Talwar explained that a number of parents come to her lab really wanting to use their kids' performance to prove to a verified expert what a terrific parent they are.

The truth bias is a painful one to overcome.

The next day, we saw that in action.

※

"My son doesn't lie," insisted Steve, a slightly frazzled father in his mid-thirties, as he watched Nick, his eager six-year-old, enthralled in a game of marbles with a McGill student. Steve was quite proud of his son, describing him as easygoing and very social. He had Nick bark out an impressive series of addition problems that Nick had memorized, as if that was somehow proof of Nick's sincerity.

Steve then took his assertion down a notch. "Well, I've never heard him lie." Perhaps that, too, was a little strong. "I'm sure he must lie, some, but when I hear it, I'll still be surprised." He had brought his son in after seeing an advertisement of Talwar's in a local parenting magazine, which had the headline, "Can your child tell the difference between the truth and a lie?" The truth was, Steve was torn. He was curious if Nick would lie, but he wasn't sure he wanted to know the answer. The idea of his son being dishonest with him was profoundly troubling.

Steve had an interesting week ahead of him, because Dr. Talwar had just asked Steve to keep a diary for the coming week, documenting every lie that his son told over the next seven days. And I knew for a fact his son did lie—I'd seen him do it.

Nick thought he'd spent the hour playing a series of games with a couple of nice women. First having played marbles in the cheery playroom, Nick then played more games with the women, one-on-one. He was in no real hurry to leave the lab, with its yellow-painted walls decorated with dozens of children's drawings and shelves full of toys. He'd won two prizes, a cool toy car and a bag of plastic dinosaurs, and everyone said he did very well.

What the first-grader didn't know was that those games—fun as they were—were really a battery of psychological tests, and the women were Talwar's trained researchers earning doctorates in child psychology. The other key fact Nick didn't know was that when he was playing games one-on-one, there was a hidden camera taping his every move and word. In an adjacent room, Ashley and I watched the whole thing from a monitor.

Nick cheated, then he lied, and then he lied again. He did so unhesitatingly, without a single glimmer of remorse. Instead, he later beamed as everyone congratulated him on winning the games: he told me he couldn't wait to come back the next weekend to play more games. If I didn't know what was going on, I'd have thought he was a young sociopath in the making. I still actually wonder if that's the case, despite Talwar's assurances to the contrary.

One of Talwar's experiments, a variation on a classic experiment known as the temptation paradigm, is known in the lab as "The Peeking Game." Courtesy of the hidden camera, we'd watched Nick play it with another one of Talwar's graduate students, Cindy Arruda. She took Nick into a very small private room and told him they were going to play a guessing game. Nick turned and straddled his chair to face the wall, while Arruda would bring out a toy that made a sound. Nick had to guess the identity of the toy based on the sound that it had made. If he was right three times, he'd win a prize.

The first toy was easy. Nick bounced in his chair with excitement when he'd figured out that the siren was from a police car. The second toy emitted a baby's cry—it took Nick a couple tries before he landed on "baby doll." He was relieved to finally be right.

"Does it get harder every time?" he asked, obviously concerned, as he pressed the baby doll's tummy to trigger another cry.

"Uh, no," Arruda stammered, despite knowing it was indeed about to get harder for Nick.

Nick turned back to the wall, waiting for the last toy. His small figure curled up over the back of the chair as if he was playing a wonderful game of hide-and-seek.

Arruda brought out a soft, stuffed soccer ball, and placed it on top of a greeting card that played music. She cracked the card for a moment, triggering it to play a music box jingle of Beethoven's "Für Elise."

Nick, of course, was stumped.

Before he had a chance to guess, Arruda suddenly said that she'd forgotten something and had to leave the room for a little bit, promising to be right back. She admonished Nick not to peek at the toy while she was gone.

Five seconds in, Nick was struggling not to peek—he started to turn around but fought the urge and looked back at the wall before he saw anything. He held out for another eight seconds, but the temptation was too great. At thirteen seconds, he gave in. Turning to look, he saw the soccer ball, then immediately returned to his "hide-and-seek" position.

When Arruda returned, she'd barely come through the door before Nick—still facing the wall as if he had never peeked—burst out with the fact that the toy was a soccer ball. We could hear the triumph in his voice—until Arruda stopped him short, telling Nick to wait for her to get seated.

That mere split-second gave Nick just enough time to realize that he should sound unsure of his answer, or else she would know he'd peeked. Suddenly, the glee was gone, and he sounded a little more hesitant. "A soccer ball?" he asked, making it sound like a pure guess.

When he turned around to face Arruda and see the revealed toy, Arruda told Nick he was right, and he acted very pleased.

Arruda then asked Nick if he had peeked when she was away.

"No," he said, quick and expressionless. Then a big smile spread across his face.

Without challenging him, or even letting a note of suspicion creep into her voice, Arruda asked Nick how he'd figured out the sound came from a soccer ball.

Nick shrank down in his seat for a second, cupping his chin in his hands. He knew he needed a plausible answer, but his first attempt wasn't close. With a perfectly straight face he said, "The music had sounded like a ball." Hunting for a better answer, but not getting any closer to it, he added, "The ball sounded black and white." His face gave no outward indication that he realized this made no sense, but he kept on talking, as if he felt he needed something better. Then Nick said that the music sounded like the soccer balls he played with at school: they squeaked. He nodded—this was the good one to go with—and then further explained that the music sounded like the squeak he heard when he kicked a ball. To emphasize this, his winning point, he brushed his hand against the side of the toy ball, as if to demonstrate the way his foot kicking the side of the ball produces a squeaking sound.

This experiment was not just a test to see if children cheat and lie under temptation. It's also designed to test children's ability to extend a lie, offering plausible explanations and avoiding what the scientists call "leakage"—inconsistencies that reveal the lie for what it is. Nick's whiffs at covering up his lie would be scored later by coders who watched the videotape. So Arruda accepted without question the fact that soccer balls play Beethoven when they're kicked and gave Nick his prize. He was thrilled.

A number of scholars have used variations of this temptation paradigm to test thousands of children over the last few years. What they've learned has turned conventional assumptions upside down.

The first thing they've learned is that children learn to lie much earlier than we presumed. In Talwar's peeking game, only a third of the three-year-olds will peek, and when asked if they peeked, most of them will admit it. But over 80% of the four-year-olds peek. Of those, over 80% will lie when asked, asserting they haven't peeked. By their fourth birthday, almost all kids will start experimenting with lying. Children with older siblings seem to learn it slightly earlier.

Parents often fail to address early childhood lying, since the lying is almost innocent—their child's too young to know what lies are, or that lying's wrong. When their child gets older and learns those distinctions, the parents believe, the lying will stop. This is dead wrong, according to Dr. Talwar. The better a young child can distinguish a lie from the truth, the more likely she is to lie given the chance. Researchers test children with elegant anecdotes, and ask, "Did Suzy tell a lie or tell the truth?" The kids who know the difference are also the most prone to lie. Ignorant of this scholarship, many parenting web sites and books advise parents to just let lies go—kids will grow out of it. The truth is, kids grow into it.

In studies where children are observed in their homes, four-year-olds will lie once every two hours, while a six-year-old will lie about once every hour. Few kids are an exception. In these same studies, 96% of all kids offer up lies.

Most lies to parents are a cover-up of a transgression. First, the kid does something he shouldn't; then, to squirm out of trouble, he denies doing it. But this denial is so expected, and so common, that it's usually dismissed by parents. In those same observational studies, researchers report that in less than one percent of such situations does a parent use the tacked-on lie as a chance to teach a lesson about lying. The parent censures the original transgression, but not the failed cover-up. From the kid's point of view, his attempted lie didn't cost him extra.

Simultaneously as they learn to craft and maintain a lie, kids also learn what it's like to be *lied to*. But children don't start out thinking lies are okay, and gradually realize they're bad. The opposite is true. They start out thinking all deception—of any sort—is bad, and slowly realize that some types are okay.

In a now classic study by University of Queensland's Dr. Candida Peterson, adults and children of different ages watched ten videotaped scenarios of different lies—from benevolent white lies to manipulative whoppers. Children are much more disapproving of lies and liars than adults are; children are more likely to think the liar is a bad person and the lie is morally wrong.

The qualifying role of intent seems to be the most difficult variable for children to grasp. Kids don't even believe a mistake is an acceptable excuse. The only thing that matters is that the information was wrong.

According to Dr. Paul Ekman, a pioneer of lying research at UC San Francisco, here's an example of how that plays out. On the way home from school on Tuesday, a dad promises his five-year-old son that he'll take him to the baseball game on Saturday afternoon. When they get home, Dad learns from Mom that earlier in the day, she had scheduled a swim lesson for Saturday afternoon and can't change it. When they tell their son, he gets terribly upset, and the situation melts down. Why is the kid so upset? Dad didn't know about the swim lesson. By the adult definition, Dad did not lie. But by the kid definition, Dad did lie. Any false statement—regardless of intent or belief—is a lie. Therefore, unwittingly, Dad has given his child the message that he condones lies.

The second lesson is that while we think of truthfulness as a young child's paramount virtue, it's lying that is the more advanced skill. A child who is going to lie must recognize the truth, intellectually conceive of an alternate reality, and be able to convincingly sell that new reality to someone else. Therefore, lying demands both advanced cognitive development and social skills that honesty simply doesn't require. "It's a developmental milestone," Talwar has concluded.

Indeed, kids who start lying at two or three—or who can control verbal leakage at four or five—do better on other tests of academic prowess. "Lying is related to intelligence," confirmed Talwar, "but you still have to deal with it."

When children first begin lying, they lie to avoid punishment, and because of that, they lie indiscriminately—whenever punishment seems to be a possibility. A three-year-old will say, "I didn't hit my sister," even though a parent witnessed the child hit her sibling. A six-year-old won't make that mistake—she'll lie only about a punch that occurred when the parent was out of the room.

By the time a child reaches school age, her reasons for lying are more complex. Punishment is a primary catalyst for lying, but as kids develop empathy and become more aware of social relations, they start to consider others when they lie. They may lie to spare a friend's feelings. In grade school, said Talwar, "secret keeping becomes an important part of friendship—and so lying may be a part of that."

Lying also becomes a way to increase a child's power and sense of control—by manipulating friends with teasing, by bragging to assert his status, and by learning that he can fool his parents.

Thrown into elementary school, many kids begin lying to their peers as a coping mechanism: it's a way to vent frustration or get attention. They might be attempting to compensate, feeling they're slipping behind their peers. Any sudden spate of lying, or dramatic increase in lying, is a sign that something has changed in that child's life, in a way that troubles him: "Lying is a symptom—often of a bigger problem behavior," explained Talwar. "It's a strategy to keep themselves afloat."

In longitudinal studies, a six-year-old who lies frequently could just as simply grow out of it. But if lying has become a successful strategy for handling difficult social situations, she'll stick with it. About one-third of kids do—and if they're still lying at seven, then it seems likely to continue. They're hooked.

In Talwar's peeking game, sometimes the researcher pauses the game with, "I'm about to ask you a question. But before I do that, will you promise to tell the truth?" (Yes, the child answers.) "Okay, did you peek at the toy when I was out of the room?" This promise cuts down lying by 25%.

In other scenarios, Talwar's researcher will read the child a short storybook before she asks about the peeking. One of the stories read aloud is *The Boy Who Cried Wolf*—the version in which both the boy and the sheep get eaten because of his repeated lies. Alternatively, they read the story of *George Washington and the Cherry Tree*, in which young George confesses to his father that he chopped down the prized tree with his new hatchet. The story ends with his father's reply: "George, I'm glad that you cut down that cherry tree after all. Hearing you tell the truth is better than if I had a thousand cherry trees."

Now if you had to guess, which story would you think reduced lying more? We ran a poll on our web site, receiving over a thousand responses to that question. Of them, 75% said *The Boy Who Cried Wolf* would work better. However, this famous fable, told all around the world, actually did not cut down lying at all in Talwar's experiments. In fact, after hearing the story, kids lied even a little more than usual.

Meanwhile, hearing *George Washington and the Cherry Tree* reduced lying a whopping 75% in boys, and 50% in girls.

We might think that the story works because Washington's a national icon—that kids are taught to emulate the honesty of our nation's founder—but Talwar's kids are Canadian, and the youngest kids have never even heard of him. To determine if Washington's celebrity was an influential factor for the older kids, Talwar re-ran the experiment, replacing Washington with a nondescript character, and otherwise leaving the story intact. The story's generic version had the same result.

Why does one fable work so well, while the other doesn't—and what does this tell us about how to teach kids to lie less?

The shepherd boy ends up suffering the ultimate punishment, but that lies get punished is not news to children. When asked if lies are *always* wrong, 92% of five-year-olds say yes. And when asked *why* lies are wrong, most say the problem with lying is you get punished for it. In that sense, young kids process the risk of lying by considering only their own self-protection. It takes years for the children to understand lying on a more sophisticated moral ground. It isn't until age eleven that the majority demonstrate awareness of its harm to others; at that point, 48% say the problem with lying is that it destroys trust, and 22% say it carries guilt. Even then, a third still say the problem with lying is being punished.

As an example of how strongly young kids associate lying with punishment, consider this: 38% of five-year-olds rate *profanity* as a lie. Why would kids think swearing is a lie? It's because in their minds, lies are the things you say that get you punished or admonished. Swearing gets you admonished. Therefore, swearing is a lie.

Increasing the threat of punishment for lying only makes children hyperaware of the potential *personal* cost. It distracts the child from learning how his lies impact others. In studies, scholars find that kids who live in threat of consistent punishment don't lie less. Instead, they become better liars, at an earlier age—learning to get caught less often. Talwar did a version of the peeking game in western Africa, with children who attend a traditional colonial school. In this school, Talwar described, "The teachers would slap the children's heads, hit them with switches, pinch them, for anything—forgetting a pencil, getting homework wrong. Sometimes, a good child would be made to enforce the bad kid." While the North American kids usually peek within five seconds, "Children in this school took longer to peek—35 seconds, even 58 seconds. But just as many peeked. Then they lied and continued to lie. They go for broke because of the severe consequences of getting caught." Even three-year-olds pretended they didn't know what the toy was, though they'd just peeked. They understood that naming the toy was to drop a clue, and the temptation of being right didn't outweigh the risk of being caught. They were able to completely control their verbal leakage—an ability that still eluded six-year-old Nick.

But just removing the threat of punishment is not enough to extract honesty from kids. In yet another variation, Talwar's researchers promise the children, "I will not be upset with you if you peeked. It doesn't matter if you did." Parents try a version of this routinely. But this alone doesn't reduce lying at all. The children are still wary; they don't trust the promise of immunity. They're thinking, *"My parent really wishes I didn't do it in the first place; if I say I didn't, that's my best chance of making my parent happy."*

Meaning, in these decisive moments, they want to know how to get back into your good graces. So it's not enough to say to a six-year-old, "I will not be upset with you if you peeked, and if you tell the truth you'll be really happy with yourself." That does reduce lying—quite a bit—but a six-year-old doesn't want to make himself happy. He wants to make the parent happy.

What really works is to tell the child, "I will not be upset with you if you peeked, and if you tell the truth, *I* will be really happy." This is an offer of both immunity *and* a clear route back to good standing. Talwar explained this latest finding: "Young kids are lying to make you happy—trying to please you." So telling kids that the truth will make a parent happy challenges the kid's original thought that hearing good news—not the truth—is what will please the parent.

That's why *George Washington and the Cherry Tree* works so well. Little George receives both immunity and praise for telling the truth.

Ultimately, it's not fairy tales that stop kids from lying—it's the process of socialization. But the wisdom in *The Cherry Tree* applies: according to Talwar, parents need to teach kids the worth of honesty just as much as they need to say that lying is wrong. The more kids hear that message, the more quickly they will take this lesson to heart.

The other reason children lie, according to Talwar, is that they learn it from us.

Talwar challenged that parents need to really consider the importance of honesty in their own lives. Too often, she finds, parents' own actions show kids an ad hoc appreciation of honesty. "We don't explicitly tell them to lie, but they see us do it. They see us tell the telemarketer, 'I'm just a guest here.' They see us boast and lie to smooth social relationships."

Consider how we expect a child to act when he opens a gift he doesn't like. We expect him to swallow all his honest reactions—anger, disappointment, frustration—and put on a polite smile. Talwar runs an experiment where children play various games to win a present, but when they finally receive the present, it's a lousy bar of soap. After giving the kids a moment to overcome the shock, a researcher asks them how they like it. Talwar is testing their ability to offer a white lie, verbally, and also to control the disappointment in their body language. About a quarter of preschoolers can lie that they like the gift—by elementary school, about half. Telling this lie makes them extremely uncomfortable, especially when pressed to offer a few reasons for *why* they like the bar of soap. They frown; they stare at the soap and can't bring themselves to look the researcher in the eye. Kids who shouted with glee when they won the peeking game suddenly mumble quietly and fidget.

Meanwhile, the child's parent is watching. They almost cheer when the child comes up with the white lie. "Often the parents are proud that their kids are 'polite'—they don't see it as lying," Talwar remarked. Despite the number of times she's seen it happen, she's regularly amazed at parents' apparent inability to recognize that a white lie is still a lie.

When adults are asked to keep diaries of their own lies, they admit to about one lie per every five social interactions, which works out to about one per day, on average. (College students are double that.) The vast majority of these lies are white lies meant to make others feel good, like telling the woman at work who brought in muffins that they taste great.

Encouraged to tell so many white lies, children gradually get comfortable with being disingenuous. Insincerity becomes, literally, a daily occurrence. They learn that honesty only creates conflict, while dishonesty is an easy way to avoid conflict. And while they don't confuse white-lie situations with lying to cover their misdeeds, they bring this emotional groundwork from one circumstance to the other. It becomes easier, psychologically, to lie to a parent. So if the parent says, "Where did you get these Pokémon cards?! I told you, you're not allowed to waste your allowance on Pokémon cards!," this may feel to the child very much like a white-lie scenario—he can make his father *feel better* by telling him the cards were extras from a friend.

Now, compare this to the way children are taught not to tattle. Children will actually start tattling even before they can talk—at around the age of fourteen months, they'll cry, point, and use their gaze to signal their mother for help when another child has stolen a toy or cookie. Appealing to grownups becomes a habit, and around the age of four, children start to hear a rule to rid them of this habit: "Don't Tell," or "Don't Tattle."

What grownups really mean by "Don't Tell" is we want children to learn to work it out with one another, first. Kids need the social skills to resolve problems, and they won't develop these skills if a parent always intrudes. Kids' tattles are, occasionally, outright lies, and children can use tattling as a way to get even. When parents preach "Don't Tell," we're trying to get all these power games to stop.

Preschool and elementary school teachers proclaim tattling to be the bane of their existence. One of the largest teachers' training programs in the United States ranks children's tattling as one of the top five classroom concerns—as disruptive as fighting or biting another classmate.

But tattling has received some scientific interest, and researchers have spent hours observing kids at play. They've learned that nine out of ten times a kid runs up to a parent to tell, that kid is being completely honest. And while it might seem to a parent that tattling is incessant, to a child that's not the case—because for every one time a child seeks a parent for help, there were fourteen other instances when he was wronged and did not run to the parent for aid.

When the child—who's put up with as much as he can handle—finally comes to tell the parent the honest truth, he hears, in effect, "Stop bringing me your problems!" According to one researcher's work, parents are *ten times* more likely to chastise a child for tattling than they are to chide a child who lied.

Kids pick up on the power of "Don't Tell" and learn they can silence one another with it. By the middle years of elementary school, being labeled a tattler is about the worst thing a kid can be called on the playground. So a child considering reporting a problem to an adult not only faces peer condemnation as a traitor and the schoolyard equivalent of the death penalty—ostracism—but he also recalls every time he's heard teachers and parents say, "Work it out on your own."

Each year, the problems kids deal with become exponentially bigger. They watch other kids vandalize walls, shoplift, cut class, and climb fences into places they shouldn't be. To tattle about any of it is to act like a little kid, mortifying to any self-respecting tweener. Keeping their mouth shut is easy; they've been encouraged to do so since they were little.

The era of holding information back from parents has begun.

For two decades, parents have rated "honesty" as the trait they most want in their children. Other traits, such as confidence or good judgment, don't even come close. On paper, the kids are getting this message. In surveys, 98% said that trust and honesty were essential in a personal relationship. Depending on their age, 96% to 98% will say lying is morally wrong.

But this is only lip service, for both parties. Studies show that 96% of kids lie to their parents, yet lying has never been the #1 topic on the parenting boards or on the benches at the playgrounds.

Having lying on my radar screen has changed the way things work around the Bronson household. No matter how small, lies no longer go unnoticed. The moments slow down, and I have a better sense of how to handle them.

A few months ago my wife was on the phone making arrangements for a babysitter. She told the sitter that my son was six years old, so that the sitter knew what age-level games to bring. Luke started protesting, loudly, interrupting my wife. Whereas before I'd have been perplexed or annoyed at my son's sudden outburst, now I understood. My son was, technically, still a week away from his sixth birthday, which he was treasuring in anticipation. So in his mind, his mom *lied*—about something *really* important to him. At his developmental stage, the benign motivation for the lie was irrelevant. The second Michele got off the phone, I explained to her why he was so upset; she apologized to him and promised to be more exact. He immediately calmed down.

Despite his umbrage at others' lies, Luke's not beyond attempting his own cover-ups. Just the other day, he came home from school having learned a new phrase and a new attitude—quipping "I don't care," snidely, and shrugging his shoulders to everything. He was suddenly acting like a teenager, unwilling to finish his dinner or complete his homework. He repeated "I don't care" so many times I finally got frustrated and demanded to know if someone at school had taught him this dismissive phrase.

He froze. And I could suddenly intuit the debate running through his head: should he lie to his dad, or rat out his friend? I knew from Talwar's research that I'd lose that one. Recognizing this, I stopped him and I told him that if he'd learned the phrase at school, he did not have to tell me *who* had taught him the phrase. Telling me the truth was not going to get his friends in trouble.

"Okay," he said, relieved. "I learned it at school." Then he told me he *did* care, and gave me a hug. I haven't heard that phrase again.

Does how we deal with a child's lies really matter, down the road in life? The irony of lying is that it's both normal and abnormal behavior at the same time. It's to be expected, and yet it can't be disregarded.

Dr. Bella DePaulo has devoted much of her career to adult lying.

In one study, she had both college students and community members enter a private room, equipped with an audiotape recorder. Promising them complete confidentiality, DePaulo's team instructed the subjects to recall the worst lie they'd ever told—with all the scintillating details.

"I was fully expecting serious lies," DePaulo remarked. "Stories of affairs kept from spouses, stories of squandering money, or being a salesperson and screwing money out of car buyers." And she did hear those kinds of whoppers, including theft and even one murder. But to her surprise, a lot of the stories told were about situations in which the subject was a mere child—and they were not, at first glance, lies of any great consequence. "One told of eating the icing off a cake, then telling her parents the cake came that way. Another told of stealing some coins from a sibling." As these stories first started trickling in, DePaulo scoffed, thinking, "*C'mon, that's the* worst *lie you've ever told?*" But the stories of childhood kept coming, and DePaulo had to create a category in her analysis just for them.

"I had to reframe my understanding to consider what it must have been like as a child to have told this lie," she recalled. "For young kids, their lie challenged their self-concept that they were a good child, and that they did the right thing."

Many subjects commented on how that momentous lie early in life established a pattern that affected them thereafter. "We had some who said, 'I told this lie, I got caught, and I felt so badly, I vowed to never do it again.' Others said, 'Wow, I never realized I'd be so good at deceiving my father; I can do this all the time.' The lies they tell early on are meaningful. The way parents react can really affect lying."

Talwar says parents often entrap their kids, putting them in positions to lie and testing their honesty unneccessarily. Last week, I put my three-and-a-half-year-old daughter in that exact situation. I noticed she had scribbled on the dining table with a washable marker. With disapproval in my voice I asked, "Did you draw on the table, Thia?" In the past, she would have just answered honestly, but my tone gave away that she'd done something wrong. Immediately, I wished I could retract the question and do it over. I should have just reminded her not to write on the table, slipped newspaper under her coloring book, and washed the ink away. Instead, I had done exactly what Talwar had warned against.

"No, I didn't," my daughter said, lying to me for the first time.

For that stain, I had only myself to blame.

FIVE

The Search for Intelligent Life in Kindergarten

Millions of kids are competing for seats in gifted programs and private schools. Admissions officers say it's an art: new science says they're wrong, 73% of the time.

Picture the little child, just turned five, being escorted into a stranger's office. Her mother helps her get comfortable for a few minutes, then departs.

Mommy might have told the girl that the stranger will help determine which school she goes to next year. Ideally, the word "test" will never be spoken; if the girl asks, "Am I going to take a test?" she will be told, "There will be puzzles and drawing and blocks and some questions to answer. Most kids think these activities are really fun."

The child is directed to a seat at a table. The test examiner sits across from her. If she grows restless after a while, they might move to the floor. (If there is a significant problem, some schools may allow a retest, but most won't allow her to return for a year or two.)

They begin each test with a series of sample questions, which the examiner demonstrates. Then they start the real test. The examiner begins with a question appropriate for the child's age. A five-year-old child might start with question no. 4 of the testing book. Each question gets a tiny bit harder, and the child keeps receiving questions until she has made several errors in a row. At this point, the "discontinue rule" is triggered—the little girl has reached the top of her ability, and they move on to a new section.

Vocabulary is tested two ways; at first, the child merely has to name what's pictured. When it gets harder, the child will be told a word, like "confine," and be asked what it means. Detailed definitions merit a 2; less detail scores a 1.

The little girl will also have to discern a word from just a few clues. "Can you tell me what I'm thinking of?" the examiner will ask. "This is something you can sit or stand on, and it is something that can be cleaned or made of dirt."

She has five seconds to answer.

On another section, the child will be shown pictures, then asked to spot what's missing. "The bear's leg!" she'll answer—hopefully within 20 seconds.

Later, the examiner will set some red and white plastic blocks out on the table. The child will be shown a card with a shape or pattern on it, and she'll be asked to assemble four blocks to mirror the shape. Blocks arranged more than one-quarter inch apart are penalized. The harder questions use blocks with bicolored sides—red and white triangles. Older kids get nine blocks.

She may also see some mazes; no lifting of the pencil is allowed, and points are taken off for going down blind alleys.

Discerning patterns is a component of all tests. For instance, the child will need to recognize that a circle is to an oval as a square is to a rectangle, while a triangle is to a square as a square is to a pentagon. Or, snow is to a snowman as a bag of flour is to a loaf of bread.

If a child is six years old, she might be read four numbers aloud (such as 9, 4, 7, 1) and asked to repeat them. If she gets them right, she'll move up to five numbers. If she can do seven numbers, she'll score in the 99th percentile. Then she'll be asked to repeat a number sequence in reverse order; correctly repeating four numbers backward counts as gifted.

Every winter, tens of thousands of children spend a morning or afternoon this way. Testing sessions like this one are the keys to admittance to elite private schools and to Gifted and Talented programs in public schools. Kids are scored against other children born in the same third of the year. Mostly based on these tests, over three million children—almost 7% of the American public school population—are in a gifted program. Another two million children won entry into private independent schools.

The tests vary by what exactly they examine. Some are forms of a classic intelligence test—for instance, the Wechsler Preschool and Primary Scale of Intelligence, known by its acronym, WPPSI. Other schools opt for an exam that doesn't strictly measure IQ; they might use a test of reasoning ability, such as the Cognitive Abilities Test, or a hybrid test of intelligence and learning aptitude, such as the Otis-Lennon School Ability Test.

Regardless of what is being tested, or which test is used, they all have one thing in common.

They're all astonishingly ineffective predictors of a young child's academic success.

While it's no surprise that not all gifted kindergartners end up at Harvard, the operating assumption has been that these screening tests *do* predict which kids will be the best at reading, writing, and math in the second and third grades. But they turn out to not even do that.

To give you a hint of the scale of the problem—if you picked 100 kindergartners as the "gifted," i.e. the smartest, by third grade only 27 of them would still deserve that categorization. You would have wrongly locked out 73 other deserving students.

Most schools don't realize how poorly the tests predict a child's elementary school academics. The few with concerns have tried to come up with other ways to test for giftedness—everything from asking a kid to draw a picture to rating a child's emotional empathy or behavior. However, scholars' analyses have shown that each of these alternatives turns out to be even *less* effective than the intelligence tests.

The issue isn't which test is used, or what the test tests. The problem is that young kids' brains just aren't done yet.

※

For decades, intelligence tests have been surrounded by controversy.

Critics have long argued that the tests have cultural or class biases. What's gone unnoticed is that, stinging from these allegations, all the testing companies have modified their tests to minimize these effects—to the point where they no longer really consider bias an issue. (While that would seem a hard pill to swallow, consider that versions of these tests are used around the world.) On top of those changes, schools with the strictest IQ requirements often make exceptions for children who come from disadvantaged backgrounds or speak something other than English as their first language.

Meanwhile, shaping the debate along the bias fault line has led us to completely ignore the larger question: how often do the tests accurately identify any bright young kids—even the mainstream children?

We asked admissions directors and school superintendents, and they all had the impression that the tests were accurate predictors. The tests come with manuals, and the first chapters of these manuals are dense with research conveying an aura of authentication. However, the statistics reported are generally not about how accurately the tests predict *future* performance. Instead, the statistics are about the accuracy of the tests at predicting current performance, and how well these tests stack up against competitors' tests.

Dr. Lawrence Weiss is the Vice President of Clinical Product Development at Pearson/Harcourt Assessment, which owns the WPPSI test. When I asked him how well his test predicts school performance just two or three years later, he explained that it's not his company's policy to assemble that data. "We don't track them down the road. We don't track predictive validity over time."

We were shocked by this, because decisions made on the basis of intelligence test results have enormous consequence. A score above 120 puts a child in the 90th percentile or higher, the conventional cutoff line for being called "gifted," and may qualify her for special classes. A score above 130 puts a child in the 98th percentile, at which point she may be placed in a separate school for the advanced.

Note, these kids aren't prodigies—a prodigy is far rarer, more like a one in a half-million phenomenon. To be classified as gifted by a school district indicates a child is bright, but not necessarily extraordinary. Half of all college graduates have an IQ of 120 or above; 130 is the average of adults with a Ph.D.

However, earning this classification when young is nothing less than a golden ticket, academically. The rarified learning environment, filled with quick peers, allows teachers to speed up the curriculum. This can make a huge difference in how much a child learns. In California, according to a state government study, children in Gifted and Talented programs make 36.7% more progress every year than the norm. And in many districts, such as New York City and Chicago, students are not retested and remain in the program until they graduate from their school. Those admitted at kindergarten to private schools will stay through eighth grade.

While the publishers of the tests aren't trying to determine how well early intelligence tests predict later achievement, the academic researchers are.

In 2003, Dr. Hoi Suen, Professor of Educational Psychology at Pennsylvania State University, published a meta-analysis of 44 studies, each of which looked at how well tests given in pre-K or in kindergarten predicted achievement test scores two years later. Most of the underlying 44 studies had been published in the mid-1970s to mid-1990s, and most looked at a single school or school district. Analyzing them together, Suen found that intelligence test scores before children start school, on average, had only a 40% correlation with later achievement test results.

This 40% correlation includes all children, at every ability level. When Suen narrowed his focus down to the studies of gifted or private schools, the correlations weren't better.

For example, one team of scholars at the University of North Carolina at Charlotte analyzed three years of scores of an upper-middle class private independent school in Charlotte. The school required all applicants take the WPPSI test prior to being admitted to kindergarten. They were identified as smart kids—the average IQ was 116. In third grade, the students took the Comprehensive Testing Battery III, a test developed to fit the advanced curricula of private schools. As a group, the students did well, averaging scores in the 90th percentile.

But did the WPPSI results forecast *which* students did well? Not really. The correlation between WPPSI scores and the achievement scores was only 40%.

For students at the *very* high end, the correlations appear to be even lower. Dr. William Tsushima looked at two exclusive private schools in Hawaii—at one school, the kids had an average IQ of 130, while at the other, just over 126. But their reading scores in second grade had only a 26% correlation with WPPSI results. Their math scores had an even poorer correlation.

The relevant question, therefore, is just how many children are miscategorized by such early testing?

As I mentioned before, using tests with that 40% correlation, if a school wanted the top tenth of students in its third-grade gifted program, *72.4% of them* wouldn't have been identified by their IQ test score before kindergarten. And it's not as if these children would have just missed it by a hair. Many wouldn't have even come close.

Fully one-third of the brightest incoming third graders would have scored "below average" prior to kindergarten.

The amount of false-positives and false-negatives is worrisome to experts such as Dr. Donald Rock, Senior Research Scientist with Educational Testing Service.

"The identification of very bright kids in kindergarten or first grade is not on too thick of ice," Rock said. "The IQ measures aren't very accurate at all. Third grade, yeah, second grade, maybe. Testing younger than that, you're getting kids with good backgrounds, essentially."

Rock did add that most kids won't fall too far. "The top one percent will certainly be in the top ten percent five years later. It is true that a kid who blows the top off that test is a bright kid, no question—but kids who do quite well might not be in that position by third grade."

According to Rock, third grade is when the public school curriculum gets much harder. Children are expected to reason through math, rather than just memorize sums, and the emphasis is shifted to reading for comprehension, rather than just reading sentences aloud using phonics. This step up in difficulty separates children.

"You see growth leveling off in a lot of kids." As a result, Rock believes third grade is when testing becomes meaningful. "Kids' rank ordering in third grade is very meaningful. If we measure reading in third grade, it can predict performance much later, in a lot of areas."

The issue isn't some innate flaw with intelligence tests. The problem is testing kids too young, with any kind of test.

"I would be concerned if high-stakes judgments such as entry to separate selective schools were based on such test results," said Dr. Steven Strand of the University of Warwick in Coventry, England. "Such structural decisions tend to be inflexible, and so kids can be locked in on the basis of an early result, while others can be locked out. It's all about having sufficient flexibility to alter provisions and decisions at a later date."

In contrast to testing children in preschool or early elementary school, Strand found that IQ tests given in middle schools are actually very good predictors of academic success in high school.

In a recent study published in the journal *Intelligence*, Strand looked at scores for 70,000 British children. He compared their results on an intelligence test at age eleven with their scores on the GCSE exam at age sixteen. Those correlated very highly. If early childhood IQ tests could predict as well as those taken at age eleven, they'd identify the gifted students about twice as accurately.

Every single scholar we spoke to warned of classifying young children on the basis of a single early test result—all advised of the necessity for secondary testing. And this caution didn't come from those who are just morally against the idea of any intelligence testing. This admonition came most strongly from those actually *writing* the tests, including: University of Iowa professor Dr. David Lohman, one of the authors of the Cognitive Abilities Test; Dr. Steven Pfeiffer, author of the Gifted Rating Scales; and Dr. Cecil Reynolds, author of the RIAS (the Reynolds Intellectual Assessment Scales).

Despite the unanimity of this view, because of the cost and time involved, kids are routinely awarded—or denied—entrance on the basis of a single test, and in many schools are never retested.

"Firm number cutoffs are ridiculous," said Reynolds. "If we were doing the same for identifying special-ed students, it would be against federal law."

※

Consider South Carolina.

A few years ago, the state hired the College of William & Mary's Center for Gifted Education to evaluate its gifted screening. South Carolina was concerned that minorities were underrepresented in the gifted programs, but—along the way—there turned out to be an even more complex problem.

Despite revamping the admissions process to increase minority participation, the program remained disproportionately white (86%). But even more disturbing was the number of kids in the gifted program—regardless their race—who were weren't functioning as gifted at all.

When William & Mary looked at the gifted kids' achievement test scores for 2002 in third, fourth, and fifth grade, the results were disastrous. In math, 12% of the gifted kids scored as having only a "basic" ability level. Another 30% were merely "proficient." In English, the numbers were far worse. You'd expect the researchers would have concluded that those children should be moved into a normal classroom, but instead William & Mary recommended the state come up with gifted interventions—basically, special programs for the kids who were remedial-yet-gifted, an oxymoronic concept if there ever was one.

We called the twenty largest public school districts in America to learn what gifted education programs they offer. Here are those twenty largest:

New York City
Los Angeles Unified
City of Chicago
Dade County (Miami)
Clark County (Las Vegas)
Broward County
   (Fort Lauderdale)
Houston ISD
Hillsborough County (Tampa)
Philadelphia City
Hawaii Dept. of Education
Palm Beach County
Orange County (Orlando)
Fairfax County (VA)
Dallas ISD
Detroit City
Montgomery County
   (MD)
Prince George's County
   (MD)
Gwinnett County (GA)
San Diego Unified
Duval County
   (Jacksonville)

All twenty had some sort of gifted program. Twelve of those districts begin their program in kindergarten. Not one district waits until third grade to screen the children—by the end of second grade, all twenty districts have anointed children as exceptional.

On paper, this flies in the face of the developmental science. "I don't have the perfect answer," said Dr. Lauri Kirsch, Supervisor of the Gifted Program at Hillsborough County School District in Tampa, Florida. "I just keep my eyes open, looking for kids. We create opportunities for kids to engage and excel. We want to give the children time to develop their giftedness."

When talking to these schools, I realized it was unfair to judge the programs solely on the basis of what age they tested the kids; it was also important to consider what the stakes were—whether the gifted program was radically better than regular classes, or only a modest supplement to regular classes. Several of those districts, like Dallas, identify the kids as early as kindergarten, but they don't make a fateful structural decision. The children identified as gifted remain in their classrooms, and once a week get to slip out and attend a two-hour enhanced class just for the gifted. That's all they get, which is almost surely not enough. It's hard to argue that Dallas is better than Detroit, which makes a fateful decision prior to kindergarten, but the kids who are identified as gifted get something far better—they're allowed to attend a full-time special academy.

In applying the science to the reality, the problem doesn't seem to lie with the age of initial screening. Even in kindergarten, a few children are clearly and indisputably advanced. Instead, what stands out as problems are: the districts who don't give late-blooming children additional chances to test in, and the lack of objective retesting to ensure the kids who got in young really belong there.

Of the top twenty school districts, *not one* requires children to score high on an achievement test or IQ test in later years to stay in the program. Children can stay in the gifted class as long as they aren't falling too far behind. Kicking kids out is not what districts prioritize—it's getting them in.

Many of the districts are still laboring under the premise that intelligence is innate and stable. By this ancient logic, retesting is not necessary, because an IQ score is presumed valid for life. The lack of reassessment is kindhearted but a double standard: the districts believe firmly in using IQ cutoffs for initial admission, but they think later tests aren't necessary.

Back in South Carolina, they've actually instituted new rules to protect low-performing kids in the gifted classes. First, students cannot be removed from the program only for falling behind in class—something else has to be going on for a kid to get kicked out. Second, if a child is moved into regular classes for the rest of a year, they are automatically allowed back into the gifted program at the beginning of the next year—without any retesting.

The Palmetto State isn't the only one that believes it is taboo to expect gifted kids to prove their merit. In Florida, a 2007 bill to reform state gifted education couldn't make it out of committee until a provision demanding retesting every three years was struck from the plan.

Once again, the test authors dispute these practices—rooted in a belief that if you're ever gifted, you're gifted for life. Explains CogAT co-author Dr. Lohman, "The classic model of giftedness—that it is something fixed—is something we've been trying to get over for some time, without much success."

Of all the districts we surveyed, none flouted the science like New York City. A single test prior to kindergarten determines entrance. Meanwhile, those who are admitted are never retested—children stay through fifth or eighth grade, depending on the school. As of 2008, the New York Department of Education had changed the tests it uses four times in four years, unable to get the results it wanted.

In 2007, a Chancellor's report noted that too few kids qualified at the 90th percentile cutoff, so the classes were filled with regular students—42% of the places for gifted kids were filled by children who tested under the *80th* percentile. Many complained the program had been watered down. Meanwhile, the district's web site warned older applicants that they would be put on wait lists in case spots became available—which the district warned would be very rare—even in fourth and fifth grade.

Private independent schools don't really have another option—almost by definition, they have to screen kids before kindergarten. But it should be recognized how fallible the screening process is—how many great kids it misses. Admission directors might already warn parents, "The admission process is more of an art than a science," but the science argues it's not 60% art, it's 60% random.

In some cities, elite feeder preschools are now using intelligence testing too. And they're not ashamed of it either: in the Seattle region, one preschool's web site boasts of being the only preschool in the state that requires IQ testing for admittance—some kids are tested at 27 months. In Detroit, one preschool waits until the kids are all of 30 months.

※

Hearing the poor accuracy of intelligence tests, it's tempting to find some other method of testing for giftedness—say, looking at a child's emotional intelligence or behavior. Dozens of web sites ask, "Is Your Child Gifted?" and then offer a checklist of behaviors to look for. And this isn't just for parents—we found schools that had adopted these checklists as part of their screening process. But are these behavioral guidelines any more valid?

Since the 1995 publication of Dr. Daniel Goleman's *Emotional Intelligence*, there has been widespread acceptance of the theory that temperament and interpersonal skills might be more important to success than cognitive intellect. In the ten-year anniversary edition of his book, Goleman praised the school districts that now mandate emotional intelligence materials be included in their curricula, and he suggested that for some students, emotional intelligence might be the linchpin to their academic success. Still other schools have incorporated the premise into their admission processes. It's increasingly popular for private schools to send preschoolers into staged play groups—administrators use checklists to quickly assess children's behavior, motivation, and personality.

So could the emotional side of children explain what IQ tests are missing?

In the last decade, several leading approaches to measuring emotional intelligence have emerged. One test, the MSCEIT, comes from the team that originally coined the term "emotional intelligence"—including Dr. Peter Salovey, Dean of Yale College. The other test, the EQ-i, comes from Dr. Reuven Bar-On, who coined the term "Emotional Quotient." Researchers around the world have been using these scales, and the results have been a shock.

In a meta-analysis of these studies, scholars concluded that the correlation between emotional intelligence and academic achievement was only 10 percent. Those studies were all done on adolescents and college students—not on kids—but one study of a prison population showed that inmates have high EQ. So much for the theory that emotionally intelligent people make better life choices.

Salovey has repeatedly slammed Goleman for misrepresenting his team's research and overstating its impact. He considers Goleman's optimistic promises not just "unrealistic" but "misleading and unsupported by the research."

In one test of emotional knowledge, kids are asked what someone would feel if his best friend moved away. The more verbal a child is, the more she's able to score high on these tests—but verbal ability is also what drives early cognitive intelligence. (In a later chapter, we'll talk about what drives that early language development.) So rather than triumphantly arguing that emotional intelligence supplants cognitive ability, one influential scholar is proving it's the other way around: higher cognitive ability increases emotional functioning.

There's also research into how children's personalities correlate with academic success. But the problem is that, at every age, different personality traits seem to matter. One study determined that in kindergarten, the extraverts are the good students, but by second or third grade, extraversion is only half as important, while other scholars found that by sixth grade, extraversion is no longer an asset. Instead, it has an increasingly negative impact. By eighth grade, the best students are conscientious and often introverted.

In 2007, Dr. Greg Duncan published a massive analysis of 34,000 children, with no less than eleven other prominent co-authors. They combed through the data from six long-term population studies—four of which were from the United States, one from Canada, and one from the United Kingdom. Prior to kindergarten, the children participating all took some variety of intelligence test or achievement test. As well, mothers and teachers rated their social skills, attention skills, and behaviors—sometimes during preschool, sometimes in kindergarten. The scholars sought out data on every aspect of temperament and behavior we recognize can affect performance in school—acting out, anxiety, aggression, lack of interpersonal skills, hyperactivity, lack of focus, et cetera.

Duncan's team had expected social skills to be a strong predictor of academic success, but, Duncan recalled, "It took us three years to do this analysis, as the pattern slowly emerged." On the whole the IQ tests showed the degree of correlations as in Suen's meta-analysis: combining math and reading together, early IQ had at best a 40% correlation with later achievement. The attention ratings, at best, showed a 20% correlation with later achievement, while the behavior ratings topped out at an 8% correlation. What this means is that

The Search for Intelligent Life in Kindergarten

many kids who turned out to be very good students were still fidgety and misbehaving at age five, while many of the kids who were well-behaved at age five didn't turn into such good students. That social skills were such poor predictors was completely unexpected: "That is what surprised me the most," confirmed Duncan.

It's tempting to imagine one could start with the 40% correlation of IQ tests, add the 20% correlation of attention skill ratings, and top it off with a social skills measure to jack the total up to a 70% correlation. But that's not how it works. The various measures end up identifying the same well-behaved, precocious children, missing the children who blossom a year or two later. For instance, motivation correlates with academic success almost as well as intelligence does. But it turns out that kids with higher IQs are more motivated, academically, so every analysis that controls for IQ shows that motivation can add only a few percentage points to the overall accuracy.

Almost every scholar has their own pet concoction of tests, like bartenders at a mixology competition. At best, these hybrids seem to be maxing out at around a 50% correlation when applied to young children.

In a later chapter of this book, we'll discuss measures that get at the skill of concentrating amid distraction—how this may be the elusive additive factor scientists are looking for. And it could be that in a few years, a scholar will emerge with a hybrid test of IQ and impulsivity that will predict a five-year-old's future performance. Until then, it needs to be recognized that no current test or teacher ratings system, whether used alone or in combination on such young kids, meets a reasonable standard of confidence to justify a long-term decision. Huge numbers of great kids simply can't be "discovered" so young.

※

With IQ test authors warning that kids' intelligence scores aren't really reliable until a child is around 11 or 12, that raises a fascinating question. What's going on in the brain that makes one person more intelligent than another? And are those mechanisms substantially in place at a young age—or do they come later?

Back in the 1990s, scientists were seeing a correlation between intelligence and the thickness of the cerebral cortex—the craterlike structure enveloping the interior of the brain. In every cubic millimeter of an adult brain, there's an estimated 35 to 70 million neurons, and as many as 500 billion synapses. If the nerve fibers in a single cubic millimeter were stretched end to end, they would run for 20 miles. So even a slightly thicker cortex meant trillions more synapses and many additional miles of nerve fibers. Thicker was better.

In addition, the average child's cortex peaked in thickness before the age of seven; the raw material of intelligence appeared to be already in place. (The entire brain at that age is over 95% of its final size.) On that basis, it could seem reasonable to make key decisions about a child's future at that stage of development.

But this basic formula, thicker is better, was exploded by Drs. Jay Giedd and Philip Shaw of the National Institutes of Health in 2006. The average smart kid does have a bit thicker cortex at that age than the ordinary child; however, the very smartest kids, who proved to have superior intelligence, actually had much thinner cortices early on. From the age of 5 to 11 they added another half-millimeter of gray matter, and their cortices did not peak in thickness until the age of 11 or 12, about four years later than normal kids.

"If you get whisked off to a gifted class at an early age, that might not be the right thing," Giedd commented. "It's missing the late developers."

Within the brain, neurons compete. Unused neurons are eliminated; the winners survive, and if used often, eventually get insulated with a layer of white fatty tissue, which exponentially increases the speed of transmission. In this way, gray matter gets upgraded to white matter. This doesn't happen throughout the brain all at once; rather, some parts of the brain can still be adding gray matter while other regions are already converting it to white matter. However, when it occurs, this upgrade can be rapid—in some areas, 50% of nerve tissue gets converted in a single year.

The result can be leaps in intellectual progress, much like a dramatic growth spurt in height. During middle childhood, faster upgrading of left hemisphere regions leads to larger gains in verbal knowledge. The area of the prefrontal cortex considered necessary for high-level reasoning doesn't even begin upgrading until preadolescence—it's one of the last to mature.

In those same years, the brain is also increasing the organization of the large nerve capsules that connect one lobe to another. Within those cerebral superhighways, nerves that run parallel are selected over ones that connect at an angle. Slight alterations here have whopping effects—a 10% improvement in organization is the difference between an IQ below 80 and an IQ above 130. Such 10% gains in organization aren't rare; on the contrary, that's normal development from age 5 to 18.

With all this construction going on, it's not surprising that IQ scores show some variability in the early years. From age 3 to age 10, two-thirds of children's IQ scores will improve, or drop, more than 15 points. This is especially true among bright kids—their intelligence is more variable than among slower children.

Dr. Richard Haier is an eminent neurologist at University of California, Irvine. When I told him that New York City was selecting gifted students on the basis of a one-hour exam at age five, he was shocked.

"I thought school districts ended that practice decades ago," Haier said. "When five-year-olds are tested, it's not clear to me that having a single snapshot in the developmental sequence is going to be that good, because not every individual progresses through development at the same rate. What about the kid who doesn't progress until after age five?"

Haier's specialty is identifying the location of intelligence in the brain. Neuroscience has always been obsessed with isolating the functions of different brain regions. Early findings came from patients with damage to discrete regions; from what they could not do, we learned where visual processing occurs, and where motor skills are stored, and where language is comprehended.

In the last decade, brain-scanning technology enabled us to decipher far more—we know what lights up when danger is imminent, and where religious sense is experienced, and where in the brain lie the powerful cravings of romantic love.

But the search for intelligence in the brain lagged. At last, neuroscientists like Haier are on the verge of identifying the precise clusters of gray matter that are used for intelligence in most adults. But during their hunt, they collectively discovered something that has made them rethink the long-held assumption that ties brain location to brain function.

As a child ages, the location of intellectual processing shifts. The neural network a young child relies on is not the same network he will rely on as an adolescent or adult. There is significant overlap, but the differences are striking. A child's ultimate intellectual success will be greatly affected by the degree to which his brain learns to shift processing to these more efficient networks.

Dr. Bradley Schlaggar, a neurologist at Washington University in St. Louis, has found that both adults and children called upon 40 distinct clusters of their gray matter when subjects performed a simple verbal test inside an fMRI scanner. However, comparing the scans of the children (age 9) to adults (age 25), Schlaggar saw that only half of those clusters were the same. The adults were utilizing their brains quite differently.

Similarly, Dr. Kun Ho Lee of Seoul National University gave IQ puzzles to two groups of Korean high schoolers inside a scanner. The brains of the smart teens had shifted processing to a network recruiting the parietal lobe; they tested in the top one percent. The brains of the normal teens had not made this shift.

Other scholars are finding this as well. Teams at Cornell, Stanford, and King's College, London, have all found that children's cognitive networks aren't the same as adults'.

"This is so contradictory to the old principles of neuroscience," remarked a gleeful Haier. "The research is going in a new direction, that intelligence moves throughout the brain as different brain areas come online."

From the unfinished cortex to the shift in neural networks, none of the critical mechanisms of intelligence are yet operational at the age most children are taking a test for entry into a gifted program or a private K through 8 school. We are making long-term structural decisions over kids' lives at a point when their brains haven't even begun the radical transformations that will determine their true intelligence.

※

Real intellectual development doesn't fit into nicely rounded bell curves. It's filled with sharp spikes in growth and rough setbacks that have to be overcome.

We need to question why this idea of picking the smart children early even appeals to us. We set this system up to make sure natural talent is discovered and nurtured. Instead, the system is failing a majority of the kids, and a lot of natural talent is being screened out.

It may sound trite to ask, "What about the late bloomers?" But in terms of truly superior cognitive development, the neuroscience suggests that "later" may be the optimal rate of development. And it's not as if society needs to wait forever for these later developers to bloom; the system of screening children would be significantly more effective if we simply waited until the end of second grade to test them.

It's common for gifted children to make uneven progress. (It's not unheard of for a gifted child's scores across verbal and nonverbal skills to be so disparate that one half of a test result could qualify for an advanced program while the other half could send the kid to special ed.)

The way most programs are currently designed, admissions officers never consider that uneven development may actually be an asset. The young child who masters cognitive skills but struggles in phonics might later approach the abstract language of poetry in a profoundly new way. A four-year-old's single-minded fascination with dinosaurs to the exclusion of anything else might not mark a deficit; instead, it might allow him to develop focus and an approach to learning that will serve him well in any other context.

Think of the little girl kept out of a gifted program—despite the fact that she'd been reading since she was two—because she wasn't manually coordinated enough to put four blocks in a perfect row.

In the meantime, the late-blooming child lives with the mistaken fact that she is not gifted—but she's bright enough to understand that the Powers That Be have decreed that it would be a waste of time and resources to develop her potential. The gifted rolls have already been filled.

SIX

The Sibling Effect

Freud was wrong. Shakespeare was right. Why siblings really fight.

In Brazil recently, a team of scholars studied the medical data from an emergency room, looking at all the cases where children had been rushed in after swallowing coins. The scholars were curious—was swallowing coins more common for children who didn't have any brothers or sisters? In the end, they decided their sample size was too small to draw any conclusion.

This was far from the first time scholars had tried to find strange side effects of being an only child. In Italy, a couple years ago, researchers tried to determine if female onlies were more likely to have an eating disorder in high school. (They weren't.) In Israel, one scholar noted that onlies had higher incidence of asthma—at least compared to children who had 15 to 20 siblings. But compared to children with a normal number of siblings, there was barely any difference in the rate of asthma. Parents of onlies could stop worrying.

Meanwhile, over in the United Kingdom, researchers were studying whether onlies get fewer warts. Not that you need to know the answer, but what the heck—onlies do have somewhat fewer warts at age 11. However, Scottish researchers have informed us that onlies get more eczema.

It seems that research on onlies has gone batty. It's no surprise why. In the last two decades, the proportion of women having only one child has about doubled in the United States, and single-child families are now more common than two-child families.

Nobody knows what this means for the children, but it seems reasonable that it must mean *something*. We have this idea because we've always stigmatized the exception, and onlies are a good example of that: way back in 1898, one of the pioneers of child psychology, G. Stanley Hall, wrote that "being an only child is a disease in itself." Many scholars today cringe at this ridiculous statement, but the studies on warts and coin swallowing suggest some are still under the influence of Hall's point of view.

Scientists have uncovered some things about onlies—where onlies measure out slightly differently than those with brothers and sisters. But these are not surprising discoveries. We know that onlies do a little bit better in school, on average—probably for the same reasons that oldest siblings do a tiny bit better than younger siblings. From a study in Australia we know that girl onlies average fifteen fewer minutes of physical activity per day, which probably explains the study in Germany that said preschool-aged onlies have slightly worse physical dexterity.

But that's not what society worries about, when it comes to onlies. What we wonder is: "Do they know how to get along?" Nowhere is this question getting more scrutiny than in China, which has limited families in urban areas to one child since 1979. (Despite this policy, 42.7% of families in China today have two or more children.) When the policy was first implemented, critics argued that a country of onlies would destroy the character of the entire nation. Despite three decades of intense study on this question, the research in China is still very mixed. One report said onlies in middle school were *less* anxious and had *better* social skills. But another report stated that in high school it was just the opposite. The research on social skills is just as conclusive in China as the coin-swallowing research in Brazil.

Why are we seeing no clear effect? It's surprising, because the *theory* that being an only child deprives a child of social skills makes so much logical sense. By growing up with siblings, a child has thousands upon thousands of interactions to learn how to get along. According to this theory, children with siblings should be massively more skilled at getting along than children with no siblings.

Yet they aren't.

Maybe the mistake here was assuming that those thousands upon thousands of interactions with siblings amount to a single positive. Perhaps the opposite is true—that children learn poor social skills from those interactions, just as often as they learn good ones.

Dr. Laurie Kramer, Associate Dean at the University of Illinois at Urbana-Champaign, is attempting to do the impossible: get brothers and sisters to be nicer to each other.

It was clear what she's up against, after just a few minutes with parents who have enrolled their children in Kramer's six-week program, "More Fun with Sisters and Brothers." We were sitting on a circle of couches in a small room, watching their children on a closed-circuit television. On the other side of the wall, in a living room wired with seven hidden cameras, the children were working with Kramer's undergraduate students.

"When they get going, it's a like a freight train. It's paralyzing," remarked one mother about the fighting between her five-year-old daughter and six-year-old son. In her professional life, she's a clinical psychiatrist working with wounded veterans. But it's seeing her kids battling that she described as "painful to watch."

Another mother sighed in frustration as we watched her seven-year-old son constantly taunt his four-year-old sister. "He knows what to say, but he just can't be nice about it." She stared into space for a moment, fighting a tear.

A mother of five-year-old twin girls felt that her kids are usually great together—but for some inexplicable reason, they can't get through cooking dinner without a nightly argument.

The families in Kramer's program are well-educated and well-off. Many of the parents are Illinois faculty, and their children attend one of the best private elementary schools in Urbana. These parents have done everything to provide their children with a positive environment. But there's one wild card in the environment that they can't control, undermining everything—how well the siblings get along.

Mary Lynn Fletcher is the program coordinator for Dr. Kramer; she's on the receiving end of the phone calls from parents who want to get their kids in the program. "Many are shaking when they call. My heart goes out to them," Fletcher said. "They are so stressed. Others, the stress isn't so bad, but they are feeling so helpless. Every day, there's a moment they have to deal with. One parent was driving her kids home from school, and she said, 'Listen to this,' then held the cell phone up to the back seat so I could hear the yelling."

It might sound like these children were the problem cases, but Ashley and I had reviewed videotapes of the children made a month earlier, in their homes. Each tape recorded a half-hour stretch of the sibling pairs playing beside each other with their toys, without any parents in the room to mediate. On these videotapes, there was definitely some tension, but what we saw looked better than normal.

Observational studies have determined that siblings between the ages of three and seven clash 3.5 times per hour, on average. Some of those are brief clashes, others longer, but it adds up to ten minutes of every hour spent arguing. According to Dr. Hildy Ross, at the University of Waterloo, only about one out of every eight conflicts ends in compromise or reconciliation—the other seven times, the siblings merely withdraw, usually after the older child has bullied or intimidated the younger.

Dr. Ganie DeHart, at State University of New York College at Geneseo, compared how four-year-old children treat their younger siblings versus their best friends. In her sample, the kids made seven times as many negative and controlling statements to their siblings as they did to friends.

Scottish researcher Dr. Samantha Punch found similar results in her interviews of ninety children. She determined that kids don't have an incentive to act nicely to their siblings, compared to friends, because the siblings will be there tomorrow, no matter what. She concluded, "Sibship is a relationship in which the boundaries of social interaction can be pushed to the limit. Rage and irritation need not be suppressed, whilst politeness and toleration can be neglected."

So do they grow out of it, by having thousands of interactions of practice? Not really, according to Kramer. Back in 1990, she and her mentor, Dr. John Gottman, recruited thirty families who were on the verge of having a second child; their first child was three or four years old. Twice a week, for months, Kramer went into their homes to observe these siblings at play until the youngest were six months old. She was back again at fourteen months, then four years. Each time, Kramer scored the sibling relationship quality, by coding how often the kids were nice or mean to each other. Nine years later, Kramer tracked these families down again. By then, the older siblings were on the verge of college. Again, she videotaped them together. To make sure they didn't ignore each other, she gave the sibling pairs some tasks—solve some puzzles together, and plan an imaginary $10,000 weekend for their family.

Kramer learned that sibling relationship quality is remarkably stable over the long term. Unless there had been some major life event in the family—an illness, a death, a divorce—the character of the relationship didn't change until the eldest moved out of the house. For the most part, the tone established when they were very young, be it controlling and bossy or sweet and considerate, tended to stay that way.

"About half of these families are still in the Urbana-Champaign area," said Kramer. "They're now into their twenties. I see their graduation and wedding announcements in the paper. I bump into their parents at the grocery store. I ask how they're getting along. It's really more of the same."

※

Kramer often hears, "But I fought with my brothers and sisters all the time, and we turned out great." She doesn't disagree. Instead, she points out that in many sibling relationships, the rate of conflict can be high, but the fun times in the backyard and in the basement more than balance it out. This net-positive is what predicts a good relationship later in life. In contrast, siblings who simply ignored each other had less fighting, but their relationship stayed cold and distant long term.

Before she began "More Fun with Sisters and Brothers," Kramer had parents fill out questionnaires about their expectations for their children's sibling interactions. The parents actually accepted conflict as a way of life for siblings; instead, what really troubled them was that their children so often just didn't seem to *care* about each other. Their feeling toward their brother or sister was somewhere between blasé ambivalence and annoyance.

So Kramer's program is unique in the field—she doesn't attempt to teach children some kinder version of conflict mediation. Grown-ups have a hard enough time mastering those techniques—attentive listening, de-escalation, avoiding negative generalizations, offering compliments. Instead, the thrust of Kramer's program is made in its title—getting siblings to *enjoy* playing together. The six hour-long sessions are meant to be a fun camp for siblings to attend. Most activities that kids have scheduled into their lives are age-segregated—siblings go off with children their own size. Here, they stick together.

In the first session, four papier-mâché hand puppets appear on a puppet stage. They announce they're alien children from the planet Xandia. The clouds on Xandia produce rain whenever brothers and sisters argue, and the planet is at risk of flooding. The aliens have come to Earth to attend the camp with the human children, in order to learn how to have more fun together. All the children—alien and earthling—spend the next six sessions playing board games, creating art projects, role playing, and dancing to a custom-made rap song. They take home bedtime books and a board game set on Xandia.

Along the way, the children adopt a terminology for how to initiate play with their siblings, how to find activities they both like to do together, and how to gently decline when they're not interested. They consciously role play these steps. What these steps are called (Stop, Think, and Talk) probably isn't important; what's crucial is the kids are given a way to bridge the age-divide, so the older child doesn't always end up in a bossy role. During one of the sessions, the children are visited by an annoying woman in trench coat named Miss Busy Bossy—she's a clownlike caricature of a boss, too busy to even put down her cell phone. The children teach her to be less bossy.

Many of the games and art projects teach the kids to recognize the feelings being broadcast in the faces of their siblings. The catchphrase they're taught is, "See it your way, see it my way." They draw these facial expressions on paper plate masks, then listen to stories and hold up the masks that correspond to how each child in the story would be feeling.

Kramer has fine-tuned her scripts for the sessions over the years, but probably the most innovative aspect of her program isn't in those details—it's that she focuses on the children at all. Other scholars assumed that four-year-olds were too young, so they directed their training at parents, trying to coach them how to respond to sibling fights. In Kramer's program, fewer fights are the *consequence* of teaching the children the proactive skills of initiating play on terms they can both enjoy. It's conflict *prevention*, not conflict *resolution*. Parents are mere facilitators; when back at home, their job is to reinforce the rule that the kids should use their steps together to work it out, *without* the parents' help.

Kramer's program is effective, by every measure. The before-and-after videotapes of the kids playing at home reveal more positive, mutual involvement, and the parent questionnaires indicate the parents spend less time breaking up arguments between the kids. The children seem to enjoy the camp, but an hour never goes by without at least one classic display of sibling tension, as the older child turns controlling, or the younger plays the provocateur. In fact, the entire premise of the camp—the idea that brothers and sisters should *enjoy* one another—is an objective not all kids are ready to accept.

"I have two special talents," seven-year-old Ethan announced to the instructors and the children in the program. "The first is soccer with my dad. The second is I'm really good at beating people up. When I beat my sister up, it makes me feel good."

His four-year-old sister, Sofia, sat not more than two feet away from him as he said this. But she didn't react to his shocking claim.

The truth was that Ethan had never actually hit his sister, who was half his size. Instead, he often fretted that she was so tiny that he might accidentally hurt her. But that session, Ethan seemed to delight in being verbally cruel to Sofia. He mocked her—loudly protesting when an instructor helped her read aloud. He said he didn't want a younger sister: "She wants to play princess, and she always wants me to be the prince, but I want to play ninja. Right now, she's really annoying, and not a worthy opponent."

At the end of the session, Ethan's mother confronted him in the hallway, demanding an explanation. Ethan made a particularly insightful point: "But Mom, it's not *cool* to like a little sister."

Ethan was convinced he had to *act* mean toward Sofia. He couldn't let the other older siblings in the program know that he liked his sister—thus the false brag about beating her up.

Curious about how Ethan and Sofia really got along, we sat down with Kramer to watch the videotape of them at home. Over the half-hour, Ethan led Sofia in the construction of a fort made of couch cushions. The tension was excruciating; it felt like a scene out of film noir—a banal little event that could explode into tragedy at any moment.

Designating himself construction manager, Ethan bossed the four-year-old around constantly. He yelled and chided her when she couldn't hold a cushion perfectly straight. When she wanted to leave for a snack, Ethan threatened, "If you do one more thing—you'll lose your job and you can't come back." When Sofia misunderstood something, the seven-year-old snapped, "No excuses! There are no excuses! You can only keep your job if you promise never, ever to make up an excuse ever again. And don't talk with your mouth full!"

However, Kramer actually saw a lot of hope in the tape. Without question, Ethan berated his sister—but the two kids had chosen, on their own, to play together, and they remained engaged in joint play the entire time. They didn't hit each other. They kept talking. Ethan threatened his sister, but he changed the rules so she could keep playing. He made an effort to help Sofia understand she had an important role in the game. When he stopped ordering her around, Sofia would ask him for guidance—which he delighted in. When Sofia tried to drag a big cushion to the fort, Ethan said, "Good job," then came over to help her.

"The kids are still connected," Kramer ultimately concluded. "There's an attempt to manage conflict. The kids like each other—they are looking out for each other. I think there's a lot to work with." She had not yet scored this tape, but at a glance she estimated it would rate a 50 out of 100—an equal balance of negative and positive moments. "I would imagine, in their tape after the program, they'll be around a 70."

So if Ethan actually liked his sister, where was he getting the message that it was uncool and he had to hide it? Ethan's mother, Rebecca, pointed out that Ethan's best friends all were nice to their little brothers and sisters. It wasn't coming from them. She believed Ethan was picking up the message from the books he was reading. He was an exceedingly gifted reader and consumed books constantly.

Rebecca was reticent to mention her theory, afraid it might come off that she was looking for a scapegoat. However, Kramer's research suggests that Rebecca may be right on target. In one of her studies, Kramer had a control group of kids come in for six weeks of reading books aloud and discussing cartoons that depicted sibling story lines. These were typical products any parent might share with his kids, hoping they would help the kids get along better—the Berenstain Bears series, *Sesame Street* books, and the like. Kramer figured these kids' relationships with their siblings would improve, but she crossed her fingers that they wouldn't improve *more* than the kids in *her* program.

But Kramer started getting complaints from parents after just a couple weeks. While the books and videos always ended on a happy note, with siblings learning to value and appreciate each other, the first half of the stories portrayed in vivid detail ways that children can fight, insult, and devalue their siblings. "From these books, the kids were learning novel ways to be mean to their younger siblings they'd never considered," Kramer recalled. Sure enough, after six weeks, the sibling relationship quality had plummeted.

Kramer went on to analyze 261 common children's books that portray sibling relationships. These ranged from picture books for preschoolers to chapter books for third graders. Kramer scored the books as she might score a videotape of kids playing together. She noted the number of times a sibling argued, threatened, excluded, and teased, as well as the positive moments of sharing, affection, problem-solving, and inclusion. The average book demonstrated virtually as many negative behaviors as positive ones. Despite all but one being overtly crafted to have a happy ending, along the way kids were constantly taunting each other, belittling a sib, and blaming others for their wrongdoing.

It turns out that Shakespeare was right, and Freud was wrong. For almost a century, Freud's argument—that from birth, siblings were locked in an eternal struggle for their parents' affection—held huge influence over scholars and parents alike. But Freud's theory turns out to be incomplete. Sibling rivalry may be less an Oedipal tale of parental love, and more King Lear.

A team of leading British and American scholars asked 108 sibling pairs in Colorado exactly what they fought about. Parental affection was ranked dead last. Just 9% of the kids said it was to blame for the arguments or competition.

The most common reason the kids were fighting was the same one that was the ruin of Regan and Goneril: sharing the castle's toys. Almost 80% of the older children, and 75% of the younger kids, all said sharing physical possessions—or claiming them as their own—caused the most fights.

Nothing else came close. Although 39% of the younger kids did complain that their fights were about...fights. They claimed, basically, that they started fights to stop their older siblings from hitting them.

Mindful of the Freudian paradigm, the scholars tempered their findings, wondering if the children were too young to understand the depths of the family psychodrama they were starring in. But these brothers and sisters weren't toddlers. The younger kids were in elementary school, and some of the older kids were already teenagers. The scholars felt that the psychological community needed to recognize that "siblings have their own repertoire of conflict issues separate from their parents." The struggle to win a greater share of parental love may be a factor, they wrote, but kids in mid-childhood don't think about it, recognize it, or articulate it.

Laurie Kramer also came to this same conclusion. She reviewed 47 popular parenting manuals, analyzing how much of their advice regarding sibling relationships was rooted in empirical research, versus how much was just unproven theory. Kramer found that every single parenting manual recited the psychodynamic paradigm, that sibling resentment stems from a loss of parental attention when the younger child is born. Kramer noted that there's certainly research making this point. For instance, one recent study showed that an older sibling's jealousy when the younger is 16 months old predicts what kind of relationship they'll have a couple years later. But Kramer feels this fixation on competition for parental love masks and distracts from a more important truth: even in families where children are given plenty of affection by both parents, "young children may fail to develop prosocial relationships with their siblings if nobody teaches them how." Less emphasis needs to be placed on the psychology, and more needs to be on skill-building.

What else is overrated? Parents imagine that the difference in age between siblings is an important factor. Some think it's preferable to have kids less than two years apart, so they are close enough in age to play together; others feel they should wait three or four years, to help each child develop independence. But the research is entirely mixed—for every study that concludes age differences matter, there's another study proving it doesn't. "Relative to other factors," said Kramer, "age spacing is not as strong a predictor. Nor is gender. There's many other things to be concerned about."

As for what does matter, Kramer's work offers one big surprise.

One of the best predictors of how well two siblings get along is determined *before* the birth of the younger child. At first glance, this is astounding—how can it be possible to predict a clash of personalities, if one of the personalities at issue doesn't even exist yet? How can their future relationship be knowable? But the explanation is quite reasonable. It has nothing to do with the parents. Instead, the predictive factor is the quality of the older child's relationship *with his best friend*.

Kramer studied young kids from families who were expecting another child. She observed these kids playing one-on-one with their best friends. The kids who could play in a reciprocal, mutual style with their best friend were the ones who had good rapport with their younger sibling, years later.

It's long been assumed that siblings learn on one another, and then apply the social skills they acquire to their relationships with peers outside the family. Kramer says it's the other way around: older siblings train on their friends, and then apply what they know to their little brothers and sisters.

After monitoring these relationships with best friends, Kramer saw that one factor stood out as especially telling: shared fantasy play. As Kramer and John Gottman explained, "Fantasy play represents one of the highest levels of social involvement for young children." In order for joint fantasy play to work, children must emotionally commit to one another, and pay attention to what the other is doing. They have to articulate what's in their mind's eye—and negotiate some scenario that allows both their visions to come alive. When one kid just announced the beginning of a ninja battle, but the other wants to be a cowboy, they have to figure out how to still ride off into the sunset together.

If, however, the child hasn't developed these good habits on friends, and the younger sibling comes along, now there's very little incentive to learn the skills of shared play (choosing an activity both can enjoy, inviting the other and/or asking to be included, recognizing when someone is busy or wants to play alone). The incentive's not there because, as Samantha Punch pointed out, the sibling will be there tomorrow no matter what. Siblings are prisoners, genetically sentenced to live together, with no time off for good behavior. There is simply no motivation to change.

Kramer also considered children's behavior in day care and preschools. The fact that kids could cooperate in class or remain engaged in a group setting didn't predict improved sibling relationships. It was that real connection between friends—that made a child care how his behavior impacted someone he liked—that was the catalyst for the difference.

"A parent is going to work hard to meet his child's needs. They are highly motivated by love," Kramer explained. "Other kids don't care if you're hungry or have a bruise on your knee—they have one, too."

In other words, getting what you need from a parent is easy. It's getting what you want from friends that forces a child to develop skills.

"It's not that parents are unimportant," Kramer has concluded. "But they are important in very different ways."

Which is why, in a sense, what Kramer is really trying to do is transform children's relationships from sibship to something more akin to a real friendship. If kids enjoy one another's presence, then quarreling comes at a new cost. The penalty for fighting is no longer just a time-out, but the loss of a worthy opponent.

SEVEN

The Science of Teen Rebellion

Why, for adolescents, arguing with adults is a sign of respect, not disrespect—and arguing is constructive to the relationship, not destructive.

Jasmine is an eighteen-year-old high school senior in Miami-Dade County, Florida. She's a natural beauty with long dark tresses and ebony eyes. Though she was raised and lives in Opa-Locka, an area known for its poverty and gangs, she attends a competitive private school across town. ("There's a lot of rich white kids who go there.") Despite a demanding courseload of honors and college prep classes, Jasmine maintains a solid 3.6 GPA and was selected for a prestigious program for children of Latin American immigrants—kids who will be the first in their families to attend college.

The youngest daughter of two in a staunchly Catholic family, Jasmine sings in her church's choir. She is often at the front of the church saying the weekly readings. Inspired by her part-time job at a local hospital, Jasmine intends to study harder this year and attend the University of Florida; she aims to become a doctor.

"I think my parents are proud of me because they know about some of the struggles I have had to go through—but I've always been very motivated," she says.

Or perhaps, if they knew the rest of Jasmine's extracurriculars, her parents might never speak to her again.

Long ago, she figured out that her parents keyed off her level of interest in a boy. When it was obvious she thought a guy was cute, they never let her be alone with him. She was allowed to go only on group outings, and dates were always chaperoned. So now she always insists that she isn't interested in a guy—they are "just friends"—then her parents will let them go out alone. She can go over to the guy's house to hang out unsupervised and have sex—sometimes planned, sometimes just a happy accident.

By the time Jasmine was fourteen, she was sneaking out of her first-floor window once a week, in the middle of the night. She was going to parties with local gangbangers—drinking enough alcohol that she was blacking out. Entire nights are gone from memory. "I'm a competitive drinker," she giggled like the schoolgirl she was. "If someone's drinking, I can drink more than them."

Still fourteen, she began dating an eighteen-year-old. Her parents knew about the guy—whom they hated and wouldn't let in the house—but Jasmine snuck out late at night to see him. They'd been having sex since their first month together. Her boyfriend secretly paid for her prescription for birth control and tried to convince Jasmine to run away with him. That had been going on for months before her mother, while putting away laundry, accidentally found the pills hidden in Jasmine's dresser.

"She went crazy," Jasmine says. "She was so upset she couldn't even talk to me. So she had my aunt come in to find out what was going on." Jasmine immediately lied that the doctor had given her the pills to regulate her hormones—and after a while, her family was convinced. As far as her family knows, she is still a virgin.

Jasmine started meeting guys in an internet chat room. They were always a few years older. One—who was at least in his twenties—came to the house to take her out. She looked out the window, ready to leave with him, but she decided he was too old for her—so she didn't go out to his car.

In four years, she was caught sneaking out only once: the police spotted her and a friend walking down the street at three a.m., hours past curfew. The police brought her home, and her parents promptly grounded her for two months. Now, at a more mature eighteen, she has cut the sneaking out down to once every other week. "I don't do those as much now…except for the random booty calls and the secret dates."

Twice, an ex-boyfriend had gotten her drunk, then forced himself on her. She sort of concedes that she'd been date-raped—but then she insists both incidents were her fault. "I drank an entire waterbottle full of vodka, and I knew if I got drunk it might happen. I was stupid. It happened 'cuz I'm not smart. Thank God I'm not pregnant." She pauses. "I sort of think God must love me, because I'm still alive."

It's not just the dating she lies about. She lies about things she doesn't really need to cover up. The lying is on autopilot. "I lie to my parents every day. I lie about homework every night. I say I finished it when I haven't even started. I finish it—but I do it at school before class. Never when I say it's done."

Jasmine explains, "I just don't want to tell my mom something if it's going to make my life difficult. She lectures me a lot—and I don't want her to stop. If she did, I would think she didn't care. So sometimes, I will tell her the truth—when I feel like being lectured. It just depends on my mood. But I only ever tell the truth when I want to."

If her parents found anything out now, it would be bad but she's less worried about it—now that she's a legal adult, looking forward to voting in her first presidential election. "Maybe I'll tell Mom someday. But not for a really long time. When she sees that I turned out okay, grown-up, so that she doesn't have to worry. After I have my career, and I'm all settled."

Until recently, we didn't really know how often teens lied to parents. The systematic accounting was nonexistent. Most parents have some sense that they're not hearing the whole truth from their teenagers. They fill the information vacuum with equal parts intuition, trust, and fear.

With other uncertainties in life, we have averages to inform a sense of what's normal. When a couple gets married, for instance, they have a 57% chance of seeing their fifteenth wedding anniversary. If you're wondering how long you might live, it's informative to know the life expectancy now averages 78 years. Those taking the New York State bar exam for the first time have an 83% chance of passing, and high school seniors applying to Harvard have a 7% chance of being admitted.

Shouldn't we have the equivalent statistics on how much teens lie to (and hide from) their parents?

Drs. Nancy Darling and Linda Caldwell thought so.

※

Darling and Caldwell both came to Penn State University around the same time, and naturally took an interest in each other's work. Darling was studying adolescent dating, which teens lie to their parents about routinely. Caldwell was researching a new field called "Leisure Studies," which sounded at first to Darling like a trivial topic, but turned out to be the study of what kids do in their free time. One of the operating theories of Leisure Studies is that adolescents turn to drinking and sex partly because they have a lot of unsupervised free time. They're bored and don't know what else to do. "When you're fourteen, everything's more interesting when you're drunk," remarked Darling.

Darling and Caldwell wondered if they could get high schoolers to cooperate in a study where they'd admit to the very things they were hiding from their parents. Darling recognized that if she sat down with a high school sophomore, she would be too imposing an authority figure to get the truth. Even her graduate students were too mature to relate to teens and gain their confidence. So she recruited from her undergraduate classes a special research team, all under age 21—a scholar's Mod Squad.

For the first semester, these eight undergrads met with Darling and were trained in research methods and interview techniques. Then Darling sent them out to the places in State College where teens hang out in public. They handed out flyers at the mall, but they were more successful at night in a little alley off Calder Way, at the back door of the video arcade. They approached teenagers and offered them a gift certificate for a free CD at the local music store in exchange for being in the study. If the teens agreed, the undergrads took down a phone number.

Darling wanted the first recruits to be the cool kids. "The idea was, if we just went to the school and asked for volunteers, we'd get the goody-two-shoes kids. Then the cool kids wouldn't join the study. We'd be oversampling the well-behaved. But if we got the cool kids, the others would follow." The core of recruits attended State College Area High School, which has 2,600 students. "It became quite the trendy thing at the high school, to be in the study," Darling recalled.

The others did follow, and soon Darling had a representative sample that matched up to national averages on a bevy of statistics, from their grades to how often they drank.

Subsequently, two of the Mod Squad researchers met with each high schooler at a place they'd feel comfortable. Often this was the Four Brothers Pizzeria on Beaver Avenue. Having only a four-dollar budget for each restaurant field trip, all they could do was buy the teen fries and a Coke, before presenting him with a deck of 36 cards. Each card in this deck described a topic teens sometimes lie to their parents about. Over the next couple hours, the teen and researchers worked through the deck, discussing which issues the kid and his parents disagreed on, and which rules the kid had broken, and how he'd pulled off the deception, and why. Because of their age similarity to their targets, the researchers never had trouble getting the high-schoolers to confide in them. Despite all the students and all the cards in the deck, only once—to a single card—did a student hold back, saying, "I don't want to talk about that."

The deck handed to the teens triggered recognition of just how pervasive their deception went. "They began the interviews saying that parents give you everything and yes, you should tell them everything," Darling observed. By the end of the interview, the kids saw for the first time how much they were lying and how many of the family's rules they had broken. Darling said, "It was something they realized—and that they didn't like about themselves."

Out of 36 potential topics, the average teen lies to her parents about 12 of them. Teens lie about what they spend their allowance on, and whether they've started dating, and what clothes they put on away from the house. They lie about what movie they went to and who they went with. They lie about alcohol and drug use, and they lie about whether they're hanging out with friends their parents disapprove of. They lie about how they spend their afternoons, if the parent is still at work. They lie whether a chaperone was in attendance at a party, or whether they rode in a car driven by a drunken teen. Even some things around the house they lie about—whether their homework is done, or what music they're listening to.

"Drinking, drug use and their sex lives are the things kids hide the most from their parents," Darling noted. "But it wasn't just the sexual acts they were hiding," she added. "They really objected to the emotional intrusiveness—being asked, 'How serious is this relationship?' and 'Do you love this person?' The kids just don't want to answer those questions."

Only one-quarter of the time do teens concoct an outright lie to pull off their deception. According to Darling's data, these direct lies are used to cover up the worst stuff. Half the time, teens execute their deception by withholding the relevant details that would upset their parent; the parent hears only half the story. And another quarter of the time, the teen manages the deception by never bringing the topic up at all, hoping the parent won't know to ask.

Rare was the kid who was completely honest with parents: 96% of the teens in Darling's study reported lying to their parents.

Being an honors student doesn't change these numbers by much, according to other research. Nor does being a really busy, overscheduled kid. No kid, apparently, is too busy to break a few rules.

"When I began this research, I would have thought the main reason teens would say they lie was, 'I want to stay out of trouble,'" Darling explained. "But actually the most common reason for deception was, 'I'm trying to protect the relationship with my parents; I don't want them to be disappointed in me.'"

Darling also mailed survey questionnaires to the parents, and it was interesting how the two sets of data reflected on each other. First, she was struck by parents' vivid fear of pushing their teens into outright rebellion. "Many parents today believe the best way to get teens to disclose is to be more permissive and not set outright rules," Darling said. Parents imagine a tradeoff between being informed and being strict. Better to hear the truth and be able to help than be kept in the dark.

Darling found that permissive parents don't actually learn more about their child's lives. "Kids who go wild and get in trouble mostly have parents who don't set rules or standards. Their parents are loving and accepting no matter what the kids do. But the kids take the lack of rules as a sign their parents don't actually care—that their parent doesn't really want this job of being the parent."

In cooperation with other scholars, Darling has done versions of her study around the world—in the Philippines, Italy, and Chile. "In Chile, the permissive parent is the norm. And kids lie to their parents there more than anyplace else."

Pushing a teen into rebellion by having too many rules was a sort of statistical myth. "That actually doesn't happen," remarked Darling. She found that most rules-heavy parents don't actually enforce them. "It's too much work," said Darling. "It's a lot harder to enforce three rules than to set twenty rules." These teens avoided rebellious direct conflict and just snuck around behind their parents' backs.

By withholding information about their lives, adolescents carve out a social domain and identity that are theirs alone, independent from their parents or other adult authority figures. According to a recent Harris Poll, 78% of parents were sure their teens could talk to them about anything. However, the teens disagreed.

To seek out a parent for help is, from a teen's perspective, a tacit admission that he's not mature enough to handle it alone. Having to tell parents about it can be psychologically emasculating, whether the confession is forced out of him or he volunteers it on his own. It's essential for some things to be "none of your business."

The big surprise in the research is *when* this need for autonomy is strongest. It's not mild at 12, moderate at 15, and most powerful at 18. Darling's scholarship shows that the objection to parental authority peaks around age 14 to 15. In fact, this resistance is slightly stronger at age 11 than at 18. In popular culture, we think of high school as the risk years, but the psychological forces driving deception surge earlier than that.

A few parents managed to live up to the stereotype of the oppressive parent, with lots of psychological intrusion, but those teens weren't rebelling. They were obedient. And depressed.

"Ironically, the type of parents who are actually most consistent in enforcing rules are the same parents who are most warm and have the most conversations with their kids," Darling observed. They've set a few rules over certain key spheres of influence, and they've explained why the rules are there. They expect the child to obey them. Over life's other spheres, they supported the child's autonomy, allowing her freedom to make her own decisions.

The kids of these parents lied the least. Rather than hiding twelve areas from their parents, they might be hiding as few as five.

※

The Mod Squad study did confirm Linda Caldwell's hypothesis that teens turn to drinking and drugs because they're bored in their free time. After the study's completion, Caldwell wondered if there was a way to help kids fend off boredom. Rather than just badgering kids with the message "Don't Do Drugs," wouldn't it be more effective to teach them how else to really enjoy their free time?

So Caldwell went about designing a program, driven by an ambitious question: "Can you teach a kid how not to be bored?"

Her research has shown that boredom starts to set in around seventh grade, and it increases all through twelfth grade. Intrinsic motivation also drops, gradually but consistently, through those same years. So Caldwell aimed her program at seventh graders in their fall semester.

She got nine middle school districts throughout rural Pennsylvania to sign up; over 600 children participated in the study. Teachers from these schools came to Penn State and received training in how to teach anti-boredom.

The program Caldwell created, TimeWise, did every detail right. Rather than some one-day intervention, this was an actual school class that lasted six weeks. Rather than being lectured to, the students enjoyed a workshop vibe, where they discussed their issues, problem-solved, and coached one another. Rather than merely testing these students after the course, Caldwell continued to test the long-term benefits of TimeWise, measuring the students' boredom levels and use of time for the next three years. Every year, the students went through a booster class, to remind them of the principles and encourage them to reapply the lessons to their changing lives.

The course began with a self-examination module. The students learned the difference between being generally bored, all day long, and being situationally bored, be it when in history class or when sitting on the couch at home, watching reruns. They learned to recognize the difference in their own motivation: "Am I doing this because I actually want to, or because my mom signed me up and I have to, or because I feel pressured by friends to follow along?" They spent the first week filling out time diaries, charting how they spent their time and how engaged they felt doing it all.

The researchers saw that it wasn't just kids with lots of free time who were bored. Even the really busy kids could be bored, for two reasons. First, they were doing a lot of activities only because their parent signed them up—there was no intrinsic motivation. Second, they were so accustomed to their parents filling their free time that they didn't know how to fill it on their own. "The more controlling the parent," Caldwell explained, "the more likely a child is to experience boredom."

The students spent a lot of time learning how to counter peer pressure. They went on to do a module on flow, based on the ideas of psychologist Mihaly Csikszentmihalyi, and did a module on understanding how the element of risk made something exciting or scary. They learned to see themselves as architects of their own experience.

When I first read of Caldwell's TimeWise, I felt jealous—I wished there had been such a program for me in seventh grade. The program was so exciting that it was simultaneously reproduced in South Africa, where children have very little to do, and it's now being reproduced in school districts in Oregon, Utah, and urban Pennsylvania. The California Parks & Recreation Society put TimeWise on the top of its list of role models for leisure education programs.

There's been only one problem. The kids came out of the class charged up, but by the end of spring, they weren't dramatically different from kids who hadn't taken the TimeWise class. "The results dissipated after the initial intervention," Caldwell noted. "You always wish for stronger results. We got some nice results, but they haven't lasted across the four years." It's really been a mystery why this great class didn't have a huge impact.

Note that her results have statistical significance; Caldwell published them in a prestigious journal and has continued to receive grants for TimeWise. But from an ordinary person's perspective, the results lack any "wow" factor. Compared to students not in the class, measurable boredom went down only about 3%. TimeWise students were only meagerly better at avoiding peer pressure, and they didn't join more clubs. Though they played sports a little more and spent more time outdoors, their intrinsic motivation was no better than regular students. These kids weren't drinking alcohol a lot—during ninth grade, they'd drank only a couple times that year, on average—but there was almost no difference on that score between the kids in the TimeWise program and the kids who weren't. The smoking of pot and cigarettes was also almost indistinguishable between the two groups.

For the seventh-graders who started out most bored, "it didn't seem to make a difference," said Caldwell. It turns out that teaching kids not to be bored is really hard—even for the best program in the country.

Why didn't TimeWise have a stronger effect?

Is it possible that teens are just neurologically prone to boredom?

According to the work of neuroscientist Dr. Adriana Galvan at UCLA, there's good reason to think so. Inside our brains is a reward center, involving the nucleus accumbens, which lights up with dopamine whenever we find something exciting or interesting or pleasurable. In a study comparing the brains of teens to the brains of adults and young kids, Galvan found that teen brains can't get pleasure out of doing things that are only mildly or moderately rewarding.

Galvan's experiment was quite ingenuous. She had kids, teens, and adults play a pirate video game while *inside* an fMRI scanner, with their heads restrained. Their arms were free to push buttons. With each successful turn of the game, they won some gold—on the screen flashed either a single gold coin, a small stack of coins, or a jackpot pile of gold.

Young kids find any sort of reward thrilling, so their brains lit up the same amount, no matter how much gold they won. Adult brains lit up according to the size of the reward: single coin, small pleasure response, big pile, big pleasure response. The teen brains did not light up in response to winning the small or medium reward—in fact, the nucleus accumbens activity dipped *below* baseline, as if they were crestfallen. Only to the big pile of gold did their reward center light up—and then it *really* lit up, signaling more activity than kids or adults ever showed.

Galvan noted that the response pattern of teen brains is essentially the same response curve of a seasoned drug addict. Their reward center cannot be stimulated by low doses—they need the big jolt to get pleasure.

But that wasn't all that Galvan saw happening in teen brains. Their prefrontal cortex seemed to be showing a diminished response whenever their reward center was experiencing intense excitement. The prefrontal cortex is responsible for weighing risk and consequences. Explaining this, Galvan said it was as if the pleasure response was "hijacking" the prefrontal cortex. At the very moment when experiencing an emotionally-charged excitement, the teens' brain is handicapped in its ability to gauge risk and foresee consequences.

In abstract situations, teens can evaluate risks just like adults. Given a scenario, they can list the pros and cons, and they can foresee consequences. But in exciting real life circumstances, this rational part of the brain gets overridden by the reward center.

All this fits the pattern we see in the real world, where adolescents seem sluggish in literature class, drink like fish on Saturday nights, and don't seem to realize it's a bad idea to put five friends on a golf cart while driving it down a steep hill with a sharp turn at the bottom.

Not all adolescents are primed like this. Galvan had her subjects fill out questionnaires that assessed how often they participated in certain risky behaviors in their own lives. She also asked them whether certain risk behaviors sounded like fun—getting drunk, shooting fireworks, and vandalizing property—or sounded merely dangerous. How they answered the questionnaires matched their neurological results: those who said risky behavior sounded like fun also had higher spikes in their brain's reward center when they won the pile of gold in the pirate video game.

The neuroscience of risk-taking is a very advanced field, but it doesn't offer many solutions; some teens are wired to take big risks, done deal. The mechanics of this brain wiring include a reduction in the density of dopamine receptors, which makes teens unable to enjoy mild rewards, and a simultaneous spurt in oxytocin receptors, which makes them highly attuned to the opinions of their peers. Surrounded by friends, they'll take stupid chances, just for the thrill.

If there's hope in this science, it comes from the few scholars who recognize that teens are only *sometimes* huge risk takers. In fact, there are all sorts of risks that terrify teens *far more* than adults. The risk of asking a girl to a dance, and getting turned down, has frozen millions of boys every year from taking that chance. Teens are so self-conscious of appearances that they wait until Christmas break to get haircuts. They feel all eyes are upon them when they raise their hand in class. They think it's risky to show up at school wearing a new shirt nobody's seen before. In many cases, the fear of embarrassment turns teens into weenies.

A series of experiments by Dr. Abigail Baird at Vassar captured this dichotomy perfectly. She put teens in an MRI scanner, then asked them to decide if certain concepts were a good idea or a bad idea. The good ideas were pleasantly mundane, such as "eating a salad," or "walking the dog." The bad ideas were grisly:

Bite down on a lightbulb
Swallow a cockroach
Light your hair on fire
Jump off a roof
Swim with sharks

When adults took this test, they answered virtually instantaneously. Their brain scans revealed that adults visualized the concept of biting a lightbulb, and then had an instinctive, physical aversion to that mental image. Areas of the brain that signal distress and danger lit up, automatically.

When teens took the test, they didn't answer differently (they didn't think swallowing a cockroach was a good idea), but it took them longer to answer. Their brain scans revealed no automatic response, nor any distress; instead, they were weighing the decision in the cognitive parts of the brain, with deliberation, as if they were momentarily agonizing over what college to attend. "They were actually *thinking* about it," Baird laughed. "They weren't *feeling* it." They didn't have painful past experiences to draw upon. Swimming with sharks simply didn't scare them.

How many times have parents said to their teens, "Why did you have to try it? Didn't you know it was a bad idea?!" Actually, the teen brain can think abstractly, but not *feel* abstractly—at least not until it's had more life experience to draw on. And *feeling* like it's a bad idea is what it would take to stop oneself from doing it.

But then Baird put some teens through another experiment. The video screen inside the MRI scanner showed a web site that was polling local teens on their opinions and tastes. The subjects created a pseudonymous user name and password to log in. They were told that they were online with other teens in the Upper Valley of New Hampshire. The poll questions were unremarkable—what style of music they liked, whether they thought Paris Hilton was cool, what local stores they shopped at. After each question, one teen's answer (and user name) would randomly display to all.

As they worked through the poll, the teens in Baird's lab did not have their answers displayed to others. In fact, there were no other teens taking the poll—that was just the pretense to scare them. And scare them it did. Just the mere *possibility* of having their preferences displayed to this imaginary audience vibrantly lit up the regions of the brain that signal distress and danger.

That's the teen brain at fifteen in a nutshell—fearless to jumping off roofs, but terrified of having its love of Nickelback exposed. Might there be a way to harness the latter to minimize the former?

※

In the dictionary, the antonym of honesty is lying, and the opposite of arguing is agreement. But in the minds of teenagers, that's not how it works. Really, to an adolescent, arguing is the opposite of lying.

That's cryptic, so let me unpack what I mean.

When Nancy Darling's researchers interviewed the teenagers from State College Area High School, they also asked the teens when and why they told the truth to their parents about things they knew their parents disapproved of. Occasionally teens told the truth because they knew a lie wouldn't fly—they'd be caught. Sometimes they told the truth because they just felt obligated, saying, "They're my parents, I'm supposed to tell them." But the main motivation that emerged was that teens told their parents the truth in hopes their parents might give in, and say it was okay. Usually, this meant an argument ensued, but it was worth it if their parents might budge.

For the average Pennsylvania teen, they told the truth only about four areas of conflict. Meaning (since they lied about twelve areas), they were three times more likely to lie than to attempt a protest.

In the families where there was less deception, there was a much higher ratio of arguing/complaining. Arguing was good—arguing was honesty. The parents didn't necessarily realize this. The arguing stressed them out.

Darling found this same pattern when she compared her results in the United States against companion studies replicated in the Philippines. She fully expected to see less arguing in the average Filipino home than in an American home. In the Philippines, family members are supposed to preserve harmony, not foment conflict; also, young people are not supposed to challenge their parents—because they are taught to believe that they owe parents a debt that can never be repaid. "A good child in the Philippines is supposed to be obedient, so because of that, we didn't think they would argue. We thought they would avoid discussion. But they had the highest rates of conflict. It was completely antithetical to our predictions."

It took further analysis for Darling to understand this counterintuitive result. The Filipino teens were fighting their parents over the rules, but not over the authority of the parents to set rules. While they might have felt the rules were too restrictive, they were far more likely to abide the rules. In American families, the teens didn't bother to argue. Instead, they just pretended to go along with their parents' wishes, but then they did what they wanted to do anyway.

Certain types of fighting, despite the acrimony, are ultimately a sign of respect—not of disrespect.

University of Rochester's Dr. Judith Smetana, a leader in the study of teen disclosure, confirms that, over the long term, "moderate conflict with parents [during adolescence] is associated with better adjustment than either no-conflict or frequent conflict."

Most parents don't make this distinction in how they perceive their arguments with their children. Dr. Tabitha Holmes studied over fifty sets of mothers and their teen daughters. Her sample was drawn from families in a program called Upward Bound, funded by the U.S. Department of Education to give high-schoolers from low income families a chance at attending college. The mothers had aspirations for their daughters and were quite protective of them—often by demanding obedience. Holmes did extensive interviews asking both mother and daughter, separately, to describe their arguments and how they felt about them. And there was a big difference.

Holmes found that 46% of the mothers rated their arguments as being destructive to the relationship. Being challenged was stressful, chaotic, and (in their perception) disrespectful. The more frequently they fought, and the more intense the fights were, the more the mom rated the fighting as harmful. But only 23% of the daughters felt that their arguments were destructive. Far more believed that fighting *strengthened* their relationship with their mother. "Their perception of the fighting was really sophisticated, far more than we anticipated for teenagers," noted Holmes. "They saw fighting as a way to see their parents in a new way, as a result of hearing their mother's point of view be articulated."

What most surprised Holmes was learning that for the teen daughters, fighting more often, or having bigger fights, did not cause the teens to rate the fighting as harmful and destructive. Statistically, it made no difference at all. "Certainly, there is a point in families where there is too much conflict. But we didn't have anybody in our study with an extreme amount of conflict." Instead, the variable that seemed to matter most was how the arguments were resolved. Essentially, the daughter needed to feel heard, and when reasonable, their mother needed to budge. The daughter had to win some arguments, and get small concessions as a result of others.

Daughters who rated arguing as destructive had parents who stonewalled, rather than collaborated. The daughters heard "Don't argue with me!" before even uttering a word. "Even the tiniest of concessions made them feel it was resolved okay," Holmes said. "One daughter told of wanting a tattoo. Her mom forbade it, but allowed the girl to buy a pair of crazy shoes that the mom had previously denied her."

"Parents who negotiate ultimately appear to be more informed," according to Dr. Robert Laird, a professor at the University of New Orleans. "Parents with unbending, strict guidelines make it a tactical issue for kids to find a way around them."

This makes sense, yet it's a very controversial finding, because in our society today we are warned not to be pushovers; we're advised that giving in breeds a nation of whiners and beggars. Even Nancy Darling's Mod Squad study showed that permissive parents are not successful parents.

So the science seems to be duplicitous—on one hand, parents have to be strict enforcers of rules, but on the other hand, parents need to be flexible or the ensuing conflict will be destructive to teens' psyche. Will the scientists please make up their minds? Or is there some finer distinction we're missing?

Well, the narrow definition of pushover parents are those who give in to their kid because they can't stand to see their child cry, or whine. They placate their children just to shut them up. They want to be their kid's friend, and they're uncomfortable being seen as the bad guy. That's not the same as a parent who makes sure her child feels heard, and if the child has made a good argument for why a rule needs to be changed, lets that influence her decision.

Nancy Darling found the same distinction. The type of parents who were lied to the least had rules and enforced them consistently, but they had found a way to be flexible that allowed the rule-setting process to still be respected. "If a child's normal curfew is eleven p.m., and they explain to their parent something special is happening, so the parent says, 'Okay, for that night only, you can come home at one a.m.'—that encourages the kid to not lie, and to respect the time." This collaboration retains a parent's legitimacy.

It has taken the psychological establishment decades to narrow in on this understanding. Dr. Laurence Steinberg at Temple University articulates this history in his books and papers. Until the early 1970s—an era when psychology was driven more by theory than by empirical studies—"parents were told to expect oppositionalism and defiance. The absence of conflict was seen as indicative of stunted development," Steinberg writes. In other words, if your child wasn't fighting and rebelling, something was wrong with him. This perspective was articulated throughout the 1950s and 1960s by theorists such as Anna Freud, Peter Blos, and Erik Erikson, who coined the term "identity crisis." But they almost exclusively studied teenagers in clinics and therapy—they were oversampling the problem teens.

In the mid-1970s, a variety of studies sampled adolescents drawn from schools, not clinics. "These studies found that 75% of teenagers reported having happy and pleasant relationships with their parents," described Steinberg. Rebellion and conflict were not normal after all. In 1976, a seminal study by Sir Michael Rutter—considered by many to be the father of modern child psychiatry—found that the 25% of teens who were fighting with their parents had been doing so long before hitting puberty. Becoming a teenager wasn't the trigger.

At that point, the narrative of adolescence bifurcated. Pop

psychology, fueled by the new explosion of self-help publishing, continued to pump out the message that the teen years are a period of storm and stress—and certainly, for many, they are. This was the dominant perspective presented in movies and in music, and there were no shortage of experts who worked with teens suffering from depression or conduct disorder to testify that angst was the norm. In the self-help aisles, Steinberg pointed out, the babies are all cuddly and the teens are all spiteful.

But for the next two decades, the social scientists kept churning out data that showed traumatic adolescence was the exception, not the norm.

Only in the last decade has the field sorted out these dual competing narratives and found an explanation for them. Essentially, the pop psychology field caters to parents, who find having a teenager in the home to be really stressful. But the social scientists were polling the teens, most of whom didn't find adolescence so traumatic. This is exactly what Tabitha Holmes learned—that parents rate all the arguing as destructive, while teens find it generally to be productive.

"The popular image of the individual sulking in the wake of a family argument may be a more accurate portrayal of the emotional state of the parent, than the teenager," Steinberg writes. "Parents are more bothered by the bickering and squabbling that takes place during this time than are adolescents, and parents are more likely to hold on to the affect after a negative interaction with their teenagers."

※

In the popular media, the dual contrasting narratives of adolescence continue. According to many news stories, teens are apathetic and unprepared. These stories mention that alcohol abuse is high, teen pregnancy is ticking back up, and huge numbers of high school seniors are failing their state exit exams even though they supposedly passed all their classes. The California State University system, for example, admits the top third of the state's high school seniors. Yet six out of ten CSU students have to take remedial classes; half are not academically prepared to be in college.

Then, to hear other stories, today's teens are so focused on success that it's alarming. The rate of kids in high school taking advanced math and science courses has leapt 20%. Colleges are drowning in applications from driven teens: the majority of teens now apply to at least four schools. In the last 35 years, enrollment in the nation's colleges has skyrocketed from 5.8 million to 10.4 million. Sure, a sizeable portion of them need remedial help—but it's a smaller portion now than in the 1980s. Their overachieving isn't limited just to their academics, either. Surveys of incoming college freshmen find that 70% of them volunteer weekly, and 60% hold down jobs while in school. Voting is up, for those eighteen and older, and the proportion who've participated in an organized demonstration is at 49%, the highest in history. The students who entered college in 2008 were engaged in more political dialogue than any class since 1968.

I suppose this split-personality is natural; both narratives exist because we need them to echo our experience at any particular time. They compete, but they both persist. We carry dual narratives whenever a phenomenon can't be characterized by a singular explanation. We now have dual narratives not just of adolescence, but of the twenty-something years and of being unmarried at forty. In the eyes of some, these reflect an unwillingness to accept reality; to others, they reflect the courage to refuse a compromised life.

The danger is when these narratives don't just reflect, they steer. Wrong from the start, comprising only half the story, these narratives nevertheless become the explanatory system through which adolescents see their life. I can only wonder how many teens, naturally prone to seeing conflict as productive, instead are being taught to view it as destructive, symptomatic of a poor relationship rather than a good one. How many like their parents just fine, yet are hearing that it's uncool to do so? How many are acting disaffected and bored, because showing they care paints them as the fool? How many can't tell their parents the truth, because honesty is just not how the story goes?

EIGHT

Can Self-Control Be Taught?

Developers of a new kind of preschool keep losing their grant money—the students are so successful they're no longer "at-risk enough" to warrant further study. What's their secret?

When I was growing up in Seattle, I participated in a sort of national rite of passage: I spent the autumn of my sophomore year in high school taking a Driver's Education class.

I vividly remember my instructor. A tall, aged gentleman who wore thick glasses, bright cardigans, and plaid pants, he was the only one of our teachers who let us address him by his first name, Claude. He doubled as the school's golf coach. I'd never thought of him as particularly kind or consoling, but he must have had the patience of a saint to teach teenagers both to drive a car and drive a golf ball.

Because I've had only one accident, I'd always credited Claude with successfully teaching me to drive. And since it's the way I learned to drive, I'd assumed that Driver's Ed *works*. I'm not alone in that presumption: seventeen states today allow those who've passed Driver's Ed to skip, outright, the driving portion of the licensing test.

But put to the test of scientific analysis, a different story emerges. Studies have compared accident data before and after schools implemented driver education. These reports have consistently found no reduction in crashes among drivers who pass a training course. At first, it was hard for me to believe the studies. After all, Driver's Ed seems like such a quintessential high school experience—there has to be a reason for it. Then I started remembering some of my friends who were in Driver's Ed with me. They'd had accidents soon after they'd gotten their licenses: Claude's careful coaching hadn't prevented them from getting into accidents. I flashed back to my own near-misses—when I was a teen who thought cutting across three lanes of traffic sounded like a really fun game.

Students who take Driver's Ed do learn the rules of the road. They learn to steer a car, apply brakes steadily, signal for turns, and park. But for the most part, mastery of the rules or motor skills isn't what prevents accidents. Instead, accidents are caused by poor *decision* skills. Teens get into a few more minor fender-benders, but many more serious accidents: statistically, teenagers get in fatal crashes at twice the rate of everyone else.

This isn't just a matter of experience at the wheel—it's really a matter of age and brain wiring in the frontal lobe. So schools can't on their own turn teens into safer drivers. Instead, they make getting a license such an easy and convenient process that they increase the supply of young drivers on the road. In 1999, the School of Public Health at Johns Hopkins University reported that nine school districts that *eliminated* Driver's Education experienced a 27% *drop* in auto accidents among 16- and 17-year-olds.

Research like that has convinced states that school driving classes aren't the answer; what really reduces auto accidents are graduated-licensing programs which delay the age at which teenagers can drive at night or with friends in the car. These decrease crashes by 20 to 30 percent.

※

In our schools, kids are subjected to a vast number of well-meaning training programs that sound absolutely great, but nevertheless fail the test of scientific analysis. Schools take seriously their responsibility to breed good citizens, not just good students—but that sometimes means that good intentions are mistaken for good ideas. The scarier the issue, the more schools hurriedly adopt programs to combat it. For example, D.A.R.E., Drug Abuse Resistance Education.

Developed originally in 1983 by the Los Angeles Police Department, D.A.R.E. sends uniformed police officers into junior high and high schools to teach about the real-life consequences of drugs and crime. And we're not talking about just a single assembly, either—in its full form, students participate in a 17-week school curriculum complete with lectures, role playing, readings, and the like. It seemed like such a promising idea, D.A.R.E. spread like wildfire. Within two decades, some form of D.A.R.E. was present in 80% of the public school districts in the United States. It claims influence over 26 million students, at an estimated annual budget of over $1 billion. As a society, we believe in the way D.A.R.E. delivers its message. Teachers support it incredibly strongly; 97% give it a "good" or "excellent" approval rating. Parents do, too: 93% believe it effectively teaches children to say no to drugs and violence.

However, any program that popular, which receives that much government support, attracts extensive scientific analysis. Throughout the 1990s and 2000s, studies randomly assigned students to a D.A.R.E. class or not. In some studies, D.A.R.E. shows a very slight decline in cigarette use, alcohol use, or drug use immediately after the training, but in all studies it shows no comparative reduction long-term.

D.A.R.E. is not alone, and it shouldn't be singled out. Hundreds of drug-prevention programs receive federal grants; the Department of Health and Human Services looked at 718 of them, and it found that only 41 had a positive effect.

Programs meant to reduce high school dropouts have a similar record. Of the 16 most well known, only one has a positive effect, even though all of these programs seem to have the details right—a high ratio of counselors to students, and a vocational bent creating a bridge to future careers.

In our research for this book, we came across dozens of school-based programs that sounded wonderful in theory, but were far from it in practice.

Among scholars, interventions considered to be really great often have an effect size of something like 15%, which means that 15% of children altered their targeted behavior, and therefore 85% did not alter it. Interventions with an effect size of only 4% can still be considered quite good, statistically—even though they have no effect on 96% of the students.

Does this mean the bar is too low for scholars? Not really. Instead, what this data indicates is that human behavior is incredibly stubborn. We're hard to budge off our habits and proclivities. While it's possible to inspire a few people to change, it's nearly impossible to change a majority of us, in any direction. Interventions for children are even more of a challenge—since developmentally, kids are by definition a moving target.

※

I explain all this to set the stage, and provide proper perspective, on something we found that *does* work. This program's success rate is marvelous on its own, but all the more astonishing in light of how difficult it is to create something that produces results with a sizeable effect. It's an emerging curriculum for preschool and kindergarten classrooms called Tools of the Mind. It requires some training for teachers, but otherwise does not cost a penny more than a traditional curriculum. The teachers merely teach differently. What's even more interesting than their results is *why* it seems to work, and what that teaches us about how young children learn.

Ashley visited pre-K and kindergarten Tools classes in two relatively affluent towns that ring Denver; I visited both types of classes in Neptune, New Jersey, which is a comparatively more-impoverished township about halfway down the Garden State Parkway between New York and Atlantic City.

Most elements of the school day are negligibly different from a traditional class. There's recess and lunch and snack time and nap time. But a typical Tools preschool classroom *looks* different—as much because of what it is missing as what is there. The wall calendar is not a month-by-month grid, but a straight line of days on a long ribbon of paper. Gone is the traditional alphabet display; instead, children use a sound map, which has a monkey next to *Mm* and a sun next to *Ss*. These are ordered not from *A* to *Z* but rather in clusters, with consonants on one map and vowels on another. *C*, *K*, and *Q* are in one cluster, because those are similar sounds, all made with the tongue mid-mouth. Sounds made with the teeth or the lips are in other clusters.

When class begins, the teacher tells the students they will be playing fire station. The previous week, they learned all about firemen, so now, the classroom has been decorated in four different areas—in one corner is a fire station, in another a house that needs saving. The children choose what role they want to take on in the pretend scenario—pump driver, 911 operator, fireman, or family that needs to be rescued. Before the children begin to play, they each tell the teacher their choice of role.

With the teacher's help, the children make individual "play plans." They all draw a picture of themselves in their chosen role, then they attempt to write it out as a sentence on a blank sheet of paper to the best of their abilities. Even three-year-olds write daily. For some, the play plan is little more than lines representing each word in the sentence. Still others use their sound map to figure out the words' initial consonants. The eldest have memorized how to write "I am going to" and then they use the sound map to figure out the rest.

Then they go play, sticking to the role designated in their plan. The resulting play continues for a full 45 minutes, with the children staying in character, self-motivated. If they get distracted or start to fuss, the teacher asks, "Is that in your play plan?" On different days of the week, children choose other roles in the scenario. During this crucial play hour, the teacher facilitates their play but does not directly teach them anything at all.

At the end, the teacher puts a CD on to play the "clean-up song." As soon as the music begins, the kids stop playing and start cleaning up—without another word from their teacher. Later, they will do what's called buddy reading. The children are paired up and sit facing each other; one is given a large paper drawing of lips, while the other holds a drawing of ears. The one with the lips flips through a book, telling the story he sees in the pictures. The other listens and, at the end, asks a question about the story. Then they switch roles.

They also commonly play games, like Simon Says, that require restraint. One variation is called graphic practice; the teacher puts on music, and the children draw spirals and shapes. Intermittently, the teacher pauses the music, and the children learn to stop their pens whenever the music stops.

The kindergarten program expands on the preschool structure, incorporating academics into a make-believe premise that's based on whatever book they're reading in class. Overall, the Tools classrooms seem a little different, but not strange in any way. To watch it in action, you would not guess its results would be so superior. In this sense, it's the opposite kind of program from D.A.R.E.—which sounded great, but had weak results. Tools has great results, despite nothing about it having intuitive, visceral appeal.

The Tools techniques were developed during the 1990s by two scholars at Metropolitan State College of Denver, Drs. Elena Bodrova and Deborah Leong. After pilot-testing the program in a few classrooms and Head Start centers, they put it to a true test in 1997, in cooperation with Denver Public Schools. Ten kindergarten teachers were randomly assigned, to teach either Tools or the regular district curriculum. In these classrooms one-third to one-half of the children were poor Hispanic students who began the year classified as having limited English-language proficiency: they were starting kindergarten effectively a grade-level behind.

The following spring, all the children took national standardized tests. The results were jaw-dropping. The children from the Tools classes were now almost a full grade-level *ahead* of the national standard. In the district, only half the kindergartners score as proficient at their grade-level. Of the Tools children, 97% scored as proficient.

Reports of the program's success began to spread within the research community. In 2001, two scholars from the National Institute for Early Education Research at Rutgers, Dr. Ellen Frede and Amy Hornbeck, visited the Tools classrooms. New Jersey was implementing free, public preschools in the neediest zones of the state. Impressed by what they saw, Frede and Hornbeck decided to test Tools in a preschool during its first year of operations, so that Hornbeck could compare the program's efficacy to that of a traditional program.

The researchers chose a site in Passaic, New Jersey, that served children from low-income families; 70% of the students came from homes where English is not the primary language. The new preschool, created in an old bank building in downtown Passaic, had eighteen classrooms. Seven on one floor were set aside as a Tools preschool; as a control, the other eleven would teach the district's regular preschool plan. Both teachers and students were randomly assigned to classrooms, and the teachers were instructed not to exchange ideas about curriculum between the two programs. At the end of the first year, the Tools scores were markedly higher on seven out of eight measures, including vocabulary and IQ.

But it was the kids' behavior ratings that really sold the school's principal on the program. From the teachers in the regular classrooms, the principal got reports of extremely disruptive behavior almost every day—preschool students kicking a teacher, biting another student, cursing, or throwing a chair. But those kinds of reports never came from the Tools classes.

The controlled experiment was supposed to last two years, but at the end of the first year the principal insisted all the classrooms switch to Tools. She decided it was unethical to deprive half the school of a curriculum that was obviously superior.

This wasn't the only time that Tools was a victim of its own success. Testing of the Tools program ended early in two other places as well: Elgin, Illinois, and Midland, Texas. The grant money funding the research was available to study children at-risk; after a year, the children no longer scored low enough to be deemed "at-risk," so the grant money to continue the analysis was no longer available. Bodrova is quick to credit the work of those schools' faculty, but added, "When it keeps happening enough times, you start to think that it may be our program that makes the difference. It's the irony of doing interventions in the real world: being too successful to study if it's successful."

Word about Tools continued to spread, and once teachers actually saw the program in action they became believers. Rutgers' Hornbeck was eventually so convinced by her own findings that she signed on to be part of the Tools team, regularly training teachers in the program. After two teachers from Neptune, New Jersey, visited the Passaic school, they were so excited that they, too, implemented Tools techniques in a new preschool they were creating in Neptune.

Sally Millaway was the principal of that Neptune school. After success with the program on the preschool level, she convinced the superintendent to try it in one class at her next post, an elementary school. When word leaked out that Millaway's school would be instituting a Tools kindergarten, the school district began getting letters from parents who wanted their children to be allowed to switch into the Tools program.

During that first year of kindergarten, Millaway had the sense it was working. But the true test would come in the standardized achievement exams all New Jersey kindergartners would take in April. A month later, Millaway got the first set of results over the fax machine. "It was unbelievable," she said. "When I saw the numbers, I laughed out loud. It was ridiculous, beyond our imaginings."

The average reading scores for the school district translated into the 65th percentile on the national spectrum. The Tools kindergartners (on average) had jumped more than 20 ticks higher, to the 86th percentile. The kids who tested as gifted almost all came from the Tools classes.

So why does this curriculum work so well? There are many interrelated factors, but let's start with the most distinctive element of Tools—the written play plans and the lengthy play period that ensues.

In every preschool in the country, kids have played firehouse. But usually, after ten minutes, the scenario breaks down. Holding a pretend fire hose on a pretend fire is a singular activity, and it grows old; needing stimulation, children are distracted by what other kids are doing and peel off into new games. Play has a joyful randomness, but it's not *sustained*. In Tools classrooms, by staging different areas of the room as the variety of settings, and by asking kids to commit to their role for the hour, the play is far more complicated and interactive. The children in the house call 911; the operator rings a bell; the firefighters leap from their bunks; the trucks arrive to rescue the family. This is considered mature, multidimensional, sustained play.

This notion of being able to sustain one's own interest is considered a core building block in Tools. Parents usually think of urging their child to pay attention, to be obedient to a teacher. They recognize that a child can't learn unless she has the ability to avoid distractions. Tools emphasizes the flip-side—kids won't be distracted because they're so consumed in the activities they've chosen. By acting the roles they've adopted in their play plans, the kids are thoroughly in the moment.

In one famous Russian study from the 1950s, children were told to stand still as long as they could—they lasted two minutes. Then a second group of children were told to *pretend* they were soldiers on guard who had to stand still at their posts—they lasted eleven minutes.

"The advantage of little kids," explained Bodrova, "is they don't yet know that they aren't good at something. When you ask a child to copy something on the board the teacher has written, he might think, 'I can't write as good as the teacher,' so then he doesn't want to do it. But hand a notepad to the child who is pretending to be a waiter in a pizza parlor. Johnny ordered cheese pizza, you ordered pepperoni. They don't know if they can write it or not—they just know that they have to do something to remember the pizza orders. They end up doing more writing than if you asked them to write a story."

It's well recognized that kids today get to play less. As pressure for academic achievement has mounted, schools around the country have cut back on recess to devote more time to the classroom. This, in turn, created a backlash; experts and social commentators opined that playtime was too valuable to cut. Their arguments were straightforward: the brain needs a break, kids need to blow off energy, cutting recess increases obesity, and it's during recess that children learn social skills. Tools suggests a different benefit entirely—that during playtime, children learn basic developmental building blocks necessary for later academic success, and in fact they develop these building blocks *better* while playing than while in a traditional class.

Take, for example, symbolic thought. Almost everything a classroom demands a child learn requires grasping the connection between reality and symbolic, abstract representation: letters of the alphabet are symbols for sounds and speech; the map on the wall is a symbol of the world; the calendar is a symbol to measure the passage of time. Words on paper—such as the word "TREE"—look to the eye nothing at all like an actual tree.

Young children learn abstract thinking through play, where a desk and some chairs become a fire engine. More importantly, when play has interacting components, as in Tools, the child's brain learns how one symbol combines with multiple other symbols, akin to high-order abstract thinking. A child masters the intellectual process of holding multiple thoughts in his head and stacking them together.

Consider high-order thinking like self-reflection, an internal dialogue within one's own mind, where opposing alternatives are weighed and carefully considered. This thought-conversation is the opposite of impulsive reaction, where actions are made without forethought. All adults can think through ideas in their heads, to differing abilities. But do kids have the same internal voice of contemplation and discussion? If so, when do they develop it? Tools is designed to encourage the early development of this Socratic consciousness, so that kids don't just react impulsively in class, and they can willfully avoid distraction.

Tools does this by encouraging that voice in the head, private speech, by first teaching kids to do it out loud—they talk themselves through their activities. When the kids are learning the capital C, they all say in unison, "Start at the top and go around" as they start to print. No one ever stops the kids from saying it out loud, but after a few minutes, the Greek chorus ends. In its place is a low murmur. A couple minutes later, a few kids are still saying it out loud—but most of the children are saying it in their heads. A few kids don't even realize it, but they've kept silently mouthing the instructions to themselves.

Kids who are doing well in school know it; when they write down their answer, they know whether or not their answer is correct. They have a subtle sense, a recognition of whether they've gotten it right. Children who are struggling are genuinely unsure; they might get the right answer, but lack such awareness. So to develop this awareness, when a Tools teacher writes a letter on the board, she writes four versions of it and asks the kids to decide which is the best *D*.

Leong explained, "This is designed to trigger self-analysis of what a good *D* looks like and what would they like their own *D*'s to look like. They think about their work, when they think about hers." Tools children are also frequently responsible for checking each other's work. In one class Ashley observed, pairs of kids were practicing their penmanship, after which they were to take turns circling which of their partner's letters were best. After one child raced through his checker duties too quickly, the other boy complained. This five-year-old actually wanted his supervisor to be more critical of his work.

Many of the exercises are chosen because they teach children to attend background cues and control their impulses. The simple game of Simon Says, for instance, entices a child to copy the leader, yet requires the kid to pay close attention and exercise intermittent restraint. Similarly, when the teacher plays the clean-up song, the children have to notice where they are in the music in order to make sure they'll be finished before the song ends. In buddy reading, the natural impulse is for every kid to want to read first; the child who holds the ears and listens patiently is learning to quell this impulse and wait.

The upshot of Tools is kids who are not merely behaved, but self-organized and self-directed. After just three months of a pilot project, Tools teachers in New Mexico went from averaging forty reported classroom incidents a month to zero. And Tools kids don't distract easily. During one lunch period in a New Jersey school cafeteria, the Tools kindergartners watched the entire rest of the student body become embroiled in a food fight. Not one Tools kid picked up as much as a scrap of food to throw, and when they returned to class, they told their teacher that they couldn't believe how out of control the older children were.

While Tools' techniques might sound fuzzy and theoretical, the program has strong support in neuroscience. In other chapters of this book, we've often touched upon the development of a child's prefrontal cortex, the part of the brain that handles executive function—planning, predicting, controlling impulses, persisting through trouble, and orchestrating thoughts to fulfill a goal. Though these are very adult attributes, executive function begins in preschool, and preschoolers' EF capability can be measured with simple computerized tests.

During the easiest stage of these tests, a child sees a red heart appear, either on the left or right side of the screen, and then pushes the corresponding button—left or right. Even three-year-olds will do this perfectly. Then the child sees a red *flower* and is instructed to press the button on the *opposite* side of the flower. The new task requires her brain to toss out the old rule and adopt a new rule—this is called "attention switching." It also requires the child to inhibit the natural urge to respond on the same side as the stimulus. For three-year-olds, this switch in rules is very hard; for four-year-olds, it's a challenge but somewhat doable. Now the real test begins. The computer begins randomly showing either a red heart or a red flower, and the child needs to hold in her working memory *both* rules: heart = press same side, flower = press opposite side. The hearts and flowers are shown for only 2.5 seconds, so the kid has to think fast, without getting switched up. It requires attentional focus and constant reorienting of the mindset. For children's brains, this is very difficult. Even thirteen-year-olds will push the wrong button 20% of the time.

The foremost expert on executive function in young children is

Dr. Adele Diamond at the University of British Columbia. A few years ago, she was approached at a conference by Bodrova, who told her about the experiment in the Passaic preschool. Diamond wondered if the success of Tools might be because it was exercising children's executive function skills. So Diamond went to Passaic to visit.

Diamond recalled, "In the regular classes, the children were bouncing off the walls. In the Tools classrooms, it was like a different planet. I've never seen anything like it." She decided to return the next year and test the children's executive functioning. "I could see the difference with my own eyes, but I wanted hard data," she said.

To do this, Diamond ran the Passaic children through a number of the executive function computer tasks. She found a huge gap between the regular kids and the Tools kids on executive function. On one task, the regular kids tested not much above chance, but the Tools kids scored at 84%. On a very difficult task, only one-quarter of the regular kids could complete the test, while over half the Tools kids completed it.

"The more the test demanded high executive function," Diamond noted, "the bigger the gap between the kids."

※

Every parent has observed a young child and wondered, with some frustration, when he'll be able to sit still (other than in front of the television). When will he be able to sustain an activity for a solid half-hour? When will he be able to stay on task, rather than be distracted by other children? When will he be able to truly apply himself? At times, it seems that a child's cognitive ability, which might be very high, is at war with his distractability.

Usually we concern ourselves only with the detrimental end of this spectrum—the kid who can't learn because he's easily distracted. What we overlook is that being at the beneficial end of the spectrum—being able to concentrate—is a skill that might be just as valuable as math ability, or reading ability, or even raw intelligence.

So why are some kids better able to direct their attention? What are the neural systems that regulate focus—and is this perhaps why Tools is getting such good results?

Dr. Silvia Bunge is a neuroscientist at the University of California, Berkeley. Her newest research is on a region of the brain called the rostral lateral prefrontal cortex. This is the part of human brains that is most different from ape brains. It's responsible for maintaining concentration and setting goals. "This is only speculative, but having kids plan their time and set weekly goals, like they do in Tools," Bunge told me, "in effect wires up the RLPFC, building it, strengthening it."

The broad term Bunge uses for a child's regulation of focus is "cognitive control." Cognitive control is necessary in many contexts. In the simplest, the child is trying to avoid distractions—not just external distractions, like another child making funny faces during class, but internal distractions. "Like the thought, 'I can't do this,'" Bunge explained.

Cognitive control is required whenever the brain has to manipulate information in the mind; this might be holding a phone number in memory just long enough to dial it, or planning chess moves in advance, or weighing the pros and cons of two choices. But it isn't just about managing information: it's also part of the process of squelching frustration and anger, and stifling an inappropriate or impulsive response.

An impulsive *social* response might be giggling in class, but there are impulsive *academic* responses, too. On multiple-choice achievement and IQ tests, there's always a "distractor" in each list of answers, a choice that is almost right. Children with weak cognitive control are tricked into selecting it. Their final score will dock them for intelligence, or reading comprehension, but they're perfectly intelligent and read just fine—they just can't regulate their impulsivity.

According to Bunge, cognitive control is not "on" all the time. Rather, the brain can allocate more or less cognitive control as it sees fit. This works as a feedback loop between two subregions in the brain. One subsystem is supposed to measure how well you're doing on whatever you're supposed to be doing. When it senses you're not doing well enough, it signals another subsystem, which allocates more cognitive control: it improves your concentration. When a child seems to be lacking in control, it's not just that her brain *can't* concentrate—she's not aware she even *needs* to concentrate. The first part of the feedback loop isn't doing its job. She's literally not paying attention to how well she's doing.

Think back to the Tools curriculum, where children are routinely asked to check and score their own work against answer sheets, and are always buddied up with a partner, checking each other's work (even in preschool). Bodrova and Leong can't emphasize enough how crucial it is for children to develop an awareness of how well they're doing and when their work is completed accurately. This sensitivity is required for the feedback system to function, and for concentration to be increased.

Bunge's specialty is putting school-aged children into fMRI scanners and monitoring brain activity while they take tests similar to the heart and flower task described above. She's found that the adult brain has a specialized region of the frontal lobe devoted to regulating rules—all sorts of rules, from heart and flower rules to the rules of grammar to the rules of driving. (When this region is damaged, people speak and write ungrammatically.) This rules region allows people to be proactive: they recognize circumstances where rules will apply, as if glancing ahead in time, preloading the brain for what to do. This proactive response is very much like private speech—telling yourself what to do, a step ahead of doing it. Decisions are made instantly, and correctly. Schoolchildren taking the same tests don't yet have this rules region to draw upon; rather than proact, their brains react. Stumbling, trying to get the rules straight, their error rate is high.

That the children in Tools choose their own work is also significant, said Bunge. "When a child gets to choose, they presumably choose activities they're motivated to do. Motivation is crucial. Motivation is experienced in the brain as the release of dopamine. It's not released like other neurotransmitters into the synapses, but rather it's sort of spritzed onto large areas of the brain, which enhances the signaling of neurons." The motivated brain, literally, operates better, signals faster. When children are motivated, they learn more.

※

This chapter began with the statistical science of Driver's Ed, and progressed to the neuroscience of preschool. The two are indeed connected, by the neural systems that regulate attention and cognitive control. Teenage drivers can score 100% on a paper test of the rules, but when driving, their reaction times are delayed because they have not yet internalized the *grammar* of driving—they have to think about it. This increases the cognitive load, and their ability to maintain attention is stressed to capacity. They are on the verge of making poor decisions. Put a friend in the car and the attention systems are easily overloaded—the driver's brain no longer proactively anticipates what could happen, glancing seconds ahead and preloading the rules. Instead, he is left to react, and can't always react accurately, no matter how fast his reflexes are.

Performing amid distractions is a daily challenge for students. In a previous chapter, we wrote about the predictive power of intelligence tests. One reason IQ tests don't predict better is that in a child's school life, academics don't take place in a quiet, controlled room, one-on-one with a teacher—the way IQ tests are administered. Academics occur among a whirlwind of distractions and pressures. Psychologists call this the difference between hot and cold cognition. Many people perform far worse under pressure, but some perform far better.

This notion comes under many names in the research: effortful control, impulsivity, self-discipline. Depending on the way it's measured, the predictive values of self-discipline in many cases are better than those of IQ scores. In simpler words, being disciplined is more important than being smart. Being both is not just a little better—it's exponentially better. In one study, Dr. Clancy Blair, of Pennsylvania State University, found that children who were above average in IQ *and* executive functioning were 300% more likely to do well in math class than children who just had a high IQ alone.

Just like the science of intelligence, the science of self-control has shifted in the last decade from the assumption that it's a fixed trait—some have it, others don't—to the assumption it's malleable. It's affected by everything from parenting styles to how recently you ate (the brain burns a lot of glucose when exercising self-control). The neural systems that govern control can get fatigued, and—according to one study—those with higher IQs suffer more from this kind of fatigue.

"Due to a multitude of empirical evidence, there is now consensus on the effectiveness of self-regulated learning on academic achievement, as well as on learning motivation," wrote Dr. Charlotte Dignath, in a recent meta-analysis of self-control interventions.

Both Ashley and I have borrowed some of the Tools of the Mind strategies. Children of every grade show up in the evenings at Ashley's tutoring facility; she now makes them write down a plan for how they'll spend their two hours, to teach them to think proactively. When they get distracted, she refers them back to their plan. She no longer simply corrects children's grammar mistakes in their homework; instead, she first points to the line containing the mistake, and asks the child to find it. This makes them think critically about what they're doing rather than mechanically completing the assignment. With kindergartners who are just learning to write, Ashley has them use private speech as they form a letter, saying aloud, "Start at the top and go around...."

I use similar techniques with my daughter. Every night, she comes home from preschool with a page of penmanship, filled with whatever letter she learned that day. I ask her to circle the best example on each line—so she'll recognize the difference between a good one and a better one. At bedtime, she and I do a version of buddy reading: after I've read her a book, I hand it to her. Then she tells the story back to me, creatively narrating from the illustrations and whatever lines she remembers verbatim. Occasionally, when she and I have the whole day together, we write up a plan for what we'll do. (I wish I did this more, because she loves it.) I also give her prompts that extend her play scenarios. For instance, she loves baby dolls; she'll collect them all, and put them to bed—this might take five or ten minutes. At that point, she no longer knows what to do. So I'll encourage her to wake the babies up, take them to school, and go on a field trip. That's usually all it takes to spark her imagination for over an hour.

In Neptune, New Jersey, one of the kids in the first Tools preschool class was Sally Millaway's own three-year-old son, George. "He had special needs," Millaway said. She was convinced Tools would work for the normal children, but would it work for George? "My son had speech and language delays, very severely—he didn't speak at all. He wasn't yet diagnosed with autism, but he had all the red flags of it." Later that fall, George was instead diagnosed with a hearing problem—he could hear tones, but it was like he was hearing underwater, the sounds blurred. "In November, his adenoids were taken out. He began talking within three days of the surgery."

"I suddenly went from thinking he would have a lifelong disability to realizing he had all this time he had to make up for," Millaway said. "Would he ever catch up to the other kids?"

Millaway's concerns were short-lived. She couldn't believe the rapid progress he made, and she attributed it entirely to Tools. After three years of the program—two in preschool, one in kindergarten—he completely overcame his early deficits. George is now in a second-grade gifted program, and Tools is taught in all Neptune kindergarten classes.

NINE

Plays Well With Others

Why modern involved parenting has failed to produce a generation of angels.

A couple years ago, an expert on preschool children's aggression, Dr. Jamie Ostrov, teamed up with Dr. Douglas Gentile, a leading expert on the effects of media exposure. The two men spent two years monitoring the kids at two Minnesota preschools, cross-referencing the children's behavior against parent reports of what television shows and DVDs the kids watched. Ranging from 2.5 to 5 years old, these were well-off children, from well-off families.

Ostrov and Gentile fully expected that kids who watched violent shows like *Power Rangers* and *Star Wars* would be more physically aggressive during playtime at school. They also expected kids who watched educational television, like *Arthur* and *Clifford the Big Red Dog*, would be not just less aggressive, but the kids would be more *prosocial*—sharing, helpful, and inclusive, etc. These weren't original hypotheses, but the study's importance was its long-term methodology: Ostrov and Gentile would be able to track the precise incremental increase in aggression over the course of the preschool years.

Ostrov had previously found that videocameras were too intrusive and couldn't capture the sound from far away, so his researchers hovered near children with clipboards in hand. The children quickly grew bored with the note taking and ignored the researchers.

The observers had been trained to distinguish between physical aggression, relational aggression, and verbal aggression. Physical aggression included grabbing toys from other children's hands, pushing, pulling, and hitting of any sort. Relational aggression, at the preschool age, involved saying things like, "You can't play with us," or just ignoring a child who wanted to play, and withdrawing friendship or telling lies about another child—all of which attack a relationship at its core. Verbal aggression included calling someone a mean name and saying things like "Shut up!" or "You're stupid"—it often accompanied physical aggression.

Ostrov cross-referenced what his observers recorded with teacher ratings of the children's behavior, the parents' own ratings, and their reports on how much television the children were watching. Over the course of the study, the children watched an average of eleven hours of media per week, according to the parents—a normal mix of television shows and DVDs.

At first glance, the scholars' hypotheses were confirmed—but something unexpected was also revealed in the data. *The more educational media the children watched, the more relationally aggressive they were.* They were increasingly bossy, controlling, and manipulative. This wasn't a small effect. It was stronger than the connection between violent media and physical aggression.

Curious why this could be, Ostrov's team sat down and watched several programs on PBS, Nickelodeon, and the Disney Channel. Ostrov saw that, in some shows, relational aggression is modeled at a fairly high rate. Ostrov theorized that many educational shows spend most of the half-hour establishing a conflict between characters and only a few minutes resolving that conflict.

"Preschoolers have a difficult time being able to connect information at the end of the show to what happened earlier," Ostrov wrote in his paper. "It is likely that young children do not attend to the overall 'lesson' in the manner an older child or adult can, but instead learn from each of the behaviors shown."

The results took the entire team by surprise. Ostrov doesn't yet have children, but his colleagues who did immediately started changing their kids' viewing patterns.

Ostrov decided to replicate the study at four diverse preschools in Buffalo, New York. (Ostrov is now a professor at the University at Buffalo, State University of New York.) "Given the fact that [the result] was so novel and so surprising, we really wanted to find out that the findings would generalize—that we weren't just finding something with this one set of kids," said Ostrov.

After the first year in Buffalo, Ostrov ran the numbers. The children in Buffalo watched a ratio of about two parts educational media to one part violent media, on average. More exposure to violent media did increase the rate of physical aggression shown at school—however, it did so only modestly. In fact, watching educational television *also* increased the rate of physical aggression, almost as much as watching violent TV. And just like in the Minnesota study, educational television had a dramatic effect on relational aggression. The more the kids watched, the crueler they'd be to their classmates. This correlation was 2.5 times higher than the correlation between violent media and physical aggression.

Essentially, Ostrov had just found that *Arthur* is more dangerous for children than *Power Rangers*.

Data from a team at Ithaca College confirms Ostrov's assessment: there is a stunning amount of relational and verbal aggression in kids' television.

Under the supervision of professor Dr. Cynthia Scheibe, Ithaca undergrads patiently studied 470 half-hour television programs commonly watched by children, recording every time a character insulted someone, called someone a mean name, or put someone down.

Scheibe's analysis subsequently revealed that 96% of all children's programming includes verbal insults and put-downs, averaging 7.7

put-downs per half-hour episode. Programs specifically considered "prosocial" weren't much better—66.7% of them still contained insults. Had the insult lines been said in real life, they would have been breathtaking in their cruelty. ("How do you sleep at night knowing you're a complete failure?" from *SpongeBob SquarePants*.) We can imagine educational television might use an initial insult to then teach a lesson about how insults are hurtful, but that never was the case, Schiebe found. Of the 2,628 put-downs the team identified, in only 50 instances was the insulter reprimanded or corrected—and not once in an educational show. Fully 84% of the time, there was either only laughter or no response at all.

※

The work of Ostrov and Schiebe are but two, of many recent studies, that question old assumptions about the causes and nature of children's aggression.

The wild kingdom of childhood can be mystifying at times. Modern involved parenting should seem to result in a sea of well-mannered, nonaggressive kids. As soon as an infant shows some indication of cognitive understanding, his parents start teaching him about sharing, kindness, and compassion. In theory, fighting and taunting and cruelty should all have gone the way of kids playing with plastic bags and licking lead paint, mere memories of an unenlightened time. Yet we read reports that bullying is rampant, and every parent hears stories about the agonies of the schoolyard. *Lord of the Flies* rings as true today as when William Golding first penned it.

Why is modern parenting failing in its mission to create a more civilized progeny? Earlier in this book, we discussed how the praised child becomes willing to cheat, and how children's experiments with lying can go unchecked, and how racial bias can resurface even in progressively-minded integrated schools. Now we turn the spotlight on children's aggressiveness—a catchall term used by the social scientists that includes everything from pushing in the sandbox to physical intimidation in middle school to social outcasting in high school.

The easy explanation has always been to blame aggression on a bad home environment. There's an odd comfort in this paradigm—as long as your home is a "good" home, aggression won't be a problem. Yet aggression is simply too prevalent for this explanation to suffice. It would imply a unique twist on the Lake Wobegon Effect—that almost every parent is *below* average.

Aggressive behavior has traditionally been considered an indicator of psychological maladaptation. It was seen as inherently aberrant, deviant, and (in children) a warning sign of future problems. Commonly cited causes of aggression were conflict in the home, corporal punishment, violent television, and peer rejection at school. While no scholar is about to take those assertions back, the leading edge of research suggests it's not as simple as we thought, and many of our "solutions" are actually backfiring.

Everyone's heard that it damages children to be witness to their parents' fighting, especially the kind of venomous screaming matches that escalate into worse. But what about plain old everyday conflict? Over the last decade, that question has been the specialty of the University of Notre Dame's Dr. E. Mark Cummings.

Cummings realized *every* child sees parents and caregivers carping at each other over such banalities as who forgot to pick up the dry cleaning, pay the bills, or whose turn it is to drive the carpool. In studies where Cummings has parents make a note of every argument, no matter how small or large, the typical married couple was having about eight disputes each day, according to the moms. (According to the dads, it was slightly less.) Spouses express anger to each other two or three times as often as they show a moment of affection to each other. And while parents might aspire to shielding their kids from their arguing, the truth is that children are witness to it 45% of the time.

Children appear to be highly attuned to the quality of their parents' relationship—Cummings has described children as "emotional Geiger-counters." In one study, Cummings found that children's emotional well-being and security are more affected by the relationship between the parents than by the direct relationship between the parent and child.

So are parents distressing their children with every bicker? Not necessarily.

In Cummings' elaborate experiments, he stages arguments for children to witness and monitors how they react, sometimes taking saliva samples to measure their stress hormone, cortisol. In some cases, two actors go at it. In others, the mother too is a confederate. While waiting with the child, the mother gets a phone call, ostensibly from the "father," and she begins arguing with him over the phone. (Her lines are mostly scripted.) In other variations of this experiment, the child just watches a videotape of two adults arguing, and she is asked to imagine the on-screen characters are her parents.

In one study, a third of the children reacted aggressively after witnessing the staged conflict—they shouted, got angry, or punched a pillow. But in that same study, something else happened, which eliminated the aggressive reaction in all but 4% of the children. What was this magical thing? Letting the child witness not just the argument, but the resolution of the argument. When the videotape was stopped mid-argument, it had a very negative effect. But if the child was allowed to see the contention get worked out, it calmed him. "We varied the intensity of the arguments, and that didn't matter," recalled Cummings. "The arguments can become pretty intense, and yet if it's resolved, kids are okay with it." Most kids were just as happy at the conclusion of the session as they were when witnessing a friendly interaction between parents.

What this means is that parents who pause mid-argument to take it upstairs—to spare the children—might be making the situation far worse, especially if they forget to tell their kids, "Hey, we worked it out." Cummings has also found that when couples have arguments entirely away from the kids, the kids might not have seen any of it but are still well aware of it, despite not knowing any specifics.

Cummings recently has shown that being exposed to constructive marital conflict can actually be good for children—if it doesn't escalate, insults are avoided, and the dispute is resolved with affection. This improves their sense of security, over time, and increases their prosocial behavior at school as rated by teachers. Cummings noted, "Resolution has to be sincere, not manipulated for their benefit—or they'll see through it." Kids learn a lesson in conflict resolution: the argument gives them an example of how to compromise and reconcile—a lesson lost for the child spared witnessing an argument.

This is obviously a very fine line to walk, but it's not as thin as the line being walked by Dr. Kenneth Dodge, a professor at Duke University. Another giant in the field, Dodge has long been interested in how corporal punishment incites children to become aggressive.

At least 90% of American parents use physical punishment on their children at least once in their parenting history. For years, the work of Dodge and others had shown a correlation between the frequency of corporal punishment and the aggressiveness of children. Surely, out-of-control kids get spanked more, but the studies control for baseline behavior. The more a child is spanked, the more aggressive she becomes.

However, those findings were based on studies of predominately Caucasian families. In order to condemn corporal punishment as strongly as the research community wanted to, someone needed to replicate these results in other ethnic populations—particularly African Americans. So Dodge conducted a long-term study of corporal punishment's affect on 453 kids, both black and white, tracking them from kindergarten through eleventh grade.

When Dodge's team presented its findings at a conference, the data did not make people happy. This wasn't because blacks used corporal punishment more than whites. (They did, but not by much.) Rather, Dodge's team had found a reverse correlation in black families—the more a child was spanked, the less aggressive the child over time. The spanked black kid was all around less likely to be in trouble.

Scholars publicly castigated Dodge's team, saying its findings were racist and dangerous to report. Journalists rushed to interview Dodge and the study's lead author, Dr. Jennifer Lansford. A national news reporter asked Dodge if his research meant the key to effective punishment was to hit children more frequently. The reporter may have been facetious in his query, but Dodge and Lansford—both of whom remain adamantly against the use of physical discipline—were so horrified by such questions that they enlisted a team of fourteen scholars to study the use of corporal punishment around the world.

Why would spanking trigger such problems in white children, but cause no problems for black children, even when used a little more frequently? With the help of the subsequent international studies, Dodge has pieced together an explanation for his team's results.

To understand, one has to consider how the parent is acting when giving the spanking, and how those actions label the child. In a culture where spanking is accepted practice, it becomes "the normal thing that goes on in this culture when a kid does something he shouldn't." Even if the parent might spank her child only two or three times in his life, it's treated as ordinary consequences. In the black community Dodge studied, a spank was seen as something that every kid went through.

Conversely, in the white community Dodge studied, physical discipline was a mostly-unspoken taboo. It was saved *only for the worst offenses*. The parent was usually very angry at the child and had lost his or her temper. The implicit message was: "What you have done is so deviant that you deserve a *special* punishment, which is spanking." It marked the child as someone who has lost his place within traditional society.

It's not just a white-black thing either. A University of Texas study of Conservative Protestants found that one-third of them spanked their kids three or more times *a week*, largely encouraged by Dr. James Dobson's Focus on the Family. The study found no negative effects from this corporal punishment—precisely because it was conveyed as normal.

Each in its own way, the work of Cummings and Dodge demonstrate the same dynamic: an oversimplified view of aggression leads parents to sometimes make it worse for kids when they're trying to do the right thing. Children key off their parents' reaction more than the argument or physical discipline itself.

If we can accept that children will be exposed to some parental conflict—and it may even be productive—can we say the same thing for interactions with their peers? Is there some level of conflict with peers that kids should learn to handle, on their own, without a parent's help?

Dr. Joseph Allen, a professor and clinician at the University of Virginia, says that many modern parents are trapped in what he calls "The Nurture Paradox."

"To protect kids is a natural parental instinct," Allen explained. "But we end up not teaching them to deal with life's ups and downs. It's a healthy instinct, and fifty years ago parents had the same instinct, just that they had no time and energy to intervene. Today, for various reasons, those constraints aren't stopping us, and we go wild."

At the Berkeley Parents Network, an online community, this struggle is vividly apparent. Parents anguish over whether jumping into the sandbox is appropriate to defend their children from a toy-grabber. Other parents confess that their once-cute child has become socially aggressive, which they find abhorrent and are at a loss to stop. The message board is full of stories of children being teased and ostracized; the responses range from coaching children to be less of a target to advocating martial arts training to reminding children they won't be invited to every birthday party in life. Nobody has the perfect answer, and it's clear just how torn the parents are.

The Nurture Paradox has moved many parents to demand "zero tolerance" policies in schools, not just for bullying, but for any sort of aggression or harassment. There is no evidence that bullying is actually on the increase, but the concern about its effects has skyrocketed.

In March 2007, the British House of Commons Education and Skills Committee convened a special inquiry on school bullying. For three days its members called a variety of witnesses, from school principals to academic scholars to support organizations. The testimony ran a full 288 pages when printed. No laws were written, and no systemwide policies were forced on all the schools, but that wasn't really the goal of the inquiry. Rather, the entire exercise was conducted to make one important categorical declaration, meant to guide the national culture: "The idea that bullying is in some way character building and simply part of childhood is wrong and should be challenged." Any sort of name-calling, mocking, gossiping, or exclusion needed to be condemned.

Most scholars have agreed that bullying can have serious effects, and that it absolutely needs to be stopped. However, they've balked on the "zero tolerance" approach.

A task force of the American Psychological Association warned that many incidents involve poor judgment, and lapses in judgment are developmentally normative—the result of neurological immaturity. All of which was a fancy way of saying that kids make mistakes because they're still young. They noted that inflicting automatic, severe punishments was causing an erosion of trust in authority figures. As the chair of the task force later explained, "The kids become fearful—not of other kids, but of the rules—because they think they'll break them by accident." During the new era of zero tolerance, levels of anxiety in students at school had gone up, not down. In Indiana, 95% of the suspensions weren't for bullying, per se—they were for "school disruption" and "other." The APA task force warned especially against over-applying zero tolerance to any sort of harassment.

Yet zero tolerance is becoming ever more common. According to one poll by Public Agenda, 68% of American parents support zero tolerance. From Florida to New York, schools are expanding their lists of what gets zero tolerance treatment to include teasing, cruelty, name-calling, social exclusion, and anything that causes psychological distress. One small Canadian town even passed a new law making these behaviors expressly illegal, punishable by fine.

According to the science of peer relations, there's one big problem with lumping all childhood aggression under the rubric of bullying. It's that most of the meanness, cruelty, and torment that goes on at schools isn't inflicted by those we commonly think of as bullies, or "bad" kids. Instead, most of it is meted out by children who are popular, well-liked, and admired.

The connection between popularity, social dominance, meanness and cruelty is hardly a surprise to any teacher—the dynamic is plainly visible at most schools. It's long been an archetype in literature and movies, from *Emma* to *Heathers* and *Mean Girls*. In some languages, there's a separate word to distinguish the kind of popular teen who diminishes others—in Dutch, for instance, the idiomatic expression *popiejopie* refers to teens who are bitchy, slutty, cocky, loud, and arrogant.

However, social scientists didn't really get around to studying the connection between popularity and aggression until this decade. That's largely due to the fact that the focus on the archetypal negative results of aggression helped papers get published and research dollars flow: grants were readily available to study the plight of aggressive kids, in the hope the findings might help society prevent aggressive kids from becoming our future prison population. The 1999 Columbine High School massacre opened more floodgates for grant dollars, as the government made it a priority to ensure students would never again open fire on their peers.

There was also a tendency, according to Dr. Allen, for social scientists to assume bad behaviors are uniformly associated with bad outcomes; aggression was considered bad behavior, so scientists were really only looking for the negative consequences of it.

Few research grants were available to study the popular kids systematically—chiefly because it was assumed popular kids are doing fine. Then, a few scholars who had been conducting long-term studies of adolescents reported on a connection between popularity and alcohol use. Lo and behold (not really any surprise), popular kids drink more and do more drugs.

For the first time, scientists were concerned about the kids who were doing well socially—they were at risk of becoming addicts, too! Suddenly, federal grant dollars began to flow into the science of popularity. Soon, the social forces of popularity were linked to aggression as well (especially relational aggression), and, finally, the social scientists caught up to the schoolteachers and screenwriters.

Today, the field of peer relations is in the process of doing an extraordinary backflip-with-twist, as scholars adapt to the new paradigm.

Ostrov's mentor, Dr. Nikki Crick of the University of Minnesota, has contradicted decades of earlier research that claimed girls weren't aggressive. She proved that girls can be just as aggressive as boys—only they're more likely to use relational aggression.

Similarly, Dr. Debra Pepler has shown that at the elementary school age, the "nonaggressive" kids are far from saintly—they still threaten to withdraw their friendship and threaten and push, just not as frequently as the more aggressive kids. So rather than the nonaggressive being the "good" kids, it might just be that they lack the savvy and confidence to assert themselves as often.

As University of Connecticut professor Dr. Antonius Cillessen explains, it's now recognized that aggressiveness is most often used as a means of asserting dominance to gain control or protect status. Aggression is not simply a breakdown or lapse of social skills. Rather, many acts of aggression require highly attuned social skills to pull off, and even physical aggression is often the mark of a child who is "socially savvy," not socially deviant. Aggressive kids aren't just being insensitive. On the contrary, says Cillessen, the relationally aggressive kid needs to be extremely sensitive. He needs to attack in a subtle and strategic way. He has to be socially intelligent, mastering his social network, so that he knows just the right buttons to push to drive his opponent crazy. Aggression comes as "early adolescents are discovering themselves. They're learning about coolness—how to be attractive to other people."

This completely changes the game for parents. When parents attempt to teach their seven-year-old daughter that it's wrong to exclude, spread rumors, or hit, they are literally attempting to take away from the child several useful tools of social dominance. "This behavior is rewarded in peer groups," observed Cillessen, "and you can say as a parent, 'Don't do this,' but the immediate rewards are very powerful." As long as the child is compulsively drawn to having class status, the appeal of those tools will undermine the parent's message. Children already know that parents think these behaviors are wrong—they've heard it since they were tots. But they return to these behaviors because of how their *peers* react—rewarding the aggressor with awe, respect, and influence.

The mystery has been why. Why don't kids shun aggressive peers? Why are so many aggressive kids socially central, and held in high regard?

Two reasons. First, aggressive behavior, like many kinds of rule breaking, is interpreted by other kids as a willingness to defy grown-ups, which makes the aggressive child seem independent and older—highly coveted traits. The child who always conforms to adults' expectations and follows their rules runs the risk of being seen as a wimp.

The other reason aggressive kids can remain socially powerful is that—just as the less-aggressive kids aren't angels—aggressive kids aren't all devils, either.

"A vast majority of behavioral scientists think of prosocial and antisocial behavior as being at opposite ends of a single dimension," explains University of Kansas professor Patricia Hawley. "To me, that oversimplifies the complexity of human behavior."

In the canon of child development, it's long been taken as gospel that a truly socially-competent child is nonaggressive. Hawley questions that orientation.

Hawley studies kids from preschool up through high school. She looks specifically at how one kid makes another do his bidding—whether it's through kind, prosocial behavior, or antisocial acts—threats, violence, teasing. Contrary to those who expected kids high in prosocial behavior to be low in antisocial acts, and vice versa, she finds that the same kids are responsible for both—the good and the bad. They are simply in the middle of everything, or, in the words of another researcher, "They're just socially busy."

Hawley calls the children who successfully use both prosocial and antisocial tactics to get their way "bistrategic controllers." These kids see that, when used correctly, kindness and cruelty are equally effective tools of power: the trick is achieving just the right balance, and the right timing. Those who master alternating between the two strategies become attractive to other children, rather than repellant, because they bring so much to the party. Not only are they popular, they're well-liked by kids, and by teachers, too (who rate them as being agreeable and well-adjusted).

Hawley's data suggests that at least one in ten children fits the bistrategic description. But inspired by her approach, several other scholars have done similar analyses. Their subsequent findings suggest that the proportion is even higher—around one in six.

Jamie Ostrov has been finding kids with a similarly mixed pattern of prosocial and aggressive behavior in his preschool research. In his television-use study, the children who watched a lot of educational television were far more relationally aggressive, but they were vastly more prosocial to classmates as well.

"The lesson from these children is that it might not make sense to look at aggression alone," Hawley stated. "Bistrategics can use unsettling levels of aggression without suffering the same consequences of those using only aggression." It's an exhibition of their nascent ambition.

For her part, Hawley's only problem is that her bistrategics are so successful, in school and in life, that she still can't get a grant to follow them long-term.

※

We began this chapter by asking why modern parenting has failed to result in a generation of kinder, gentler kids. It turns out that many of our enlightened innovations have had unintended consequences.

When we changed the channel from violent television to tamer fare, kids just ended up learning the advanced skills of clique formation, friendship withdrawal, and the art of the insult.

In taking our marital arguments upstairs to avoid exposing the children to strife, we accidentally deprived them of chances to witness how two people who care about each other can work out their differences in a calm and reasoned way.

We thought that aggressiveness was the reaction to peer rejection, so we have painstakingly attempted to eliminate peer rejection from the childhood experience. In its place is elaborately orchestrated peer interaction. We've created the play date phenomenon, while ladening older kids' schedules with after-school activities. We've segregated children by age—building separate playgrounds for the youngest children, and stratifying classes and teams. Unwittingly, we've put children into an echo chamber. Today's average middle schooler has a phenomenal 299 peer interactions a day. The average teen spends sixty hours a week surrounded by a peer group (and only sixteen hours a week surrounded by adults). This has created the perfect atmosphere for a different strain of aggression-virus to breed—one fed not by peer rejection, but fed by the need for peer status and social ranking. The more time peers spend together, the stronger this compulsion is to rank high, resulting in the hostility of one-upmanship. All those lessons about sharing and consideration can hardly compete. We wonder why it takes twenty years to teach a child how to conduct himself in polite society—overlooking the fact that we've essentially left our children to socialize themselves.

※

One more factor that contributes to children's aggression needs to be mentioned.

Dr. Sarah Schoppe-Sullivan did a study of parenting styles, and how they relate to aggressiveness and acting out at school. The fathers in her study fell into three camps—the Progressive Dads, the Traditional Dads, and the Disengaged Dads.

We might expect that the Progressive Dads would smoke their competition. No longer inhibited by gender roles, and very involved in child rearing from the moment of birth, Progressive Dads are regularly shown in the research to be an almost universally good phenomenon. Children of these coparenting fathers have better sibling relationships, feel good about themselves, and do better academically.

And at first, in Schoppe-Sullivan's study, the Progressive Dads far outshone the other two groups. In the lab, they were more engaged with both spouses and kids. At home, they shared responsibility for the children. While the Traditional Dads were involved parents, their involvement was usually at their wives' direction. The Progressive Dads, on the other hand, were adept parents on their own. These dads figured out what the kid should be wearing for school and the rest of the morning routine and then put the child to bed. They played more with the kids, and they were more supportive when they did so. They were just as likely as the moms to stay home from work if the kid was sick.

However, Schoppe-Sullivan was surprised to discover that the Progressive Dads had poorer marital quality and rated their family functioning lower than the fathers in couples who took on traditional roles. Their greater involvement may have lead to increased conflict over parenting practices—which in turn would affect their kids.

At the same time, the Progressive Dad was inconsistent in what forms of discipline he ultimately used: he wasn't as strong at establishing rules or enforcing them. Extrapolating from earlier research showing that fathers often doubt their ability to effectively discipline a child, Sullivan has hypothesized that the Progressive Dad may know how *not* to discipline a child (i.e., hit the kid, scream), but he doesn't know what to do instead. Indeed, the whole idea that he would actually need to discipline a child—that the kid hasn't simply modeled the father's warm, compassionate ways—may throw him for a loop. Moreover, he finds punishing his kid acutely embarrassing. Therefore, one day it'd be no dessert; the next day the silent treatment; the third it would be a threat of no allowance if the infraction happened again; the fourth it'd be psychological criticism meant to induce guilt. He's always trying something new, and caving at the wrong time.

This inconsistency and permissiveness led to a surprising result in Sullivan's study: the children of Progressive Dads were aggressive and acted out in school nearly as much as the kids with fathers who were distant and disengaged.

There's an old word in the Oxford English Dictionary that means "one skilled in the rearing of children." The word is pedotrophist. We sometimes assume that today's progressive coparents who can set up a portable crib in sixty seconds and can change a diaper one-handed are the contemporary pedotrophists.

But at least in one dimension, the progressive parent appears to come with a natural weakness.

TEN

Why Hannah Talks and Alyssa Doesn't

Despite scientists' admonitions, parents still spend billions every year on gimmicks and videos, hoping to jump-start infants' language skills. What's the right way to accomplish this goal?

In November 2007, a media firestorm erupted.

The preeminent journal *Pediatrics* published a report out of the University of Washington: infants who watched so-called "baby videos" had a quantifiably smaller vocabulary than those who had not watched the videos. With sales of baby videos estimated to be as high as $4.8 billion annually, the industry went on red alert.

Robert A. Iger, Chief Executive Officer of Disney—which owns the Baby Einstein brand—took the unusual step of publicly disparaging the scholars' work, describing their findings as "doubtful" and the study methodology as "poorly done." He complained the university statement in support of the study was "reckless" and "totally irresponsible."

Parents, many of whom had these DVDs on their shelves, were similarly disbelieving. One of the big reasons for their skepticism was an inexplicably wacky result within the study. According to the data, almost all other kinds of television and movies infants were exposed to—from Disney's own *The Little Mermaid* to *American Idol*—were fine for kids. It was baby DVDs—and only baby DVDs—to watch out for. Iger described the findings as nothing less than "absurd."

How could these DVDs, beloved by infants around the world, possibly be bad for them?

The report was actually a follow-up to an earlier study the researchers had done to examine if parents used the television as an electronic babysitter. Most academics had assumed that was true—parents were parking the kids in front of a video while they went to make a phone call or cook dinner—but no one had tried to find out if there was a basis to the hypothesis.

In that study, parents did confirm that some babysitting was going on, but the main reason infants were watching television—especially videos such as those in the Baby Einstein and Brainy Baby series—was because parents believed the programs would give their children a cognitive advantage.

"We had parents with kids in front of the TV for as many as twenty hours a week 'for their brain development,'" recalled Dr. Andrew Meltzoff, one of the authors of both studies. "Parents told us that they couldn't provide much for their children, and that troubled them, so they had saved up and bought the videos hoping that would make up for everything else. Then they had faithfully strapped their kids into place to watch for four to six hours a week. They said they thought that was the best thing they could do for their babies."

Moved by parents' dramatic efforts to shore up their children's intellectual development, the scholars conducted the second study—in order to quantify the actual impact of such television exposure.

The research team called hundreds of families in Washington and Minnesota, asking parents to report the amount of television their children were watching, by each type of program. Then, they had the parents complete what's known as the MacArthur Communicative Development Inventory. Quite simply, the CDI is a list of 89 common words infants may know, and, if they are old enough, say themselves. The words represent a range of vocabulary sophistication, from "cup" and "push" to "fast" and "radio." The CDI is an internationally accepted measure of early language—translated versions of it are used around the world.

Analyzing the data, the scholars found a dose-response relationship, meaning the more the children watched, the worse their vocabulary. If infants watched the shows one hour per day, they knew 6 to 8 fewer of the 89 CDI words than infants who did not watch any baby DVDs. That might not sound like a big deficit, but consider that the average eleven-month-old boy recognizes only 16 of the CDI words in the first place. Understanding 6 fewer of the CDI words would drop him from the 50th percentile to the 35th.

The results couldn't have been further from the statements made in the very first press release from Baby Einstein, in March 1997:

> Studies show that if these neurons are not used, they may die. Through exposure to phonemes in seven languages, Baby Einstein contributes to increased brain capacity.

Baby Einstein creator Julie Aigner-Clark specifically credited one professor, Dr. Patricia Kuhl, as the inspiration for much of the video's content. In an interview, Aigner-Clark explained, "After reading some of the research by Patricia Kuhl of the University of Washington, I decided to make the auditory portion of the video multilingual, with mothers from seven different countries reciting nursery rhymes and counting in their native languages."

Kuhl and other scholars had determined that, at birth, babies are sensitive to any language's phonemes—unique sound combinations that make up a word. (Each language has about 40 phonemes, such as "kuh" or "ch.") Once babies are around six to nine months old, they gradually lose that generalist sensitivity. Their brains become specialized, trained to recognize the phonemes of the language (or languages) they hear most. Kuhl describes this process as becoming "neurally committed" to a language. Commonly-used neural pathways in the brain strengthen, while unused pathways weaken.

Aigner-Clark's hope was that her audio track would train children's brains to recognize phonemes in a wide assortment of languages—

essentially, preventing neural specialization. Hearing these languages early in life would allow them to learn multiple foreign languages later.

Back in 1997, Aigner-Clark's product seemed to piggyback on Kuhl's research. But that's quite ironic, because in the years since, Patricia Kuhl's ongoing findings have helped explain why baby DVDs *don't* work.

First, in a longitudinal study, Kuhl showed that neural commitment to a primary language isn't a bad thing. The more "committed" a baby's brain is, at nine months old, the more advanced his language will be at three years old. With a weaker connection, children don't progress as quickly, and this seems to have lasting impact.

Second, Kuhl went on to discover that babies' brains do not learn to recognize foreign-language phonemes off a videotape or audiotape—at all. They absolutely do learn from a live, human teacher. In fact, babies' brains are so sensitive to live human speech that Kuhl was able to train American babies to recognize Mandarin phonemes (which they'd never heard before) from just twelve sessions with her Chinese graduate students, who sat in front of the kids for twenty minutes each session, playing with them while speaking in Mandarin. By the end of the month, three sessions per week, those babies' brains were virtually as good at recognizing Mandarin phonemes as the brains of native-born Chinese infants who'd been hearing Mandarin their entire young lives.

But when Kuhl put American infants in front of a videotape or audio recording of Mandarin speech, the infants' brains absorbed none of it. They might as well have heard meaningless noise. This was true *despite* seeming to be quite engaged by the videos. Kuhl concluded: "The more complex aspects of language, such as phonetics and grammar, are not acquired from TV exposure."

By implication, we can conclude that baby DVDs *don't* delay neural commitment; rather, they have virtually no effect on auditory processing.

The irony here only deepens. One might have noticed that all of these scholars are at the University of Washington. Kuhl and Meltzoff are Co-Directors of the same lab. So when Disney CEO Iger attacked the *Pediatrics* scholars, he was attacking the very laboratory and institution that Baby Einstein had hailed, when its Language Nursery DVD was first released.

So why does an infant need a live human speaker to learn language from? Why are babies learning nothing from the audio track of a baby DVD, while their language isn't impaired by exposure to regular TV?

The evidence suggests one factor is that baby DVDs rely on disembodied audio voice-overs, unrelated to the abstract imagery of the video track. Meanwhile, grown-up television shows live actors, usually close up—kids can see their faces as they talk. Studies have repeatedly shown that seeing a person's face makes a huge difference.

Babies learn to decipher speech partly by lip-reading: they watch how people move their lips and mouths to produce sounds. One of the first things that babies must learn—before they can comprehend any word meanings—is when one word ends and another begins. Without segmentation, an adult's words probably sound about the same to an infant as does his own babbling. At 7.5 months, babies can segment the speech of people they see speaking. However, if the babies hear speech while looking at an abstract shape, instead of a face, they can't segment the sounds: the speech once again is just endless gibberish. (Even for adults, seeing someone's lips as he speaks is the equivalent of a 20-decibel increase in volume.)

When a child sees someone speak and hears his voice, there are two sensory draws—two simultaneous events both telling the child to pay attention to this single object of interest—this moment of human interaction. The result is that the infant is more focused, remembers the event, and learns more. Contrast that to the disconnected voice-overs and images of the baby videos. The sensory inputs don't build on each other. Instead, they compete.

Would baby DVDs work better if they showed human faces speaking? Possibly. But there's another reason—a more powerful reason—why language learning can't be left to DVDs. Video programming can't interact with the baby, responding to the sounds she makes. Why this is so important requires careful explanation.

※

Wondering what parents' prevailing assumptions about language acquisition were, we polled some parents, asking them why they thought one kid picked up language far faster than another. Specifically, we were asking about two typically-developing kids, without hearing or speech impairments.

Most parents admitted they didn't know, but they had absorbed a little information here and there to inform their guesses. One of these parents was Anne Frazier, mother to ten-month-old Jon and a litigator at a prestigious Chicago law firm; she was working part-time until Jon turned one. Frazier had a Chinese client base and, before having Jon, occasionally traveled to Asia. She'd wanted to learn Mandarin, but her efforts were mostly for naught. She had decided that she was too old—her brain had lost the necessary plasticity—so she was determined to start her son young. When she was dressing or feeding her baby, she had Chinese-language news broadcasts playing on the television in the background. They never sat down just to watch television—she didn't think that would be good for Jon—but Frazier did try to make sure her child heard twenty minutes of Mandarin a day. She figured it couldn't hurt.

Frazier also assumed that Jon would prove to have some level of innate verbal ability—but this would be affected by the sheer amount of language Jon was exposed to. Having a general sense that she needed to constantly talk to her child, Frazier was submitting her kid to a veritable barrage of words.

"Nonstop chatter throughout the day," she affirmed. "As we run errands, or take a walk, I describe what's on the street—colors, everything I see. It's very easy for a mother to lose her voice."

She sounded exhausted describing it. "It's hard to keep talking to myself all the time," Frazier confessed. "Infants don't really contribute anything to the conversation."

Frazier's story was similar to many we heard. Parents were vague on the details, but word had gotten out that innate ability wasn't the only factor: children raised in a more robust, language-intensive home will hit developmental milestones quicker. This is also the premise of popular advice books for parents of newborns, which usually devote a page to reminding parents to talk a lot to their babies, and around their babies. A fast-selling new product being sold to parents is the $699 "verbal pedometer," a sophisticated gadget the size of a cell phone that can be slipped into the baby's pocket or car seat. It counts the number of words the baby hears during an hour or day.

The verbal pedometer is actually used by many researchers who study infants' exposure to language. The inspiration behind such a tool is a famous longitudinal study by Drs. Betty Hart and Todd Risley, from the University of Kansas, published in 1994.

Hart and Risley went into the homes of a variety of families with a seven- to nine-month-old infant. They videotaped an hour of interactions while the parent was feeding the baby or doing chores with the baby nearby—and they repeated this once a month until the children were three. Painstakingly breaking down those tapes into data, Hart and Risley found that infants in welfare families heard about 600 words per hour. Meanwhile, the infants of working-class families heard 900 words per hour, and the infants of professional-class families heard 1,500 words per hour. These gaps only increased when the babies turned into toddlers—not because the parents spoke to their children more often, but because they communicated in more complex sentences, adding to the word count.

This richness of language exposure had a very strong correlation to the children's resulting vocabulary. By their third birthday, children of professional parents had spoken vocabularies of 1,100 words, on average, while the children of welfare families were less than half as articulate—speaking only 525 words, on average.

The complexity, variety, and sheer amount of language a child hears is certainly one driver of language acquisition. But it's not scientifically clear that merely hearing lots of language is the crucial, dominant factor. For their part, Hart and Risley wrote pages listing many other variables at play, *all* of which had correlations with the resulting rate at which the children learned to speak.

In addition, the words in the English language that children hear most often are words like "was," "of," "that," "in," and "some"—these are termed "closed class" words. Yet children learn these words the most slowly—usually not until after their second birthday. By contrast, children learn nouns first, even though nouns are the least commonly-occurring words in parents' natural speech to children.

The basic paradigm, that a child's language output is a direct function of the enormity of input, also doesn't explain why two children, both of whom have similar home experiences (they might both have highly educated, articulate mothers, for instance) can acquire language on vastly divergent timelines.

A decade ago, Hart and Risley's work was the cutting edge of language research. It's still one of the most quoted and cited studies in all of social science. But in the last decade, other scholars have been flying under the radar, teasing out exactly what's happening in a child's first two years that pulls her from babble to fluent speech.

If there's one main lesson from this newest science, it's this: the basic paradigm has been flipped. The information flow that matters most is in the opposite direction we previously assumed. The central role of the parent is not to push massive amounts of language *into* the baby's ears; rather, the central role of the parent is to notice what's coming *from* the baby, and respond accordingly—coming from his mouth, his eyes, and his fingers. If, like Anne Frazier, you think a baby isn't contributing to the conversation, you've missed something really important.

In fact, one of the mechanisms helping a baby to talk isn't a parent's speech at all—it's not what a child *hears* from a parent, but what a parent accomplishes with a well-timed, loving caress.

※

Dr. Catherine Tamis-LeMonda, of New York University, has spent the last decade looking specifically at parent-responsiveness to infants, and its impact on language development. Along with Dr. Marc Bornstein of the National Institutes of Health, she sent teams of researchers into homes of families with nine-month-old babies. For the most part, these were affluent families with extremely well-educated parents living in the New York City area. The researchers set some age-appropriate toys down on the floor and asked the mother to play with her child for ten minutes.

These interactions were videotaped, and the ten-minute tapes were later broken down second by second. Every time the baby looked to the mother, or babbled, or reached for a toy was noted. The children did this, on average, about 65 times in ten minutes, but some kids were very quiet that day and others very active. Every time the mother responded, immediately, was also noted. The moms might say, "Good job," or "That's a spoon," or "Look here." The moms responded about 60 percent of the time. Responses that were late, or off-timed (outside a five-second window), were categorized separately.

The researchers then telephoned the mothers every week, for the next year, to track what new words the child was using that week—guided by a checklist of the 680 words and phrases a toddler might know. This created a very accurate record of each child's progression. (They also repeated the in-home videotape session when the infant was thirteen months old, to get a second scoring of maternal responsiveness.)

On average, the children in Tamis-LeMonda's study said their first words just before they were thirteen months old. By eighteen months, the average toddler had 50 words in her vocabulary, was combining words together, and was even using language to talk about the recent past. But there was great variability within this sample, with some tots hitting those milestones far earlier, others far later.

The variable that best explained these gaps was how often a mom rapidly responded to her child's vocalizations and explorations. The toddlers of high-responders were a whopping six months ahead of the toddlers of low-responders. They were saying their first word at ten months, and reaching the other milestones by fourteen months.

Remember, the families in this sample were all well-off, so *all* the children were exposed to robust parent vocabularies. All the infants heard lots of language. How often a mother initiated a conversation with her child was not predictive of the language outcomes—what mattered was, if the infant initiated, whether the mom responded.

"I couldn't believe there was that much of a shift in developmental timing," Tamis-LeMonda recalled. "The shifts were hugely dramatic." She points to two probable mechanisms to explain it. First, through this call-and-response pattern, the baby's brain learns that the sounds coming out of his mouth affect his parents and get their attention—that voicing is important, not meaningless. Second, a child needs to associate an object with a word, so the word has to be heard just as an infant is looking at or grabbing it.

In one paper, Tamis-LeMonda compares two little girls in her study, Hannah and Alyssa. At nine months old, both girls could understand about seven words, but weren't saying any yet. Hannah was vocalizing and exploring only half as often as Alyssa—who did so 100 times during the ten minutes recorded. But Hannah's mom was significantly more responsive. She missed very few opportunities to respond to Hannah, and described whatever Hannah was looking at twice as often as Alyssa's mother did with Alyssa. At thirteen months, this gap was confirmed: Hannah's mom responded 85% of the time, while Alyssa's mom did so about 55% of the time.

Meanwhile, Hannah was turning into a chatterbox. Alyssa progressed slowly. And the gap only increased month by month. During their eighteenth month, Alyssa added 8 new words to her productive vocabulary, while in that same single-month period, Hannah added a phenomenal 150 words, 50 of which were verbs and adjectives.

At twenty-one months, Alyssa's most complicated usages were "I pee" and "Mama bye-bye," while Hannah was using prepositions and gerunds regularly, saying sentences like: "Yoni was eating an onion bagel." By her second birthday, it was almost impossible to keep track of Hannah's language, since she could say just about anything.

This variable, how a parent responds to a child's vocalizations—right in the moment—seems to be the most powerful mechanism pulling a child from babble to fluent speech.

Now, if we take a second look at the famous Hart and Risley study, in light of Tamis-LeMonda's findings, this same mechanism is apparent. In Hart and Risley's data, the poor parents initiated conversations just as often with their tots as affluent parents (about once every two minutes). Those initiations were even slightly richer in language than those of the affluent parents. But the real gap was in how parents *responded* to their children's actions and speech.

The affluent parents responded to what their child babbled, said, or did over 200 times per hour—a vocal response or a touch of the hand was enough to count. Each time the child spoke or did something, the parent quickly echoed back. The parents on welfare responded to their children's words and behavior less than half as often, occupied with the burden of chores and larger families. (Subsequent analysis by Dr. Gary Evans showed that parent responsiveness was also dampened by living in crowded homes; crowding leads people to psychologically withdraw, making them less responsive to one another.)

Tamis-LeMonda's scholarship relies on correlations—on its own, it's not actually proof that parent-responsiveness *causes* infants to speed up their language production. To really be convinced that one triggers the other, we'd need controlled experiments where parents increase their response rate, and track if this leads to real-time boosts in infant vocalization.

Luckily, those experiments have been done—by Dr. Michael Goldstein at Cornell University. He gets infants to change how they babble, in just ten minutes flat.

The first time a mother and her infant arrive for an appointment at Michael Goldstein's lab in the psychology building on the Cornell University campus, they're not tested at all. They're simply put in a quiet room with a few toys, for half an hour, to get used to the setting. The walls are white, decorated with Winnie the Pooh stickers. The carpet is light brown and comfortable to sit on. On the floor are many of the same playthings the infant might have at home—a brightly colored stuffed inchworm, stacking rings, a play mat with removable shapes, and a toy chest to explore. At three points around the room, videocameras extend from the wall, draped in white cloth to be inconspicuous. The mom knows full well that she is being watched, both on camera and through a large one-way glass pane. But this is otherwise a nice moment to interact with her baby—she can't be distracted by the cell phone or household chores. Her baby pulls himself to his mom's lap, puts the toys nearby in his mouth, and if he can crawl, perhaps pulls himself up to look inside the toy chest.

The next day, mother and baby return. In Goldstein's seminal experiment, the nine-month-old infant is put in denim overalls that carry a very sensitive wireless microphone in the chest pocket. The mother is given a pair of wireless headphones that still allow her to hear her baby. They are put back in the playroom, and again asked to play together naturally. After ten minutes, a researcher's voice comes over the headphones with instructions. When the mom hears the prompt "Go ahead," she's supposed to lean in even closer to her baby, pat or rub the child, and maybe give him a kiss.

The mom doesn't know what triggers this cue. The mom just knows that, over the next ten minutes, she hears "Go ahead" a lot, almost six times a minute. She might notice that her baby is vocalizing more—or that he's waving his arms or flapping his feet—but she won't know what's triggering this. For the final ten minutes, she's asked to simply play and interact naturally with her child again.

When mother and infant leave, she has almost no idea what the researchers might have been up to. For two half-hour periods, she merely played and talked with her child.

But here's what it was like on the other side of the one-way glass: during those middle ten minutes, every time the child made a voiced sound (as opposed to a cough, grunt, or raspberry), it could be heard loudly over speakers in the observation room. Immediately, the researcher told the mother to "go ahead," and within a second the mother had affectionately touched the child. Later that night, a graduate student would sit down with the session videotape and take notes, second by second, tracking how often the baby babbled, and what quality of sounds he made.

While all baby babble might sound like gibberish, there's actually a progression of overlapping stages, with each type of babble more mature and advanced than the one prior. "No less than eighty muscles control the vocal tract, which takes a year or more to gain control of," Goldstein explained. From birth, children make "quasi-resonant" vowel sounds. They use the back of the vocal tract with a closed throat and little breath support. Because the larynx hasn't yet descended, what breath there is passes through both the mouth and nose. The result is nasal and creaky, often sounding like the baby is fussy (which it's not).

While the child won't be able to make the next-stage sound for several months, there's still a very important interaction with parents going on. They basically take turns "talking," as if having a mock conversation. The baby coos, and the daddy responds, "Is that so?" The baby babbles again, and the daddy in jest returns, "Well, we'll have to ask Mom."

While most parents seem to intuit their role in this turn-taking pattern spontaneously—without being told to do so by any handbook—they don't all do so equally well. A remarkable study of vocal turn-taking found that when four-month-old infants and their parents exhibited better rhythmic coupling, those children would later have greater cognitive ability.

According to Goldstein, "Turn-taking is driving the vocal development—pushing the babies to make more sophisticated sounds."

Parents find themselves talking to their baby in the singsongy cadence that's termed "parentese," without knowing why they're strangely compelled to do so. They're still using English, but the emotional affect is giddily upbeat and the vowels are stretched, with highly exaggerated pitch contours. It's not cultural—it's almost universal—and the phonetic qualities help children's brains discern discrete sounds.

Around five months, a baby has gained enough control of the muscles in the vocal tract to open her throat and push breath through to occasionally produce "fully resonant" vowels. "To a mother of a five-month-old," Goldstein said, "hearing a fully resonant sound from her baby is a big deal. It's very exciting." If her response is well-timed, the child's brain notices the extra attention these new sounds win. At this point, parents start to phase out responding to all the old sounds, since they've heard them so often. That selective responsiveness in turn further pushes the child toward more fully-resonant sounds.

Soon the baby is adding "marginal syllables," consonant-vowel transitions—rather than "goo" and "coo," more like "ba" and "da," using the articulators in the front of the mouth. However, the transition from the consonant to the vowel is drawn out, since the tongue and teeth and upper cleft can't get out of the way fast enough, causing the vowel to sound distorted. (This is why so many of a baby's first words start with *B* and *D*—those are the first proper consonants the muscles can make.)

As early as six months, but typically around nine months, infants start producing some "canonical syllables," the basic components of adult speech. The consonant-vowel transition is fast, and the breath is quick. The child is almost ready to combine syllables into words. "We used nine-month-olds in our study because at that age, they are still commonly expressing all four types of babble," Goldstein said. Quasi-resonant vowel babble might still be in the majority, and canonical syllables quite rare.

With this developmental scale in mind, it's shocking to hear the difference in how the baby vocalizes over the course of Goldstein's experiment. In the first ten minutes (that baseline natural period when the mom responded as she might at home), the average child vocalized 25 times. The rate leapt to 55 times in the middle ten minutes, when the mom was being coached to "go ahead" by Goldstein. The complexity and maturity of the babble also shot up dramatically; almost all vowels were now fully voiced, and the syllable formation improved. Canonical syllables, previously infrequent, now were made half the time, on average.

To my ear, it was stunning—the children literally sounded five months older, during the second ten-minute period, than they had in the first.

"What's most important to note here is that the infant was not mimicking his parent's sounds," Goldstein noted.

During those middle ten minutes, the parent was only caressing the child, to reward the babble. The child wasn't hearing much out of his mother's mouth. But the touching, by itself, had a remarkable effect on the frequency and maturity of the babble.

Goldstein reproduced the experiment, asking parents to speak to their children as well as touch them. Specifically, he told half the parents what vowel sound to make, the other half he fed a consonant-vowel syllable that was wordlike, such as "dat." Not surprisingly, the tots who heard vowels uttered more vowels, and those who heard syllables made more canonical syllables. Again though, the babies weren't repeating the actual vowel or consonant-vowel. Instead, they adopted the phonological pattern. Parents who said "ahh" might hear an "ee" or an "oo" from their baby, and those who said "dat" might hear "bem." At this tender age, infants aren't yet attempting to parrot the actual sound a parent makes; they're learning the consonant-vowel transitions, which they will soon generalize to *all* words.

To some degree, Goldstein's research seems to have unlocked the secret to learning to talk—he's just given eager parents a road map for how to fast-track their infants' language development. But Goldstein is very careful to warn parents against overdoing it. "Children need breaks for their brain to consolidate what it's learned," he points out. "Sometimes children just need play time, alone, where they can babble to themselves." He also cites a long trail of scholarship, back to B.F. Skinner, on how intermittent rewards are ultimately more powerful than constant rewards.

And lest any parent pull her infant out of day care in order to ensure he's being responded to enough, Goldstein says, "The mix of responses a baby gets in a high-quality day care is probably ideal."

Tamis-LeMonda also warns against overstimulation. Her moms weren't responding at that high rate *all day*. "In my study, the mothers were told to sit down and play with their infant and these toys. But the same mom, when feeding the baby, might respond only thirty percent of the time. When the child is playing on the floor while the mom is cooking, it might be only ten percent. Reading books together, they'd have a very high response rate again."

Goldstein has two other points of caution, for parents gung-ho on using his research to help their babies. His first concern is that a parent, keen to improve his response rate, might make the mistake of over-reinforcing less-resonant sounds when a baby is otherwise ready to progress, thereby slowing development. This would reward a baby for immature sounds, making it too easy for the baby to get attention. The extent to which parents, in a natural setting, should phase out responses to immature sounds, and become more selective in their response, is thus far unknown.

Goldstein's second clarification comes from a study he co-authored with his partner at Cornell, Dr. Jennifer Schwade. As Goldstein's expertise is a tot's first year of life, Schwade's expertise is the second year, when children learn their first 300 words. One of the ways parents help infants is by doing what's called "object labeling"—telling them, "That's your stroller," "See the flower?," and "Look at the moon." Babies learn better from object-labeling when the parent waits for the baby's eyes to naturally be gazing at the object. The technique is especially powerful when the infant both gazes *and* vocalizes, or gazes *and* points. Ideally, the parent isn't intruding, or directing the child's attention—instead he's following the child's lead. When the parent times the label correctly, the child's brain associates the sound with the object.

Parents screw this up in two ways. First, they intrude rather than let the child show some curiosity and interest first. Second, they ignore what the child is looking at and instead take their cues from *what they think the child was trying to say.*

The baby, holding a spoon, might say "buh, buh," and the zealous parent thinks, "He just said 'bottle,' he wants his bottle," and echoes to the child, "Bottle? You want your bottle? I'll get you your bottle." Inadvertently, the parent just crisscrossed the baby, teaching him that a spoon is called "bottle." Some parents, in Goldstein and Schwade's research, make these mismatches of speech 30% of the time. "Beh" gets mistaken by parents as "bottle," "blanket," or "brother." "Deh" is interpreted as "Daddy" or "dog," "kih" as "kitty," and "ebb" as "apple." In fact, at nine months old, the baby may mean none of those—he's just making a canonical syllable.

Pretending the infant is saying words, when he can't yet, can really cause problems.

Proper object-labeling, when the infants were nine months, had an extremely strong positive correlation (81%) with the child's vocabulary six months later. Crisscrossed labeling—such as saying "bottle" when the baby was holding a spoon—had an extremely negative correlation with resulting vocabulary (−68%). In real life terms, what did this mean? The mother in Schwade's study who was best at object labeling had a fifteen-month-old daughter who understood 246 words and produced 64 words. By contrast, the mother who crisscrossed her infant the most had a fifteen-month-old daughter who understood only 61 words and produced only 5.

※

According to Schwade's research, object labeling is just one of any number of ways that adults scaffold language for toddlers. Again, these are things parents tend to do naturally, but not equally well. In this section, we'll cover five of those techniques.

For instance, when adults talk to young children about small objects, they frequently twist the object, or shake it, or move it around—usually synchronizing the movements to the singsong of parentese. This is called "motionese," and it's very helpful in teaching the name of the object. Moving the object helps attract the infant's attention, turning the moment into a multisensory experience. But the window to use motionese closes at fifteen months—by that age, children no longer need the extra motion, or benefit from it.

Just as multisensory inputs help, so does hearing language from multiple speakers.

University of Iowa researchers recently discovered that fourteen-month-old children failed to learn a novel word if they heard it spoken by a single person, even if the word was repeated many times. The fact that there was a word they were supposed to be learning just didn't seem to register. Then, instead of having the children listen to the same person speaking many times, they had kids listen to the word spoken by a variety of different people. The kids immediately learned the word. Hearing multiple speakers gave the children the opportunity to take in how the phonics were the same, even if the voices varied in pitch and speed. By hearing what was different, they learned what was the same.

A typical two-year-old child hears roughly 7,000 utterances a day. But those aren't 7,000 unique sayings, each one a challenge to decode. A lot of that language is already familiar to a child. In fact, 45% of utterances from mothers begin with one of these 17 words:

what, that, it, you, are/aren't, I, do/don't, is, a, would, can/can't, where, there, who, come, look, and let's.

With a list of 156 two- and three-word combinations, scholars can account for the beginnings of two-thirds of the sentences mothers say to their children.

These predictably repeating word combinations—known as "frames"—become the spoken equivalent of highlighting a text. A child already knows the cadence and phonemes for most of the sentence—only a small part of what's said is entirely new.

So you might think kids need to acquire a certain number of words in their vocabulary before they learn any sort of grammar—but it's the exact opposite. Grammar teaches vocabulary.

One example: for years, scholars believed that children learned nouns before they learned verbs; it was assumed children learn names for objects before they can comprehend descriptions of actions. Then scholars went to Korea. Unlike European languages, Korean sentences often end with a verb, not a noun. Twenty-month-olds there with a vocabulary of fewer than 50 words knew more verbs than nouns. The first words the kids learned were the last ones usually spoken—because they heard them more clearly.

Until children are eighteen months old, they can't make out nouns located in the middle of a sentence. For instance, a toddler might know all of the words in the following sentence: "The princess put the toy under her chair." However, hearing that sentence, a toddler still won't be able to figure out what happened to the toy, because "toy" came mid-sentence.

The word frames become vital frames of reference. When a child hears, "Look at the ___," he quickly learns that ___ is a new thing to see. Whatever comes after "Don't" is something he should stop doing—even if he doesn't yet know the words "touch" or "light socket."

Without frames, a kid is just existing within a real-life version of *Mad Libs*—trying to plug the few words he recognizes into a context where they may or may not belong.

This key concept—using some repetition to highlight the variation—also applies to grammatical variation.

The cousin to frames are "variation sets." In a variation set, the context and meaning of the sentence remain constant over the course of a *series* of sentences, but the vocabulary and grammatical structure change. For instance, a variation set would thus be: "Rachel, bring the book to Daddy. Bring him the book. Give it to Daddy. Thank you, Rachel—you gave Daddy the book."

In this way, Rachel learns that a "book" is also an "it," and that another word for "Daddy" is "him." That "bring" and "give" both involve moving an object. Grammatically, she heard the past tense of "give," that it's possible for nouns to switch from being subjects to being direct objects (and vice versa), and that verbs can be used as an instruction to act ("Give it") or a description of action taken ("You gave").

Variation sets are the expertise of a colleague of Schwade's at Cornell, Dr. Heidi Waterfall. Simply put, variation sets are really beneficial at teaching both syntax and words—and the greater the variations (in nouns, verbs, conjugation and placement) the better.

From motionese to variation sets—each element teaches a child what is signal and what is noise. But the benefits of knowing what to focus on and what to ignore can hardly be better illustrated than by the research on "shape bias."

For many of the object nouns kids are trying to learn, the world offers really confusing examples. Common objects like trucks, dogs, telephones, and jackets come in every imaginable color and size and texture. As early as fifteen months old, kids learn to make sense of the world by keying off objects' commonality of shape, avoiding the distraction of other details. But some kids remain puzzled over what to focus on, and their lack of "shape bias" holds back their language spurt.

However, shape bias is teachable. In one experiment, Drs. Linda Smith and Larissa Samuelson had seventeen-month-old children come into the lab for seven weeks of "shape training." The sessions were incredibly minimal—each was just five minutes long and the kids learned to identify just four novel shapes ("This is a wug. Can you find the wug?"). That's all it took, but the effect was amazing. The children's vocabulary for object names skyrocketed 256%.

A nine-month-old child is typically-developing if he can speak even 1 word. With the benefit of proper scaffolding, he'll know 50 to 100 words within just a few months. By two, he will speak around 320 words; a couple months later—over 570. Then the floodgates open. By three, he'll likely be speaking in full sentences. By the time he's off to kindergarten, he may easily have a vocabulary of over 10,000 words.

※

It was one thing to learn about these scaffolding techniques from Goldstein and Schwade—but it was another thing to actually see their power in action.

Ashley had that chance shortly after we returned from Cornell, when she met her best friends, Glenn and Bonnie Summer, and their twelve-month-old daughter Jenna, for a casual dinner in Westwood, a shopping area in West Los Angeles. Ashley thinks of Jenna as her niece, and she had brought a tiny, red Cornell sweatshirt for the baby. During dinner, Ashley also couldn't help but try some of the scaffolding techniques on Jenna.

Every time Jenna looked at something, Ashley instantly labeled it for her. "Fan," Ashley pronounced, when Jenna's gaze landed on the ceiling fan that beat the air. "Phone," she chimed, whenever Jenna's ears led her eyes to the pizza joint's wall-mounted telephone, ringing off the hook. Whenever Jenna babbled, Ashley immediately responded with a word or touch. Ashley clearly noticed the different babble stages in Jenna's chatter.

Jenna turned to her mother and made the baby sign gesture "More," tapping her fingertips together. She wanted another piece of the nectarine Bonnie had brought for her.

After giving the little girl the fruit, Bonnie complained: "It's the one baby sign she knows—a friend of mine taught it to her—and now I can't get Jenna to say 'More.' She used to try saying the word out loud, but now she only signs it. I hate it."

Ashley felt a little guilty; she too was messing with Jenna's language skills. But her guilt vanished when she realized that Jenna was babbling noticeably more than before. Jenna was looking straight at Ashley when she talked, using more consonant-vowel combinations, right on cue. Ash was ecstatic. There, in a Westwood dive, she and her niece had replicated Goldstein's findings, even down to the same fifteen-minute time frame.

Emboldened, Ashley asked Jenna's parents if she could try something. Jenna had about ten words in her spoken vocabulary—"milk," "book," "mama," and "bye bye," among others. But her parents had not yet been able to directly teach her a new word, on the spot. Since Goldstein's experiment had worked so well, Ashley decided to try Schwade's lesson on motionese. She took a small piece of the nectarine and danced it through the air, while saying, "Fr-uu-ii-t, Jen-na, fr-uu-ii-t." Jenna looked wide-eyed.

"Now, you do it," Ashley instructed Glenn and Bonnie.

"Froo-oooo-ooottt," Glenn said, bobbing the next piece of nectarine up and down. His attempt sounded more like a Halloween ghost than parentese. Ashley coached him—a little more singsong, a little more rhythm in the hand movement. Glenn tried it a second time: "Fro-ooo-oo-ttt." He set the nectarine chunk in front of Jenna.

"Oooot!!" piped Jenna, picking the piece up from the table.

Glenn started laughing, turned to Ashley and said, "I didn't think it was going to work quite that fast."

Ashley hadn't expected so either. Jenna kept repeating her new word until the baggie was empty. Needless to say, Jenna's parents were doing twice as much object-labeling and motionese by the time dinner was over. The next day, they used motionese to teach her "sock" and "shoe." Since then, they've increased their responsiveness to Jenna's babbles, and they've seen the difference.

In the 1950s and 1960s, Massachusetts Institute of Technology linguist Dr. Noam Chomsky altered the direction of social science with his theory of an innate Universal Grammar. He argued that what children hear and see and are taught, in combination, is just too fractured and pattern-defying to possibly explain how fast kids acquire language. The stream of input couldn't account for the output coming from kids' mouths. Chomsky highlighted the fact that young children can do far more than merely repeat sentences they've heard; without ever having been taught grammar, they can generate unique novel sentences with near-perfect grammar. Therefore, he deduced that infants must be born with "deep structure," some underlying sense of syntax and grammar.

By the 1980s, Chomsky was the most quoted living scholar in all of academia, and remained at the top through the millennium.

However, in the intervening decades, each step of language acquisition has been partially decoded and, in turn, dramatically demystified. Rather than language arising from some innate template, each step of language learning seems to be a function of auditory and visual inputs, contingent responses, and intuitive scaffolding, all of which steer the child's attention to the relevant pattern. Even Chomsky himself has been considering the import of the newly discovered mechanisms of language learning. In 2005, Chomsky and his colleagues wrote, somewhat cryptically: "Once [the faculty of language] is fractionated into component mechanisms (a crucial but difficult process) we enter a realm where specific mechanisms can be empirically interrogated at all levels.... We expect diverse answers as progress is made in this research program."

This doesn't rule out the possibility that some portion is still innate, but the portion left inexplicable—and therefore credited to innate grammar—is shrinking fast.

A similar argument can be applied to the notion held by our society that having better or lesser verbal skills and reading skills is a function of innate verbal ability. To a parent, these skills *seem* innate, because from the moment their daughter could talk, she was precocious—speaking full sentences by two, reading words by three and books by four. But the parent's unaware of his own influence in those first two years.

"When parents see development in their kids, they are only seeing the output—not the mechanisms underneath," said Goldstein. "We just see significant changes, so parents tend to say, 'It must be built in.' I don't think people are aware of what they are bringing to babies."

According to an extensive study comparing identical twins to fraternal twins, headed by University of New Mexico's Dr. Philip Dale, only 25% of language acquisition is due to genetic factors.

So do kids who get a head start keep their advantage, over time? Does being an early talker really mean the child will be a better reader, in elementary school? Or do other kids quickly catch up, once they hit the language spurt, too?

Scientists tend to say that *both* are true. The advantage is real, yet many kids do catch up, and show no long-term consequences. Dr. Bruce Tomblin, Director of the Child Language Research Center at the University of Iowa, noted that language measures are highly stable once children are in elementary school, but prior to that age, they're not stable. "The trajectories of their future results look like spaghetti," he said. "The only thing typical about typical language development was variability."

According to Tamis-LeMonda, this is especially true for toddlers who spoke late, but still understood a lot of words early. "Sometimes a kid who seems to catch up wasn't actually behind in the first place; their receptive vocabulary was proceeding apace, but they weren't talking much because they were shy or didn't quite have the motor control yet."

Harvard University's Dr. Jesse Snedeker has studied how international adoptees fare in the United States. These children often spend their first year, or years, in orphanages and with foster families, then come to American families that are quite well-off. Some adoptees do have learning difficulties, but "the adoptees who were typically developing…they caught up to their American-born peers within three years," concluded Snedeker. This was true whether they were adopted at age one or age five—even up to age ten.

Nevertheless, the general trend is apparent: an early advantage in language can be quite meaningful, at least through the first several years of elementary school. Going back to the famous Hart and Risley study from the University of Kansas, Dr. Dale Walker analyzed how those children were doing academically six years later—in third grade, at age nine. The measures taken at age three, of how long kids' average spoken sentences were, and how big their spoken vocabulary was, strongly predicted third-grade language skills. The correlation was strongest for their spoken language ability, and it was still quite strong for their reading, spelling, and other measures of verbal ability. It didn't help with math, which wasn't a surprise; presumably, this head start in language wouldn't drive all cognitive functions.

It's important to characterize early language precocity for what it is: a head start, but far from a guarantee. "It's not like the infancy period is the only critical period," said Tamis-LeMonda. "New skills are emerging in every period, and vocabulary development has to continually expand."

Conclusion

The Myth of the Supertrait.

When Ashley and I began this book, we adamantly chose not to focus just on children's intellectual prowess. Brainy prodigies were not our goal; rather, we were interested in a more complete perspective of children, including the development of their moral compasses, their behavior around peers, their self-control, and their honesty.

We chose this subject at what seemed a fortuitous time. Over the last ten years, a new branch of psychology has emerged. Rather than studying clinical patients with pathologies, these scientists have applied their skills to studying healthy, happy people who thrive, in order to discern what were the habits, values, and neuroscience of those with greater well-being. This new starting-point has led to insights about the strengthening of positive emotions such as resilience, happiness, and gratitude.

In one celebrated example, Dr. Robert Emmons, of the University of California at Davis, asked college students to keep a gratitude journal—over ten weeks, the undergrads listed five things that had happened in the last week which they were thankful for. The results were surprisingly powerful—the students who kept the gratitude journal were 25% happier, were more optimistic about the future, and got sick less often during the controlled trial. They even got more exercise.

Emmons repeated his study, this time with undergrads writing in a gratitude journal every day for two weeks—and he also sent questionnaires about the participants to their close friends, asking them to rate their friend on a variety of measures. He wanted to see if the subjects' improved sense of well-being was more than just an internal state of mind; did it actually affect how they interacted with others? The answer was a confident yes. Their friends had noticed them being more helpful and emotionally supportive.

Philosophers have long written about the importance of gratitude. Cicero called it the parent of all other virtues. Shakespeare described ingratitude as a marble-hearted fiend, and he decried ingratitude in children as being more hideous than a sea monster. But until Emmons' research, we couldn't really say whether gratitude triggered well-being, or whether gratitude was merely the by-product of well-being. Certainly the two rise and fall together, but Emmons showed that gratitude could be enhanced, independently, and greater well-being would result.

By itself, this wasn't exactly extraordinary, but in the context of happiness theories, it was significant. Back in 1971, two scholars, Philip Brickman and Donald Campbell, described the human condition as a "hedonic treadmill." Essentially, we have to keep working hard just to stay in the same relative place in society. Even when our situation improves, the sense of achievement is only temporary, because our hedonistic desires and expectations rise at the same rate as our circumstances. Brickman and Campbell noted that lottery winners are not any happier, long-term, than non-winners, and paraplegics are not less happy than those of us with all our limbs. They argued that this plight was inescapable, due to our neural wiring. Our brains are designed to notice novel stimuli, and tune out everyday, predictable stimuli. What we really notice, and are affected by, are relative and recent changes. As soon as those become static, we return to a baseline level of well-being.

That we are so adaptive can be a good thing. When life falls apart, we'll soon get used to it—such changes in circumstance don't have to become incapacitating. But when our lives are blessed, and things are going well, there seems something morally decrepit in how we so easily overlook how good we have it.

In the last forty years, a lot of cracks have been discovered in Brickman and Campbell's theory of the hedonic treadmill. First, while most people might have a happiness set point, it's not a flat neutral—it's actually a fairly positive state. Around the world, 80 percent of people report being quite happy or very happy. Also, while paraplegics and lottery winners might return to their baseline, other classes of people (on average) never quite recover—such as widows, divorcees, and the long-term unemployed.

Emmons' work was yet another crack in the hedonic treadmill theory. Effectively, he demonstrated that our default wiring can be consciously tricked; by forcing college students to pay attention to the bounty in their everyday lives, he got them to escape the perception-trap of the treadmill.

One of the many scholars inspired by Emmons' research was Dr. Jeffrey Froh, a psychology professor at Hofstra University on Long Island. Froh also served as the psychologist for the Half Hollow Hills school district, spending a fair amount of time in the local grammar schools and high schools. Froh had been struck by the rampant materialism and sense of entitlement within the affluent Long Island youth culture.

"At the high school, there were BMWs in the parking lot, and E-Class Mercedes," Froh said. "And they really wanted to look a certain way. They dressed immaculate. They wore two-hundred-dollar jeans, and hundred-dollar T-shirts. They wanted peers to know they didn't get these on sale, and they weren't knockoffs. There was also a lot of focus on where they'd been admitted to college—not for the educational value, but for the status and prestige, for the name brand of certain universities."

He saw in Emmons' work a possible antidote to all that.

Froh certainly wasn't alone in that view. Educational institutes, newspaper columnists, and parenting coaches began advocating that children keep gratitude journals. Many schools started incorporating gratitude exercises into their curricula.

Froh, however, thought these efforts warranted scientific testing and real analysis. So with Emmons' consultation, Froh began the first randomly assigned, controlled trial of gratitude in schoolchildren.

Hoping to help these kids before they turned into materialistic high schoolers, he went into the Candlewood Middle School in Dix Hills, New York, and enlisted the cooperation of the three teachers who taught "Family and Consumer Science" to sixth and seventh graders. All told, eleven classrooms were involved, amounting to 221 students; this included a cross-section of the whole school, with some gifted children and special education children. Four of the classes were given gratitude journals; daily, for two weeks, the students were asked to "think back over the last day and write down on the lines below up to five things in your life that you are grateful for or thankful for."

This took just a few minutes at the start of each class. Some responses were quite specific ("I am grateful my mom didn't go crazy when I accidentally broke a patio table"); some hinted at a specific event but didn't explain it in detail ("My coach helped me out at baseball practice"); far more were all-encompassing ("My grandma is in good health, my family is still together, my family still loves each other, and we have fun every day"). Froh was particularly excited by how few of the kids' items had anything to do with their possessions. Very little materialism emerged, and even then, it was eccentric, such as the child who was grateful for all the *Star Wars* books. The gratitude inventories, it seemed, were recalibrating the kids' focus.

Before, during, and after the two-week period, teachers also passed out and collected questionnaires that measured students' life satisfaction, gratitude, and emotions. This was repeated three weeks later, to see if the benefits lasted. The teachers were never told the purpose of the study, so they couldn't bias the results; for the most part, they stuck to scripts Froh had written.

At the same time, three classrooms were assigned as control groups; all these students did were the questionnaires, with no other writing. The last four classes were instructed to complete the questionnaires, and also to complete their own daily writing assignment: the students in these classes listed five hassles that had occurred each day. Froh considered these four classes as a kind of alternative control group, to check for effects of dwelling on the negative.

So what was the impact of counting blessings?

There was none.

The four classes of students who counted their blessings didn't experience more gratitude than the control group—not during the two-week exercise, immediately after, or three weeks later. The journal writing simply didn't have the intended effect. At all stages, the three classes in the control group—which did nothing but take the mood questionnaires—experienced the most gratitude of the three groups. As a result, the kids who did the exercise weren't friendlier or more helpful to their friends. They didn't have greater all-around life satisfaction.

Strangely, though, these lackluster results didn't slow down the excitement around Froh's study. The gratitude journal sounded like exactly the sort of exercise kids *should* do. Everyone involved wanted it to work and fully expected it to work. With that kind of momentum built up, everyone was predisposed to consider the intervention a success, no matter what the data determined.

The study results were published in a notable journal. Candlewood Middle School itself was so happy with the exercise that the administrators had all the thousand-plus students repeat it.

Newspapers then wrote feature stories about Froh's study, clearly creating the impression that his study had effectively reproduced the results of Emmons' studies on college students. In none of the articles was there a single mention about the flimsiness of the results. A year later, when Thanksgiving rolled around again—triggering a new round of coverage—these same claims were repeated.

One explanation for the press accounts could be the distraction created by the data on the alternative control group—the four classes who dwelled on the negative every day. Not surprisingly, those kids looked a little worse, statistically, than the other groups. But there was scant evidence that writing in the gratitude journal improved one's well-being more than doing nothing. The only thing the study proved was that dwelling on the negative can bum you out.

Why were the results so different from Emmons' work on college students?

Froh wasn't sure, and he was troubled. He set the quantitative analysis aside, to go reread the kids' actual diary entries. Quickly, he realized that a fair number of the middle schoolers suffered gratitude fatigue.

"They wrote the same thing, day after day—'my dog, my house, my family,'" Froh recalled. "In hindsight, it might have been ideal for the teachers to encourage the kids to vary their answers, think harder, and really process it—rather than let them complete it in a hurry so they could get back to their classwork."

He realized his next experiment would have to address this.

At first glance, Froh's study appears to be another classic case where good intentions were mistaken for a good idea. But his story didn't end there.

For Froh to really figure out what happened, he needed to drop two of his main assumptions.

First, he had to drop his expectation that middle schoolers should react the same way as college students to the gratitude intervention. As long as he held that expectation, he was thinking that something had gone wrong in his study—and that if he could find his error, he could get the intended result.

But maybe nothing had gone wrong. Maybe he'd made no mistakes, and his results were completely accurate. And because he wasn't thinking broadly enough, he was unable to glean what his results actually proved.

There are eight years of development from middle school to college. Was there something about those intervening years that could explain why the middle-schoolers didn't benefit from the exercise? As we learned from Nancy Darling's research on teenagers, the need for autonomy peaks at age 14, and is stronger in a 12-year-old than in a college student (largely because a college student has already established the autonomy she desires). Were the middle-schoolers reacting differently, because of their need for independence?

Or could it be a difference in cognitive capabilities? Digging deeper into gratitude's effects, Froh learned that children will not experience gratitude unless they recognize three things about the various bounties in their lives: that they are *intentional, costly,* and *beneficial.* Children need to comprehend that this nice life of theirs isn't by accident, it's the gift of hardworking parents and teachers who make sacrifices for the good of children—who in turn truly benefit from it.

Were younger kids capable of understanding all that?

Froh began to design a new study, working with a K–12 parochial school, where he could test a gratitude intervention on kids from grades 3, 8, and 12, to look for the effects of age.

That Froh had chosen a parochial school was an interesting choice. The school's religious teachings on sacrifice could have already given its students an increased awareness of gratitude. Froh knew that these kids were already regularly taught to count their blessings in the context of prayer.

To give them something new, Froh didn't ask these children to list five things every day. Instead, they were to pick one person in their lives—someone they'd never fully expressed their appreciation for—and write them a letter of thanks. They worked on this letter in class, three times a week, for two weeks, elaborating on their feelings and polishing their prose. On the final Friday, they were to set up a time with that person and read the letter to them, out loud, face-to-face.

Their letters were heartbreaking and sincere, demonstrating a depth of thoughtfulness not seen in the previous study. "It was a hyperemotional exercise for them," Froh said. "Really, it was such an intense experience. Every time I reread those letters, I choke up."

But when Froh analyzed the data, again he ran into the same problem—overall, the kids hadn't benefited from the intervention. What was going on?

To solve it, Froh had to extract himself from another assumption.

He'd assumed that positive emotions, like gratitude, are inherently protective—they ward off problem behavior and prevent troubled moods. He wasn't alone in this assumption; in fact, it is the core premise of every scholar working in the field of positive psychology.

Because of this, Froh had expected to find an inverse relationship between gratitude and negative emotions, such as distress, shame, nervousness, hostility, and fear. Meaning, even if he couldn't change the amount of kids' gratitude the way Emmons had, Froh still expected that some kids would feel a lot of gratitude, and others less or none at all. And he figured that kids who felt very grateful and appreciative would be spared from the brunt of troubled moods. It should protect them. But the data from his multiple studies didn't support this. Kids high in gratitude suffered storms of emotion just as commonly as the kids low in gratitude.

At that point, Froh's thinking was sparked by a few scholars who were rethinking the hedonic treadmill.

"They argued that happiness is not a unitary construct," Froh explained. "You can feel good and have well-being, but still be nervous, still be stressed. You can feel better overall, but the daily stressors haven't necessarily gone away. For a scholar, this means that when you measure for positive affect, negative affect, and life satisfaction, they won't all move in the same direction."

Froh looked very carefully at each band of data measuring the kids' emotions during the second study. Overall, writing the thank-you letters had little benefit, just like his prior study. But this aggregation masked what was really going on. It turned out that some kids *were* benefiting from the exercise, while others weren't. Together, their scores canceled each other out.

Those who benefited from the exercise were kids low in positive affect—kids who rarely experienced emotions like excitement, hope, strength, interest, and inspiration. Writing the thank-you letter, and presenting it to a parent, coach, or friend, did indeed fill them with gratitude and make them feel better about their lives. "Those are the kids who would really benefit from gratitude exercises," said Froh. "The children who usually appear unengaged, or not very alert. They're rarely cheerful or content."

However—and this is the important twist—for those kids who normally experienced a lot of hope and excitement, Froh's exercise had the opposite outcome. It made them feel less happy, hopeful, and grateful.

Why was the gratitude exercise making them feel *worse?* What could possibly be *bad* about gratitude?

Well, for kids with a strong need for autonomy and independence, it might be demoralizing to recognize how much they are dependent upon grownups. They might already feel like adults are pulling all the strings in their lives—controlling what they eat, what they study, what they're allowed to wear, and who they hang out with. And they'd rather feel self-reliant than beholden. Their sense of independence might be an illusion, but it's a necessary illusion for their psychological balance and future growth into genuine independence. Their lack of gratitude might be the way they maintain the illusion that they are in control of their own lives.

Froh is considering that his intervention led those children to realize just how much of their lives depended on someone else's whim or sacrifice. They didn't feel happy that people were always there doing things for them. Instead, it made them feel powerless.

※

The lesson of Jeffrey Froh's work is *not* that society should simply give up on teaching children about gratitude. Certainly, some children do benefit from the exercises. (In fact, Froh remains so committed to the idea that one of his grad students recently began pilot-testing a five-week gratitude school curriculum.) However, for most kids, gratitude is not easily manufactured, and we can't take it for granted that gratitude should supersede other psychological needs just because we want it to.

The real value in Froh's story, however, isn't limited to his insight on gratitude. We're including it here because we think that his entire process is also illustrative of a much larger point.

When we looked back at all the enormity of research that this book was built on, an interesting pattern was apparent. Most of the noteworthy insights into child development were revealed when scholars dropped the same two assumptions as Froh had.

Or, to restate that with more emphasis: a treasure trove of wisdom about children is there for the grasping after one lets go of those two common assumptions.

The first assumption is that things work in children in the same way that they work in adults. To put a name to this reference bias, let's call it the Fallacy of Similar Effect.

In chapter after chapter of this book, great insights were gained when scholars set that assumption aside. Consider the research into sleep. It was, for a long time, all too convenient to assume kids are affected by sleep loss the same way as adults—it's tiring but manageable. But when scholars decided to test that, they found that the magnitude of effect on kids was exponentially damaging.

In the same way, we presumed that because measured intelligence is stable in adults, it's also stable in young children. It's not—it plateaus and spurts. And because adults can pick up the implicit message of multiculturally diverse environments, we assumed kids can, too. They can't—they need to hear explicit statements about how wrong it is to judge people for their skin color.

Here's yet another example of this fallacy in operation. In our chapter about Tools of the Mind, we described how pretend play is the way young kids master symbolic representation, which soon becomes necessary for all academic coursework. But this crucial point never comes up when society debates the purpose of kids' free time, or the necessity of school recess. Instead, the arguments are always about exercise and social skills. That's because for adults, playtime is a chance to blow off steam and relax with friends. While those are certainly relevant to children too, our adult frame of reference has caused us to overlook a crucial purpose of play.

The Fallacy of Similar Effect also helps explain why society got it wrong on praising children. In a variety of studies, praise has been shown to be effective on adults in workplaces. Grownups like being praised. While praise can undermine a child's intrinsic motivation, it doesn't have this affect on adults. It has the opposite effect: being praised by managers *increases* an adult's intrinsic motivation, especially in white-collar professional settings. (Only in a few circumstances, such as some blue-collar union workplaces, is praise interpreted as untrustworthy and manipulative.) It's because we like praise so much that we intuited lavishing it upon kids would be beneficial.

The second assumption to drop, as illustrated in Froh's story, is that positive traits necessarily oppose and ward off negative behavior in children. To name this bias, let's call it the Fallacy of the Good/Bad Dichotomy.

The tendency to categorize things as either good for children or bad for children pervades our society. We tend to think that good behavior, positive emotions, and good outcomes are a package deal: together, the good things will protect a child from all the bad behaviors and negative emotions, such as stealing, feeling bored or distressed, excluding others, early sexual activity, and succumbing to peer pressure.

When Ashley and I first began this book, we wrote out a wish list of Supertraits we wanted for kids—gratitude, honesty, empathy, fairness. If we could sufficiently arm children with Supertraits such as these, we hoped that problems would bounce off them just as easily as bullets bounced off Superman.

Then Victoria Talwar taught that us that a child's dishonesty was a sign of intelligence and social savvy. Nancy Darling explained how teens' deception was almost a necessary part of developing one's adolescent identity. Laurie Kramer's research showed us how blind devotion to fairness can derail sibling relationships. Patricia Hawley and Antonius Cillessen revealed how empathy may be evil's best tool: the popular kids are the ones who are the best at reading their friends—and using that perception for their gain. And of course, there was that study about imprisoned felons having higher emotional intelligence than the population as a whole.

It isn't as if we've now abandoned our desire for children to acquire honesty and other virtues. (And we're still telling kids to "play nice" and say thank you.) But we no longer think of them as Supertraits—moral Kevlar.

The researchers are concluding that the good stuff and the bad stuff are not opposite ends of a single spectrum. Instead, they are each their own spectrum. They are what's termed orthogonal—mutually independent.

Because of this, kids can seem to be walking contradictions. A child can run high in positive emotions *and* high in negative emotions—so the fact that a teen can be happy about a new boyfriend won't negate her stress over school. There can be wild disconnects between children's stated opinions and their actions. Kids can know that fruit tastes good and that it's good for them—but that doesn't mean kids will eat any more apples.

And many factors in their lives—such as sibling interactions, peer pressure, marital conflict, or even gratitude—can be both a good influence *and* a bad influence.

Despite these contradictions, the goal of having a deeper understanding of children is not futile. In fact, it's by studying these apparent contradictions very closely that deeper understanding emerges.

It's when children are at their most mysterious that we, their caretakers, can learn something new.

ACKNOWLEDGMENTS

We wish to thank Adam Moss and Hugo Lindgren at *New York Magazine* for encouraging us to "geek out" in our stories, trusting that readers would be turned on, not turned off, by the depth of science we covered. Many others at *New York* also deserve credit—especially Lauren Starke, Serena Torrey, and our former editor, Adam Fisher.

At our publisher, Twelve, special thanks go to Jon Karp, Jamie Raab, and Cary Goldstein. Peter Ginsberg, at Curtis Brown Ltd., played a huge role in guiding us. We are also indebted to Nathan Bransford, Shirley Stewart, and Dave Barbor.

Of course, we're enormously grateful to many scholars and others who were instrumental in helping us with our research. Our praise chapter—the catalyst for our first piece for *New York* on the science of kids—would not have been possible without the cooperation of Stanford University's Carol S. Dweck. Our chapter on "Why Kids Lie" just wouldn't have been the same without the cooperation of McGill University's Victoria Talwar and her entire lab—especially Cindy M. Arruda, Simone Muir, and Sarah-Jane Renaud. Similarly, our language chapter is particularly indebted to Michael H. Goldstein and Jennifer A. Schwade of Cornell University and the rest of the B.A.B.Y. Lab. Deborah J. Leong, Elena Bodrova, and Amy Hornbeck showed us Tools of the Mind in action. University of Illinois at Urbana-Champaign's Laurie Kramer and Mary Lynn Fletcher spent snowy days driving us around, while explaining their work on sibling relationships. We are also indebted to the many families who spoke with us and allowed us to observe their children's participation in lab experiments.

Dozens of researchers kindly agreed to be interviewed. Countless others sent advanced drafts of papers and presentations. We hounded scholars at conferences. We made pests of ourselves with endless rounds of e-mails and so sorry to call again but if you could clarify that number just one more time.... Despite all that, they were uniformly gracious.

Thanks to Brown University's Mary A. Carskadon, Judith Owens, and Monique K. LeBourgeois; Douglas K. Detterman at Case Western Reserve University; and, also at Cornell University, B.J. Casey, Marianella Casasola, Gary W. Evans, Jeffrey T. Hancock, and Heidi R. Waterfall; Columbia University's Jeanne Brooks-Gunn and Geraldine Downey; at Duke University, Kenneth A. Dodge, Jennifer E. Lansford, and James Moody; Florida State University's Roy F. Baumeister and Stephen I. Pfeiffer; David S. Crystal, Georgetown University; Harvard University's Mahzarin R. Banaji, Kurt W. Fischer, and Jesse Snedeker; Linda B. Smith, Indiana University; Douglas A. Gentile of Iowa State University; Cynthia L. Scheibe of Ithaca College; Kent State University's A. Margaret Pevec and Rhonda A. Richardson; Robert D. Laird, Louisiana State University; Kay Bussey, Macquarie University; Dan Ariely at Massachusetts Institute of Technology; Judith S. Brook and Catherine S. Tamis-LeMonda of New York University; Northwestern University's Frederick W. Turek; Oberlin College's Nancy Darling; Christopher Daddis and Sarah J. Schoppe-Sullivan of Ohio State University; Jeane Coperhaven-Johnson of Ohio State University at Mansfield; Marjorie Taylor, University of Oregon; Duane F. Alwin, Clancy Blair, Linda L. Caldwell, Pamela M. Cole, and Douglas M. Teti of Pennsylvania State University; Shawn Whiteman at Purdue University; Rutgers University's W. Steven Barnett; Jean M. Twenge, San Diego State University; Jamie M. Ostrov, State University of New York, University at Buffalo; Tabitha R. Holmes at State University of New York, New Paltz; Avi Sadeh at Tel Aviv University; Texas A&M University's Cecil R. Reynolds; Birgitte Vittrup, Texas Women's University; Laurence Steinberg at Tufts University; Noel A. Card and Stephen T. Russell of the University of Arizona; University of British Columbia's Adele Diamond; Silvia A. Bunge, Elliot Turiel, and Matthew P. Walker of University of California, Berkeley; Greg J. Duncan and Richard J. Haier, University of California, Irvine; Abigail A. Baird, Adriana Galvan, Michael Prelip, and Gary Orfield at the University of California, Los Angeles; University of California, Santa Barbara's Bella M. DePaulo; Claire Hughes, University of Cambridge; Susan Goldin-Meadow, University of Chicago; Antonius H. N. Cillessen, University of Connecticut; David F. Lohman and Larissa K. Samuelson at the University of Iowa; University of Kansas' Patricia H. Hawley and Dale Walker; Frederick W. Danner of the University of Kentucky; Rochelle S. Newman and Nan Bernstein Ratner at the University of Maryland; Linda R. Tropp, University of Massachusetts, Amherst; Ronald D. Chervin, Jennifer Crocker, Denise Kennedy, and Louise M. O'Brien of the University of Michigan; Kyla L. Wahlstrom at University of Minnesota; Alan L. Sillars, University of Montana; E. Mark Cummings at the University of Notre Dame; April Harris-Britt and Jane D. Brown of the University of North Carolina at Chapel Hill; David F. Dinges of University of Pennsylvania; University of Pittsburgh's Ronald E. Dahl; Judith G. Smetana, University of Rochester; at the University of Texas, Austin, Rebecca S. Bigler, Elizabeth A. Vandewater, and Mark Warr; Joseph P. Allen at the University of Virginia; Steven Strand, University of Warwick; Andrew N. Meltzoff at the University of Washington; C. Robert Cloninger of Washington University in St. Louis; and Peter Salovey of Yale University.

We'd also like to express our appreciation to: Deborah Linchesky at the American Academy of Pediatrics; Stephen C. Farrell of Choate-Rosemary Hall; Brian O'Reilly of the College Board; Donald A. Rock at Educational Testing Service; Anna Hogrebe at Elsevier B.V.; Lawrence G. Weiss of Harcourt Weiss / Pearson; Lauri Kirsch of Hillsborough County Public Schools; Lisa Smith and Stacy Oryshchyn of Jefferson County Public School District, Denver, Colorado; Gigi Ryner and Jackie Gleason of Stony Creek Preschool in Littleton, Colorado; Minnesota Regional Sleep Disorders Center's Mark W. Mahowald; Thomas D. Snyder, National Center for Education Statistics; Jay N. Giedd and Marc Bornstein at the National Institutes of Health; Lisa Sorich Blackwell, New Visions for Public Schools; Richard L. Atkinson, Obetech LLC; Sally Millaway and Kathleen Thomsen of Neptune, New Jersey schools; Erin Ax at Effective Educational Practices; Judy Erickson, Sage Publications; the entire staff of the Society for Research in Child Development; Jessica Jensen and Debbie Burke of Van Arsdale Elementary School, Arvada, Colorado; and Bethany H. Carland of Wiley-Blackwell. Additionally, thanks to Joan Lawton, the staff and members of the Magic Castle in Hollywood, California, and Rose M. Kreider at the United States Census Bureau.

NOTES

Preface

Cary Grant as doorman: A number of Magic Castle members recall Cary Grant acting as the doorman, either having been there during Grant's tenure or having heard it from other members at the time. Outside the club membership, the story has become more elaborate over the years; some versions even claim that Grant occasionally donned a doorman costume when at its entrance. Our account is based on Joan Lawton's recollection of the events, which she kindly relayed to us in interviews. (And no, Lawton doesn't recall him ever wearing a costume. He was usually in a suit, sometimes a tuxedo.)

Introduction

Neural network activated in parenting: Parts of the brain involved in paternal attachment, love, and responsiveness include: anterior cingulate cortex; anterior insula; mesial prefrontal cortex; right orbitofrontal cortex; periaqueductal gray; hypothalamus; thalamus; caudate nucleus; nucleus accumbens; and putamen. Bartels and Zeki (2004); Lorberbaum et al. (2002); Noriuchi et al. (2008); and Swain et al. (2007).

Prose throughout is our mutual collaboration: From start to finish, the book has been a joint effort, from the research to the writing. However, at times in the text when recalling personal experiences, we needed to identify ourselves individually. Therefore, when the pronoun "I" is used, it refers to Po's personal experiences; when "Ashley" is employed, this refers to her personal experiences. These passages of text, though, are jointly composed and edited.

Chapter 1, The Inverse Power of Praise

Categorization of gifted students: The exact requirements for gifted programs vary, but most start calling children gifted based on scores on an intelligence test or achievement test at the 90th percentile.

Advanced students' poor self-assessment of competence: That gifted students frequently underestimate their abilities has been reported in a number of studies, including: Cole et al. (1999); Phillips (1984); and Wagner and Phillips (1992). Note that in these studies, a common method of assessment is to ask students to describe their proficiency in a school subject and then compare the students' self-reports to their actual achievement scores.

Columbia University survey: Dweck (1999).

Brightest girls collapse after failure round: One of the things that Dweck's research suggests is that there is nothing inherently fragile or dramatic about being blessed with an advanced brain, but it's the praise that makes intelligent children more vulnerable.

Interestingly, in one of her studies, Dweck found that after the failure round of tests, all the girls were collapsing, but the higher their IQ, the more they collapsed—to the remarkable point where girls who had the highest IQs in the first round of tests performed even worse than the low IQ girls in the last round. Explaining this, Dweck conjectured: "Girls are used to being perfect. Girls feel other people's opinions and feedback are valid ways to learn about their abilities. Boys always call each other morons. Nobody else is going to give you the final verdict on your abilities."

This may explain findings by Henderlong: she has seen age and gender differences in her own renditions of praise experiments, indicating that boys may respond differently to person-oriented praise such as "You're smart." Henderlong Corpus and Lepper (2007).

Baumeister's assessment of self-esteem findings: Baumeister's expressed disappointment at the results of his findings was originally reported by Ahuja (2005).

Higher self-esteem leads to higher aggression: Since Baumeister's review, the relationship between high self-esteem and aggression has been expressly seen in the study of children. In 2008, scholars reported on a study where children were to play computer games—believing that they were playing against other children, but in reality playing only against the computer—with a predetermined, losing outcome. After studying how the children attacked their believed opponents, the researchers concluded that there was no empirical support for a claim that children with low self-esteem were aggressive, but there was support that those with high self-esteem were more aggressive and more narcissistic. They even suggested that efforts to boost self-esteem "are likely to increase (rather than to decrease) the aggressive behavior of youth at risk." Thomaes et al. (2008).

Review of 150 praise studies: Henderlong and Lepper (2002).

Cloninger's location of the persistence circuit in the brain: Cloninger put people inside an fMRI scanner to measure their brain activity while they looked through a series of 360 photographs, like car accidents and people holding children. He asked them to rate the photographs as pleasant, neutral, or unpleasant. Those who were most persistent (scored on a seven-factor personality test) had the highest activity in their lateral orbital and medial prefrontal cortex, as well as their ventral striatum. Interestingly, they also rated more neutral photographs as pleasant, and unpleasant photographs as neutral. In other words, persistent individuals actually experience the world as more pleasant—less bothers them.

Chapter 2, The Lost Hour

Parents' poor accuracy in assessing the sufficiency of their children's sleep: Several scholars have tried to figure out how accurate parents are at assessing their children's amount of sleep, comparing parental reports with kids' reports and scientific measures (actigraphy). Parents frequently overestimate the time their kids are asleep by at least a half-hour—even as much as an hour and a half. See, for example, National Sleep Foundation (2006a) and Werner et al. (2008).

High school students reporting sleep deprivation: Teens' lack of sleep is a problem that by no means is limited to American youth: teens around the world are exhausted. In a study of Singaporean high-schoolers, 96.9% said they weren't getting enough sleep. And only 0.5% of them had discussed their sleep difficulties with a physician. Lim et al. (2008).

Basis of "lost hour" of kids' sleep: There seems to be universal agreement as to the fact that kids are getting less sleep today than in years past. However, there's less agreement in just how much sleep kids have lost. We base our "one lost hour" on research we did in sleep studies and general time use studies: our determination is probably a conservative assessment.

According to one report, in 1997, children age 3 to 5 were found to be getting just over 10.8 hours of sleep per night, while children 6 to 8 years old were getting 10.1 hours of sleep. In 2004, the National Sleep Foundation found that the 3- to 5-year-olds were down to 10.4 hours of sleep, and the 6- to 8-year-olds were down to 9.5 hours. (Compare Hofferth and Sandberg [2001] to the National Sleep Foundation's 2004 Sleep in America Poll.)

Over the same time period, Brown University found that, in 1997, nine- to twelve-year-olds were getting about 9.6 hours of sleep, but in 2004, sixth graders were getting 8.3 of sleep—a difference of 1.3 hours. Carskadon (2004) and Sleep in America poll (2006).

Further support for the hour loss of sleep can be found in an influential and widely cited study of Swiss children. In that study, throughout the 1990s, sleep duration for children fell across all ages—meaning that a two-year-old slept less in 1986 than he would have in 1974, and a fourteen-year-old slept less in 1986 than he did in 1974. The youngest children actually saw the most severe drop in sleep duration. Six-month-old infants born in 1993 were sleeping 2.5 hours less than those born in 1978, while there was a 1.0 hour difference for sixteen-year-olds. Iglowstein et al. (2003).

In 2005, the American Academy of Pediatrics' Working Group on Sleepiness in Adolescents/Young Adults and the AAP Committee on Adolescence issued a technical report that opined that the Iglowstein study was an "impressive work" and a valuable guideline as to trends in youth sleep in the United States; if anything, the American scholars believed that the US results would be more "extreme" than the Swiss results. Millman et al. (2005). And Landhuis et al. believe that a two-hour drop in the past two decades is also a supportable claim. Landhuis et al. (2008).

Other studies addressing the international downward trend in sleep duration include: Van Cauter et al. (2008) and Taheri (2006).

Rhode Island study on teens setting bedtimes: Wolfson and Carskadon (1998).

Sleep deprivation and its effects on emotional stability and development: For ADHD, authors' interviews with Ronald Chervin and Louise O'Brien; Chervin et al. (2005); Chervin et al. (2002); and Chervin et al. (1998). For emotional stability of adolescents, authors' interviews with Ronald Dahl, David Dinges, and Frederick Danner, as well as Dahl (1999); Danner and Phillips (2008).

Experimental manipulation of children's sleep duration and test performance:

Since Sadeh's experiment, Tzischinsky et al. (2008) essentially replicated his findings—having eighth graders sleep an hour more than normal. The students who slept the extra time scored significantly higher on math tests and attention measures.

Effects of sleep loss akin to lead exposure: McKenna (2007).

Studies reporting a sleep/grade correlation: See, e.g., Danner and Gilman (2008); Warner et al. (2008); Bachmann and Ax (2007); and Fredriksen et al. (2004).

Sleep deprivation's interference with brain mechanisms: Durmer and Dinges (2005).

Slow-wave sleep and kids' learning vocabulary: Backhaus et al. (2008).

Edina, Minn. SAT scores: The *New York Times* previously reported on Edina's SAT gains; however, the article reported incorrect scores. The *Times* reported lower figures than the students had actually achieved. Wahlstrom had requested a correction at the time; however, no one responded to her query. Per our request to Wahlstrom, Wahlstrom retrieved the information that she had previously provided the *Times*, and then re-analyzed the data to confirm the accuracy of the increase.

O'Reilly of the College Board explained to us in an interview that the increase is even more extraordinary on two points. First, the scores we include in the text were based on the 1600-point test: a 212-point increase would essentially account for 14% of a total score. Second, most Minnesota students take the ACT: only the most competitive students take the SAT. Accordingly, O'Reilly says that students in the top 10% of an Edina SAT class would be in the *top 1%* nationally. We also note that the increase in scores after the later start time is roughly equivalent to the increase promised by professional SAT prep courses.

Later school start times result in improved quality of life: Htwe et al. (2008); Danner and Phillips (2008) and Wahlstrom interviews.

Prevalence of early morning high school start times: Wolfson and Carskadon (2005).

McMaster review of obesity prevention programs: Thomas (2006). British officials completed a similar large-scale review of obesity prevention programs and also concluded that there was "scant" evidence that such programs were effective. See "Obesity 'Not Individuals' Fault" (2007). Stice et al. (2006) also considered the efficacy of most programs to be "trivial."

Kids' TV watching and other sedentary activity: Vandewater isn't the only scholar who disputes the premise that kids limit their physical activity because they are watching television. Taveras et al. (2007) concluded that if a kid watched an hour less of television each week, there would be no increase in his physical activity. And other researchers have measured the time spent on homework, computer use, reading, hobbies, hanging out with friends, even sitting in a car on the way to school. When those are considered, television is as little as one-third of a teen's sedentary activity. Biddle et al. (2009); Biddle (2007); and Utter et al. (2003).

Studies showing relationships between sleep deprivation and children's obesity: In addition to the American, Australian, Canadian, and Japanese studies finding a connection between children's shortened sleep and obesity, this same relationship has now also been found by scholars in France, Germany, Portugal, Tunisia, China, Hong Kong, Taiwan, Brazil, and New Zealand—where scholars found that shortened sleep in elementary school children predicted obesity at age 32. Studies reporting a connection include: Landhuis et al. (2008); Nixon et al. (2008); Taveras et al. (2008); Lumeng et al. (2007); Eisenmann et al. (2006); Chaput et al. (2006); Gupta et al. (2002); and Sekine et al. (2002).

Two meta-analyses also have found a relationship between children's sleep and obesity: Cappuccio et al. (2008) and Chen et al. (2008).

While some scholars—e.g., Hassan et al. (2008) and Horne (2008)—are still unsure about the relationship between sleep and kids' obesity, *Pediatrics* has determined that enough data supports short-sleep's relationship to overweight in children, that sleep should be considered in assessing an individual child's weight issues. Krebs et al. (2007). And other scholars believe that the data is now persuasive enough that kids' sleep and obesity should be considered a public health issue. Young (2008).

CDC/USDA positions on kids and sleep: Park (2008); Schoenborn and Adams (2008); Redding (2007); and Hensley (2007).

Chapter 3, Why White Parents Don't Talk About Race

Infants' perception of racial differences: Kelly et al. (2007) have determined that infants begin to notice the visually apparent aspects of racial differences somewhere between the third and sixth months.

Experiment with cross-race groups: Rooney-Rebeck and Jason (1986).

Subgroupism in Japanese schools: Based in part on authors' interview and correspondence with David Crystal and Crystal et al. (2000).

Shushing kids' discussion of race: In one case we learned about, a kindergarten teacher began her lecture on Martin Luther King Jr. only to have one of the children cut her off with: "Mommy says we shouldn't talk about color." Polite and Saenger (2003).

Study of Detroit high school students: Oyserman et al. (2006).

Black Santa and White Santa: Account is based on authors' interviews, correspondence with Coperhaven-Johnson, and her report, Coperhaven-Johnson (2007).

Chapter 4, Why Kids Lie

100,000 children testifying: Following Talwar's discoveries about children's understanding of lying, and under what circumstance they are more likely to lie, the Canadian legislature revised its procedure to determine if children should be allowed to testify. Talwar et al. (2002) and Bill C-2 (2004).

Lie-detection systems: In an extensive review of 150 studies on lie detection, University of Portsmouth professor Aldert Vrij concluded: "[T]here is not a single verbal, nonverbal or physiological cue uniquely related to deception. In other words, nothing similar to Pinocchio's growing nose actually exists." Vrij (2004). Perhaps the most common belief about lie detection is that people avert their gaze when telling a lie. However, study after study show that gaze aversion has little if any relation to a person's lying. Gaze aversion is even less of a signal for children: they frequently look away from a conversation partner when they are concentrating. See, e.g., Talwar and Lee (2002a) and Vrij et al. (2004).

Fascinatingly, in a 2006 study of over 11,000 survey responses from 57 countries, 64% of respondents said that gaze aversion signaled lying. Scholars hypothesize that the myth of gaze aversion comes from a different emotional state altogether: around the world, people look down at the ground as an indication of shame. Therefore, the scholars suggest there's an (errant) assumption that liars are ashamed of their falsehood and thus look away. Global Deception Research Team (2006).

Parents' inability to detect children's lies: Talwar has been regularly studying parents' failure to identify children's lying, first publishing results in 2002. She isn't alone in her findings, either: scholars Angela M. Crossman and Michael Lewis found similar results, with parents again performing at levels lower than chance in identifying children's lying in their study. Crossman and Lewis (2006).

In Talwar's newest study, she's been looking to see if some people are just better at lie detection than others. She's found that only 4% were repeatedly significantly better at lie detection. Leach et al. (2009).

Prevalence of children who peek and lie: The percentages of children who will cheat and lie during the peeking game we've reported come from Talwar's first 2002 study. Talwar and Lee (2002a). However, Talwar has since replicated this pattern in many subsequent studies: the percentage of children who peek and those who lie remain amazingly consistent. Additionally, other scholars have since replicated her work in their own versions of the peeking game.

Lying's connection with intelligence: Talwar has found that children with more advanced executive functioning and working memory are better liars. She's also seen relationships between children's lying and "theory of mind"—the ability to understand and keep track of multiple people's points of view.

Children's lying to make a parent happy: Along with Talwar's research, Bussey's work fleshes out this insight. When Bussey has presented children with anecdotes, and asked them to predict if the protagonist would be truthful or not, the children's responses were in part determined by whether or not the story had said if the protagonist would be punished for a misdeed or its admission. Bussey has also shown that it isn't until children are eight years old that they begin to believe that truth telling may make the truth teller himself feel better. Bussey (1999) and Wagland and Bussey (2005).

Additionally, a 2007 University of Texas, El Paso, study offers an intriguing twist for both Talwar's conclusion that children lie to make an adult happy and Dweck's praise-addicted children. In the UT study, young children were asked if they'd seen anyone take an examiner's toy. Some children were told, "Thank you, you've been a big help," every time they answered "Yes" to *any* of the examiner's questions. Within four minutes, half of the children who had heard that praise had begun making false confessions. They actually lied about wrongs they weren't a part of, so that the praise could continue. Billings et al. (2007).

Frequency of children's lies: Wilson et al. (2003) and Wilson et al. (2004).

Tattling: The primary work on children's tattling comes from den Bak and Ross (1996) and Ross and den Bak-Lammers (1998). Friman et al. (2004) is also informative, particularly on his point that fourth-graders consider tattling an aggressive act on par with stealing or destruction of another's property.

Frequency of adult lies: There are popularized claims that the average adult lies at least three times in a ten-minute conversation. However, that statistic is based on an experiment in a highly manipulated situation—where two strangers were told to sit in a room and at least one had been instructed to say things that would make the other like him. Even in that artificial environment, 40% of the test subjects never lied at all. The data from DePaulo and Hancock on the frequency of lies is based not on an experimental manipulation, but on diary studies—where people kept track, on a daily basis, of every lie that they told. In the DePaulo and Hancock studies, people in the general population lied only about once a day—college students twice a day. DePaulo et al. (1996) and Hancock et al. (2004).

Adults' treasuring of children's honesty: Indeed, in an analysis of twenty years of parents' responses to a national survey on asking what trait parents wanted most for their children, "honesty" was the clear winner—nothing else came close. Alwin (1989).

Chapter 5, The Search for Intelligent Life in Kindergarten

The model intelligence test: Our version of the intelligence test is based on publicly available training manuals, presentations, and sample questions: the questions we used draw from a variety of both intelligence and achievement tests. The actual tests themselves are held under close guard: the publishers generally sell them only to licensed psychologists and school administrators. (There are a few underground test guides out there, as well.)

The correlation between pre-K testing and third-grade achievement: This is a mathematical determination, based on a 40% correlation—the typical statistical relationship between children's performance on an IQ test at preschool or kindergarten to their scores on the same test in third grade. Lohman (2006); Lohman and Korb (2006); and Lohman (2003).

Regarding how well WPPSI scores predict *later* achievement, previous research has shown that WPPSI scores (at ages 4 to 6) account for only 7% to 24% of a child's SAT scores, 11 or 12 years later. Thus, at least 76% of a child's SAT score is not determined by their early intelligence. Spinelli (2006) and Baxter (1988).

Intelligence test authors and publishers working to eliminate racial/ethnic bias: Dietz (undated); Rock and Stenner (2005); and Lohman and Lakin (2006).

International efficacy of intelligence tests: See, for example, Barber (2005).

IQs of college graduates and Ph.D.s: Colom (2004).

Rate of progress for California gifted students: "Windows and Classrooms" (2003).

North Carolina study comparing early intelligence tests with later achievement: Kaplan (1996).

Fully one-third of the brightest incoming third graders score below average prior to kindergarten: Lohman (2006).

Use of a single test for gifted placement: In addition to the scholars' unanimity that a single test should not be the sole determinant for placement in a gifted program, such admonitions come from the publishers of the tests themselves. In a clinical guide edited by the president and CEO of Pearson's Assessment division, practitioners are warned that "a single test must never be used in isolation to assess a gifted child or to make recommendations regarding a child's school placement." Sparrow and Gurland (1998).

Reynolds' statement on gifted versus special ed. assessment: Reynolds is referring to federal requirements that students who are being considered for placement within special education programs be tested and retested, prior to placement, and their progress in the programs is continually reassessed.

South Carolina's assessment of gifted students: VanTassel-Baska et al. (2007); VanTassel-Baska et al. (2002); and "Removal of Students" (2004).

Thwarted Florida legislative effort to retest: "Legislative Update" (2008).

New York City gifted programs: "Chancellor Proposes Change" (2008) and "Gifted and Talented Proposal" (2007).

Emotional intelligence / Salovey vs. Goleman: The team that first coined the term "emotional intelligence" included: John D. Mayer, Peter Salovey, and David R. Caruso.

In a packed-to-the-rafters room at the 2008 convention of the American Psychological Association, Salovey called his colleagues' attention to this line from Goleman's 1995 book, "...what data exist, suggest [EI] can be as powerful, and at times more powerful, than IQ." Salovey explained that "what existed" in 1995 was "zero"—there was no data at all when Goleman had written that claim. At the time, Salovey's team had just come up with the theory that emotional intelligence might exist: they hadn't even come up with a way to measure it. Goleman's 1998 claim that "nearly 90% of the difference between star performers at work and average ones is due to EI" was also unsupported at the time. Since then, Salovey and others have found that in some fields, emotional intelligence may be a benefit, but, in others, it's a liability. Among insurance adjusters, for example, those with higher emotional sensitivity are less efficient and productive, because they get too emotionally involved with their clients.

Obviously, Salovey, Mayer, and Caruso remain firm believers that there is such a thing as emotional intelligence, and that it's likely an asset. But they are still working out just what it is, and what it means to have it. In the meantime, they are frustrated that they've been repeatedly taken to task by other scientists for claims that Goleman and others—not the scholars themselves—have made.

And as for schools' training children in emotional intelligence, the first real study on whether it can be taught, and if that would have an academic benefit, is just under way. Author notes on 2008 APA Conference; Mayer, Salovey, and Caruso (2008); and Salovey (2008).

Emotional intelligence in a prison population: Hemmati et al. (2004).
"In one test of emotional knowledge": Izard et al. (2001).
Academic success and personality traits: Newsome et al. (2000).
Brain cortex and synapses development: To give you a sense of the furious amount of organization that is going on within the brain, as many as 30,000 synapses may be lost *every second* until a child hits adolescence. For overviews of the brain's cortical and synaptic development, see Shaw (2007); Giedd (2008); Shaw et al. (2006); Lenroot and Giedd (2006); and Lerch et al. (2006). See also Spear (2000) in Chapter 7 sources.
Brain's organization: Myelination—the process in which gray matter becomes

white matter—affects more specific cognitive processes, such as the development of working memory. Organization of brain fibers, known as axons, dramatically impacts the brain's speed of processing. Lerch et al. (2006); Nagy et al. (2004); Barnea-Gorlay et al. (2005); Schmithorst and Holland (2007); Schmithorst et al. (2002); and Schmithorst et al. (2006).

Two-thirds of children's IQ scores will improve, or drop, more than 15 points: The work of Sontag and McCall analyzed data from the Fels Longitudinal Study; the individuals in the Fels study had their IQ measured every half year from age 2.5 to age 6, then every year until age 12, and then again at 14, 15, and 17. McCall found that the IQ of normal middle-class children changed an average of 28.5 points between age 2.5 and age 17. In addition, more than one out of three children displayed performance jumps of more than 30 IQ points during that same age span. Some argue that IQ is stable over childhood, especially after age 6; however, McCall explains that the high stability correlations offered as evidence are somewhat misleading. Those formulas compare the variation in an individual's scores against the much wider variation in all people's IQs. Thus, when reported as a correlation, the variance in an individual's scores looks relatively small—but the raw scores over an individual's childhood years tell a different story. See Sontag et al. (1958); McCall et al. (1973); and Sternberg et al. (2001).

Another early study of children from infancy to age 16 found that more than half of them saw their IQs change significantly—not once but *three times* during that period. Schwartz and Elonen (1975).

Gifted kids' IQs are more variable: Sparrow and Gurland determined, "Of the kids in the standardization sample of the WISC-III, 45.8% of the kids with [Full Scale IQs] greater than 125 had discrepancies between [the two main sections of the test] of 11 or more points." Sparrow and Gurland (1998). Others reporting variance for gifted children's performance on intelligence tests include: Robinson and Clinkenbeard (1998) and Robinson and Weimer (1991).

Locating love, religion, and danger in the brain: Danger is most keenly observed in the amygdala, as well as in the hippocampus, insula, prefrontal cortex, premotor cortex, striatum and anterior cingulate. Recitation of biblical passages activates the dorsolateral prefrontal, dorsomedial frontal and medial parietal cortex. Romantic love is present in the medial insula, anterior cingulate cortex, dentate gyrus, hypothalamus, hippocampus, putamen, globus pallidus, and, for women, in the genu. Phelps et al. (2001); Williams et al. (2001); Azari et al. (2001); Bartels and Zeki (2000); and Bartels and Zeki (2004) in the sources for the introduction.

Developmental shifts of brain's processing: Some of reports on this developmental shift include: Casey et al. (2005); Colom et al. (2006a); Colom et al. (2006b); Haier (1990); Johnson et al. (2008); Paus et al. (2005); Paus et al. (1999); Rubia et al. (2006); Scherf et al. (2006); Schlaggar et al. (2002); and Thomas et al. (2008).

Chapter 6, The Sibling Effect

Increase in one-child families: Interestingly, despite the increase in only-child families, only 3% of Americans believe that a single-child family is ideal. Mancillas (2006).

Frequency of sibling arguments: Kramer et al. (1999).

Kramer's findings on parents' acceptance of sibling conflict: Kramer and a number of scholars complain that parental acceptance of sibling conflict actually contributes to its prevalence: seeing it as inevitable, parents do less to prevent it from occurring. The scholars also reject the idea that sibling conflict is a certainty, pointing to more congenial sibling relationships in other cultures, where elder siblings are expected to be caregivers to younger children.

Parents' role in conflict prevention and conflict resolution: Another reason why Kramer's approach is so innovative is that the research on parents' attempts at conflict resolution are decidedly mixed. Smith and Ross (2007) had some success in training parents how to mediate sibling disputes. (The program was Smith's doctoral dissertation—and Kramer was on the review panel.) But without that training, Ross and other scholars have found that parents' intervention in an argument can actually make things worse. Often, their focus is on forcing children to share a fought-over toy, or to divert one child from the conflict—but then they deprive the kids of an opportunity to learn negotiation or respect for others' needs. Even worse is when a parent just ends the argument with something like, "That's enough—I've had it with you two." Because there, the parent is exhibiting the same sort of self-centered, unilateral power play that the children are attempting. See, e.g., Kramer et al. (1999); Perlman et al. (2007); Ross et al. (2006); and Ross (1996).

Causes of sibling disputes: McGuire et al. (2000).

Chapter 7, The Science of Teen Rebellion

Certainties of life statistics: For marriage disruption probabilities, see Bramlett and Mosher (2002). For life expectancy in the United States, see the National Center for Health Statistics' Fastats. The 2008 New York State bar pass rate for first-time takers was 83%, up from 79.1% the previous year, while Harvard's record number of applicants in 2008 (27,462), made its 7% acceptance rate the lowest in the school's history. McAlary (2008) and "A Record Pool" (2008).

Boredom and alcohol / drug use: The National Center for Addiction and Substance Abuse found that adolescents who were bored were 50% more likely to smoke, get drunk, or use illegal drugs. Caldwell and Smith (2006).

Harris poll of the parents of teens: "Wake Up Moms and Dads!" (2008).

A teen saying "none of your business" / the drive for autonomy: An adolescent's drive for autonomy isn't universal—kids don't usually demand across-the-board control of their lives. Instead, scholar Judith Smetana has determined that adolescents divide the world into certain spheres of control: they believe there are things that parents have the right to have control over, but there are also things that are rightly under a kid's own control. The tension comes in that parents and adolescents don't always agree what goes in which category.

For example, both father and daughter might agree that he can set rules about driving, because those are safety-related. But the father might also believe that he should have a right of approval over his daughter's friends, and his daughter adamantly disagrees, believing that who her friends are should be up to her alone. Another example: parents might be furious about a child's refusal to clean his room or take care of his things, but he sees his sloppiness as something that affects only him, so he doesn't understand what they are so upset about.

One might assume that early adolescents accept more parental governance, but Darling has actually found it's the other way around: early adolescents want more control over their lives than late adolescents.

Brain's reward center: Galvan's experiment was specifically designed to assess how rewards are processed within the nucleus accumbens and the orbital frontal cortex, because those areas of the brain are particularly sensitive to the amount of rewards. The brain's ventral striatum and thalamus are also involved in the brain's perception and response to rewards. See Izuma et al. (2008) in Chapter 1 sources and Galvan et al. (2005).

Arguing with parents: Arguing with parents peaks when kids are in early adolescence—from 11 to 14 years old. However, that's true for older siblings; for a younger sibling, that peak period of conflict occurs between a second child and his mother at ages 9 to 11, and with a dad, earlier still—at just 7 to 9 years. Shananan et al. (2007).

The myth of the rebellious teen years: Our review of the flawed early research into teen rebellion is based on Steinberg (2001). Current estimates are that real rebellion against parents occurs only about 5–15% of the time. Smetana, Campione-Barr, and Metzger (2006). The myth of teen rebellion isn't the only lore around teens: there's no support that teens are driven by "raging hormones," either. Spear (2000).

College students in remedial programs: California isn't the only state with college students in remedial programs. Pennsylvania estimates that one-third of its state college students were also in remedial classes. "Analysis of the 2003–04 Budget" (2003), "Early Assessment Program" (2008), and Barnes (2007).

But there's a hidden story in those remediation numbers: nationally, fewer students are in remedial programs now than since the 1980s. 42% of the Class of 1982 needed remedial courses in college—including 29% of the students in the nation's top quintile. By 1992, the remediation rate was down to 26% overall, and just 9% of the nation's best needed remediation. The rate's been hovering around 28% ever since. There are actually fewer colleges and universities offering remedial courses now than there were in the 1980s. Adelman (2004) and Pasard and Lewis (2003).

Increase in students taking advanced math and science / increase in college applications: The 20% increase in students' participation in math and science occurred from 1990 to 2004. That isn't the only indicator that students are taking more advanced courses: from 1996 to 2007, the number of students taking Advanced Placement exams (trying to obtain college credit while still in high school) tripled—to 1.5 million. More students are also meeting or exceeding the recommended years of high school study in key subjects. Morisi (2008) and "The American Freshman: Forty-Year Trends" (2007).

Of course, there is room for improvement—the nation's failure and dropout rates are unacceptable. But, on average, millions more kids are better academically prepared than ever before.

Enrollment data for colleges: "Percentage of High School Completers" (2008).

Surveys of college freshmen: We drew our data from the Higher Education Research Institute's annual survey, "The American Freshman," for the years 2007 and 2009.

Chapter 8, Can Self-Control Be Taught?

Inefficacy of Driver's Ed: Mayhew et al. (1998); Vernick et al. (1999); and Williams (2006).

Failure of drug-prevention and dropout programs: The General Accounting Office reported on the ineffectiveness of D.A.R.E. and a review of other drug-prevention programs in a report presented to Senator Richard J. Durbin (D-Illinois). Kanof (2003). Similar assessments were included in a Report to Congress from National Institute of Justice. Sherman et al. (1998). Scholarly analyses include Lynam et al. (1999) and Shepard (2001).

Interventions and effect sizes: For a perspective on how effect sizes play out in specific interventions, see Ammerman et al. (2002); Snyder et al. (2004); Welsh and Farrington (2003); Stice et al. (2006); and Wilfley et al. (2007).

Learning through use of private speech: A study at Vanderbilt University recently demonstrated the power of teaching private speech. Four- and five-year-olds had to pick up a color and shape pattern, then predict what the next object in the pattern would be. The control group was taught how to see a pattern, but the experimental groups were taught to talk themselves out loud through the pattern. The kids taught the private speech were 300% better at the task than the control kids. Rittle-Johnson et al. (2008).

The malleability of self-control: Masicampo and Baumeister (2008) and Baumeister et al. (2007).

Study finding a correction between high IQ and glucose-related fatigue: Shamosh and Gray (2007).

Chapter 9, Plays Well With Others

Scholars' responses to Dodge's findings: Based on author notes of remarks by Dodge, Lansford, and members of the audience during Dodge et al.'s presentation at the Society for Research in Child Development Biennial meeting in Boston, 2007.

Ethnic/cross-cultural differences in use of corporal punishment: It's important to note that, even for most families who use corporal punishment, it's usually a rare occurrence, and that we are talking about spanking only as a reprimand. We aren't talking about abuse. And, to restate one more time what's in the text, Dodge and his colleagues do *not* believe that their work should encourage anyone to use corporal punishment. Instead, they believe that the parents' and cultural meanings attached to punishment (whatever form it takes) must be considered when understanding its effects on a child.

Conservative Protestants' and other religious denominations' use of corporal punishment: Gershoff et al. (1999); Gershoff (2002); and Regnerus et al. (2003).

British inquiry on bullying: House of Commons (2007).

Rise of zero tolerance: Skiba et al. (2006) and author interviews with the chairman of the APA's zero tolerance task force, Cecil Reynolds.

popie-jopie: Author interviews with Cillessen; and deBruyn and Cillessen (2006).

Studies connecting popularity and alcohol use: See, for example, Allen et al. (2006) and Allen and McFarland (2008).

Kids who are "socially busy": Author interview with Claire Hughes.

Estimate that bistrategic controllers could be as many as one out of six children: Jacobs et al. (2007).

Adolescents' time spent in interactions with adults and peers: Spear (2000) in Chapter 7 sources; authors' interviews and correspondence with Baird and Allen.

Chapter 10, Why Hannah Talks and Alyssa Doesn't

University of Washington studies on babies' language and video use: Zimmerman et al. (2007a) and Zimmerman et al. (2007b).

Infant language measure/CDI: The Zimmerman et al. studies employed what's known as the "Short-form CDI"—a list of 89 words that are considered highly indicative of the breadth of a young child's vocabulary. The full-form CDI is a list of every word—it's meant to create a real-time index of a child's entire vocabulary—but, depending on the age of the child, it can take trained researchers as much as two to three hours to administer the full CDI. Therefore, in phone surveys such as those conducted by the University of Washington, the Short-form CDI is really the only practical alternative—and its results are reliable enough to satisfy scholars in the field. Indeed, some consider the full-CDI to be ideal for the scientist, but overkill for the parent and child. Author notes from IASCL Conference, Edinburgh, Scotland (2008); and Fenson et al. (2000).

Aigner-Clark credits Kuhl: Burr (1997) and Morris (1997).

Infant segmentation of language: Jusczyk (1999); Newman et al. (2006); and Newman et al. (2003).

Simultaneity of sensory input: Bahrick and Lickliter (2002); Bahrick and Lickliter (2000); Gogate and Bahrick (1998); and Hollich et al. (2005)

Acquisition of nouns and "closed class" words: Goodman et al. (2008).

Infant/parent verbal turn-taking predicts cognitive ability: Tamis-LeMonda and Bornstein (2002).

Motionese and word learning: Schwade et al. (2004).

Value of multiple speakers for word learning: Rost and McMurray (2008).

45% of utterances to a two-year-old begin with one of 17 words: Cameron-Faulkner et al. (2003).

Comparison of word acquisition in European and Korean languages: Bornstein et al. (2004).

Use of frames and variation sets: In a two-year-long study of children 14 to 30 months of age, by 30 months, those children whose parents had used more variation sets had more advanced language—both in the number of words they knew and the structure of their syntax. Fernald and Hurtado (2006); Bornstein et al. (1999); Waterfall (2009); and Waterfall (2006).

Shape bias: Author interviews with Samuelson and Smith; also Samuelson (2008); Samuelson and Horst (2004); Samuelson (2002); Samuelson (2000); Smith (2008); and Smith et al. (2002).

Growth of a child's vocabulary: Goodman et al. (2008)

Conclusion

Scholars' reassessment of the hedonic treadmill: Diener et al. (2006).

Effects of praise on adults: See, for example, McCausland et al. (2007) and Earley (1986).

Children's orthogonal development of virtue and vice: Another example comes from Padilla-Walker—she's seen that parents' efforts to inculcate children with prosocial values impacts the children's prosocial attitudes and behavior—but it doesn't seem to change their antisocial behavior or attitudes. Padilla-Walker (2007) and Padilla-Walker and Carlo (2007).

Kids who know they like the taste of fruit don't eat more apples: Unfortunately, we aren't speaking hypothetically here. A team from the University of California, Los Angeles was hired to evaluate the efficacy of the Nutrition Network, a program 325 schools within the Los Angeles Unified School District were using in their classrooms to promote better eating habits. The researchers surveyed nearly a thousand third, fourth, and fifth graders. They found that almost all kids—in or out of the program—knew that fruit tastes good and that it's good for them. (The kids also knew the benefits of vegetables—even if they didn't like the taste.) But despite knowing that, the kids ate about one piece of fruit a day, and slightly less than one serving of vegetables. The scholars had wondered if the cost of fresh produce might be the obstacle to eating more, but less than one percent of students said their parents couldn't afford fresh goods. Instead, the number one reason kids didn't fulfill their daily requirement was that they simply wanted something else to eat. Prelip et al. (2006).

SELECTED SOURCES AND REFERENCES

In addition to the numerous interviews we conducted, the following is a list of significant research materials and conference presentations that directly informed the text.

Introduction

Bartels, Andreas, and Semir Zeki, "The Neural Correlates of Maternal and Romantic Love," *NeuroImage*, vol. 21, no. 3, pp. 1155–1166 (2004).

Lorberbaum, Jeffrey P., John D. Newman, Amy R. Horwitz, Judy R. Dubno, R. Bruce Lydiard, Mark B. Hamner, Daryl E. Bohning, and Mark S. George, "A Potential Role for Thalamocingulate Circuitry in Human Maternal Behavior," *Biological Psychiatry*, vol. 51, no. 6, pp. 431–445 (2002).

Noriuchi, Madoka, Yoshiaki Kikuchi, and Atsushi Senoo, "The Functional Neuroanatomy of Maternal Love: Mother's Response to Infant's Attachment Behaviors," *Biological Psychiatry*, vol. 63, no. 4, pp. 415–423 (2008).

Swain, James E., Jeffrey P. Lorberbaum, Samet Kose, and Lane Strathearn, "Brain Basis of Early Parent-Infant Interactions: Psychology, Physiology, and In Vivo Functional Neuroimaging Studies," *Journal of Child Psychology and Psychiatry*, vol. 48, nos. 3–4, pp. 262–287 (2007).

Chapter 1, The Inverse Power of Praise

Ahuja, Anjana, "Forget Self-Esteem and Learn Some Humility," *The Times* (London), p. A1 (May 17, 2005).

Anderson, D. Chris, Charles R. Crowell, Mark Doman, and George

S. Howard, "Performance Posting, Goal Setting, and Activity-Contingent Praise as Applied to a University Hockey Team," *Journal of Applied Psychology*, vol. 73, no. 1, pp. 87–95 (1988).

Baumeister, Roy F., Jennifer D. Campbell, Joachim I. Krueger, and Kathleen D. Vohs, "Does High Self-Esteem Cause Better Performance, Interpersonal Success, Happiness or Healthier Lifestyles?" *Psychological Science in the Public Interest*, vol. 4, no. 1, pp. 1–44 (2003).

Baumeister, Roy F., Jennifer D. Campbell, Joachim I. Krueger, and Kathleen D. Vohs, "Exploding the Self-Esteem Myth," *Scientific American*, vol. 292, pp. 84–92 (2005).

Baumeister, Roy F., Debra G. Hutton, and Kenneth J. Cairns, "Negative Effects of Praise on Skilled Performance," *Basic and Applied Psychology*, vol. 11, no. 2, pp. 131–148 (1990).

Blackwell, Lisa Sorich, Kali H. Trzesniewski, and Carol S. Dweck, "Implicit Theories of Intelligence Predict Achievement Across an Adolescent Transition: A Longitudinal Study and an Intervention," *Child Development*, vol. 78, no. 1, pp. 246–263 (2007).

Campanella Bracken, Cheryl, Leo W. Jeffres, and Kimberly A. Neuendorf, "Criticism or Praise? The Impact of Verbal Versus Text-Only Computer Feedback on Social Presence, Intrinsic Motivation, and Recall," *CyberPsychology & Behavior*, vol. 7, no. 3, pp. 349–357 (2004).

"Chat Wrap-Up: Student Motivation, What Works, What Doesn't," *Education Week*, vol. 26, no. 3, p. 38 (2006).

Cole, David A., Joan M. Martin, Lachlan A. Peeke, A. D. Seroczynski, and Jonathan Fier, "Children's Over- and Underestimation of Academic Competence: A Longitudinal Study of Gender Difference, Depression and Anxiety," *Child Development*, vol. 70, no. 2, pp. 459–473 (1999).

Crocker, Jennifer, Interview with Neal Conan, *Talk of the Nation*, National Public Radio. WashingtonDC (Aug. 3, 2005).

Dweck, Carol S., "Caution—Praise Can Be Dangerous," *American Educator*, vol. 23, no. 1, pp. 4–9 (1999).

Dweck, Carol S., *Mindset*. New York: Ballantine (2006).

Dweck, Carol S., "The Perils and Promise of Praise," *Educational Leadership*, vol. 65, no. 2, pp. 34–39 (2007).

"Empty Praise: A Generation Ill-Prepared for Real World," *San Diego Union-Tribune*, p. B.10.2 (2005).

Gusnard, Debra A., John M. Ollinger, Gordon L. Shulman, C. Robert Cloninger, Joseph L. Price, David C. Van Essen, and Marcus E. Raicule, "Persistence and Brain Circuitry," *Proceedings of the National Academy of Sciences*, vol. 100, no. 6, pp. 3476–3484 (2003).

Hancock, Dawson R., "Influencing Graduate Students' Classroom Achievement, Homework Habits and Motivation to Learn With Verbal Praise," *Educational Research*, vol. 44, no. 1, pp. 83–95 (2002).

Henderlong, Jennifer, and Mark R. Lepper, "The Effects of Praise on Children's Intrinsic Motivation: A Review and Synthesis," *Psychological Bulletin*, vol. 128, no. 5, pp. 774–795 (2002).

Henderlong Corpus, Jennifer, and Mark R. Lepper, "The Effects of Person Versus Performance Praise on Children's Motivation: Gender and Age as Moderating Factors," *Educational Psychology*, vol. 27, no. 4, pp. 487–508 (2007).

Henderlong Corpus, Jennifer, Kelly E. Love, and Christin M. Ogle, "Social-Comparison Praise Undermines Intrinsic Motivation When Children Later Doubt Their Ability," Paper and poster presented at Biennial Meeting, Society for Research in Child Development, Atlanta (2005).

Henderlong Corpus, Jennifer, Christin M. Ogle, and Kelly E. Love-Geiger, "The Effects of Social-Comparison Versus Mastery Praise on Children's Intrinsic Motivation," *Motivation and Emotion*, vol. 30, no. 4, pp. 335–345 (2006).

Izuma, Keise, Daisuke N. Saito, and Norihiro Sadato, "Processing of Social and Monetary Rewards in the Human Striatum," *Neuron*, vol. 58, no. 2, pp. 284–294 (2008).

Kennedy Manzo, Kathleen, "Student Ambition Exceeds Academic Preparation," *Education Week*, vol. 24, no. 30, p. 6 (2005).

Kutner, Lawrence, "Parents and Child," *New York Times* (June 6, 1991), p. c.2.

Lepper, Mark R., David Greene, and Richard E. Nisbett, "Undermining Children's Intrinsic Interest With Extrinsic Reward: A Test of the 'Overjustification' Hypothesis," *Journal of Personality and Social Psychology*, vol. 28, no. 1, pp. 129–137 (1973).

May, J. Christopher, Mauricio R. Delgado, Ronald E. Dahl, V. Andrew Stenger, Neal D. Ryan, Julie A. Fiez, and Cameron S. Carter, "Event-Related Functional Magnetic Resonance Imaging of Reward-Related

Brain Circuitry in Children and Adolescents," *Biological Psychiatry*, vol. 55, no. 4, pp. 359–366 (2004).

McHoskey, John W., William Worzel, and Christopher Szyarto, "Machiavellianism and Psychopathy," *Journal of Personality and Social Psychology*, vol. 74, no. 1, pp. 192–210 (1998).

Meyer, Wulf-Uwe, Rainer Reisenzein, and Oliver Dickhauser, "Inferring Ability From Blame: Effects of Effort Versus Liking-Oriented Cognitive Schemata," *Psychology Science*, vol. 46, no. 2, pp. 281–293 (2004).

Mueller, Claudia M., and Carol S. Dweck, "Praise for Intelligence Can Undermine Children's Motivation and Performance," *Journal for Personality and Social Psychology*, vol. 75, no. 1, pp. 33–52 (1998).

Ng, Florrie Fei-Yin, Eva M. Pomerantz, and Shui-fong Lam, "European American and Chinese Parents' Responses to Children's Success and Failure: Implications for Children's Response," *Developmental Psychology*, vol. 43, no. 5, pp. 1239–1255 (2008).

Niiya, Yu, Jennifer Crocker, and Elizabeth N. Bartmess, "From Vulnerability to Resilience Learning Orientations Buffer Contingent Self-Esteem From Failure," *Psychological Science*, vol. 15, no. 12, pp. 801–805 (2004).

Peikin, David, "Praising Children for Their Intelligence May Leave Them Ill-Equipped to Cope With Failure" [Press release], American Psychological Association, Washington DC (1998).

Phillips, Deborah, "The Illusion of Incompetence Among Academically Competent Children," *Child Development*, vol. 55, no. 6, pp. 2000–2016 (1984).

Pomerantz, Eva M., Wendy S. Grolnick, and Carrie E. Price, "The Role of Parents in How Children Approach Achievement." In: Andrew J. Elliot and Carol S. Dweck (Eds.), *The Handbook of Competence and Motivation*, pp. 259–278. New York: Guilford Press (2005).

Reynolds, John, Mike Stewart, Ryan MacDonald, and Lacey Sischo, "Have Adolescents Become Too Ambitious? U.S. High School Seniors' Career Plans, 1976 to 2000," Department of Sociology, Florida State University (2005).

Ryan, Richard M., and Edward L. Deci, "Self-Determination Theory and the Facilitation of Intrinsic Motivation, Social Development, and Well-Being," *American Psychologist*, vol. 55, no. 1, pp. 68–78 (2000).

Strickler, Jane, "What Really Motivates People?" *Journal for Quality and Participation*, pp. 26–28 (2006).

Swanbrow, Diane, "Shame on Us: Shaming Some Kids Makes Them More Aggressive" [Press release], University of Michigan, Ann Arbor (2008).

Thomaes, Sander, Brad J. Bushman, Hedy Stegge, and Tjeert Olthof, "Trumping Shame by Blasts of Noise: Narcissism, Self-Esteem, Shame, and Aggression in Young Adolescents," *Child Development*, vol. 79, no. 6, pp. 1792–1801 (2008).

Wagner, Barry M., and Deborah A. Phillips, "Beyond Beliefs: Parent and Child Behaviors and Children's Perceived Academic Competence," *Child Development*, vol. 63, no. 6, pp. 1380–1391 (1992).

Webster, Robert L., and Harry A. Harmon, "Comparing Levels of Machiavellianism of Today's College Students With College Students of the 1960s," *Teaching Business Ethics*, vol. 6, no. 4, pp. 435–445 (2002).

Willingham, Daniel T., "How Praise Can Motivate—or Stifle," *American Educator*, vol. 29, no. 4, pp. 23–27, (2005–2006).

Chapter 2, The Lost Hour

Acebo, Christine, Avi Sadeh, Ronald Seifer, Orna Tzischinsky, Abigail Hafer, and Mary A. Carskadon, "Sleep/Wake Patterns Derived From Activity Monitoring and Maternal Report for Healthy 1- to 5-Year-Old Children," *Sleep*, vol. 28, no. 12, pp. 1568–1577 (2005).

Anderson, Patricia M., and Kristin F. Bucher, "Childhood Obesity: Trends and Potential Causes," *Future of Children*, vol. 16, no. 1, pp. 19–45 (2006).

Arcia, Emily, Peter A. Ornstein, and David A. Otto, "Neurobehavioral Evaluation System (NES) and School Performance," *Journal of School Psychology*, vol. 29, no. 4, pp. 337–352 (1991).

Arcuri, Jim, "AASM to School-Bound: Sleep Is the Right Ingredient for Academic Success" [Press release], American Academy of Sleep Medicine, Westchester, IL (2007).

Arcuri, Jim, "Children With Sleep Disorders Symptoms Are More Likely to Have Trouble Academically" [Press release], Associated Professional Sleep Societies, LLC, Westchester, IL (2007).

Arcuri, Jim, "Sleep Deprivation Can Lead to Smoking, Drinking" [Press release], Associated Professional Sleep Societies, LLC, Westchester, IL (2007).

Bachmann, Alissa, and Erin Ax, "The Relationship Between the Prevalence of Sleep Disorders Symptoms and Academic Performance in Lower Elementary School Students," *Journal of Sleep and Sleep Disorders Research*, vol. 30, 2007 Abstract Supplement, p. A99 (2007).

Backhaus, Jutta, Ralf Hoeckesfeld, Jan Born, Fritz Hohagen, and Klaus Junghanns, "Immediate as Well as Delayed Post Learning Sleep but Not Wakefulness Enhances Declarative Memory Consolidation in Children," *Neurobiology of Learning and Memory*, vol. 89, no. 1, pp. 76–80 (2008).

Bartolic, Silvia K., Sook-Jung Lee, and Elizabeth A. Vandewater, "Relating Activity Involvements to Child Weight Status: Do Normal and Overweight Children Differ in How They Spend Their Time?," Paper presented at the Population Association of America Annual Meeting, New York (2007).

Bass, Joseph, and Fred W. Turek, "Sleepless in America," *Archives of Internal Medicine*, vol. 165, no. 1, pp. 15–16 (2005).

Beebe, D. W., D. Rose, and R. Amin, "Effect of Chronic Sleep Restriction on an Adolescents' Learning and Brain Activity in a Simulated Classroom: A Pilot Study," *Journal of Sleep and Sleep Disorders Research*, vol. 31, 2008 Abstract Supplement, p. A77 (2008).

Biddle, Stuart J. H., "Sedentary Behavior," *American Journal of Preventive Medicine*, vol. 33, no. 6, pp. 502–504 (2007).

Biddle, Stuart J. H., Trish Gorely, Simon J. Marshall, and Noel Cameron, "The Prevalence of Sedentary Behavior and Physical Activity in Leisure Time: A Study of Scottish Adolescents Using Ecological Momentary Assessment," *Preventive Medicine*, vol. 48, no. 2, pp. 151–155 (2009).

Bogan, Lisa, Louise Herot, Amy Harris Hoermann, Catharine Kempson, Helen Martin, Janice Whitney, and Carole Young-Kleinfield, "School Start Time Study Report," League of Women's Voters, Wilton, CT (2002).

Born, Jan, "Sleep Enforces the Temporal Sequence in Memory" [Press release], Public Library of Science, University of Lübeck, Germany (2007).

Brandt, Michelle, "Stanford Study Links Obesity to Hormonal Changes From Lack of Sleep" [Press release], Stanford University, Stanford, CA (2004).

Burtanger, Donna, "Practice Makes Perfect, if You Sleep on It" [Press release], Harvard University, Cambridge, MA (2002).

Cappuccio, Francesco P., Frances M. Taggart, Ngianga-Bakwin Kandala, Andrew Currie, Ed Peile, Saverio Stranges, and Michelle A. Miller, "Meta-analysis of Short Sleep Duration and Obesity in Children and Adults," *Sleep*, vol. 31, no. 5, pp. 619–626 (2008).

Carins, A., J. Harsh, and M. LeBourgeois, "Napping in Children Is Related to Later Sleep Phase," *Journal of Sleep and Sleep Disorders Research*, vol. 30, 2007 Abstract Supplement, p. A100 (2007).

Chaput, J-P., M. Brunet, and A. Tremblay, "Relationship Between Short Sleeping Hours and Childhood Overweight/Obesity: Results From the 'Québec en Forme' Project," *International Journal of Obesity*, vol. 30, no. 7, pp. 1080–1085 (2006).

Chen, Xiaoli, May A. Beydoun, and Youfa Wang, "Is Sleep Duration Associated With Childhood Obesity? A Systematic Review and Meta-analysis," *Obesity*, vol. 16, no. 2, pp. 265–274 (2008).

Chervin, Ronald D., Kristen Hedger Archbold, James E. Dillon, Parviz Panahi, Kenneth J. Pituch, Ronald E. Dahl, and Christian Guilleminault, "Inattention, Hyperactivity, and Symptoms of Sleep-Disordered Breathing," *Pediatrics*, vol. 109, no. 3, pp. 449–456 (2002).

Chervin, Ronald D., James E. Dillon, Claudio Bassetti, Dara A. Ganoczy, and Kenneth J. Pituch, "Symptoms of Sleep Disorders, Inattention, and Hyperactivity in Children," *Sleep*, vol. 20, no. 12, pp. 1185–1192 (1997).

Chervin, Ronald D., Deborah L. Ruzicka, Kristen Hedger Archbold, and James E. Dillon, "Snoring Predicts Hyperactivity Four Years Later," *Sleep*, vol. 28, no. 7, pp. 885–890 (2005).

Crosby, Brian, Michelle Gryczkowski, Monique K. LeBourgeois, D. Joe Olmi, Brian Rabian, and John R. Harsh, "Mid-Sleep Time and Psychosocial Functioning in Black and White Preschool Children," Paper presented at the Associated Professional Sleep Societies' 21st Annual Meeting, Salt Lake City (2007).

Dahl, Ronald E., "The Consequences of Insufficient Sleep for Adolescents," *Phi Delta Kappan*, vol. 80, no. 5, pp. 354–359 (1999).

Dahl, Ronald E., "Sleep, Learning, and the Developing Brain: Early-to-Bed as a Healthy and Wise Choice for School Aged Children," *Sleep*, vol. 28, no. 12, pp. 1498–1499 (2005).

Danner, F. W., and R. Gilman, "Sleep Habits, Emotional Disturbance, and ADHD in High School Freshmen," *Journal of Sleep and Sleep Disorders Research*, vol. 31, 2008 Abstract Supplement, p. A107 (2008).

Danner, F. W., and R. R. Staten, "Disturbed Sleep, Psychological Distress, and Life Satisfaction in a College Sample," *Journal of Sleep and Sleep Disorders Research*, vol. 31, 2008 Abstract Supplement, p. A112 (2008).

Danner, Fred, "Sleep Deprivation and School Performance," Presentation at Academy of Professional Sleep Societies Annual Meeting, Las Vegas (2000).

Danner, Fred, and Barbara Phillips, "Adolescent Sleep, School Start Times, and Teen Motor Vehicle Crashes," *Journal of Clinical Sleep Medicine*, vol. 4, no. 6, pp. 533–535 (2008).

Danner, Frederick, "Disturbing Trends in the Sleep of 'Normal' Children and Adolescents," Paper presented at 17th annual meeting of the Associated Professional Sleep Societies, Chicago (2003).

Dollman, James, K. Ridley, T. Olds, and E. Lowe, "Trends in the Duration of School-Day Sleep Among 10- to 15-year-old South Australians Between 1985 and 2004," *Acta Pædiatrica*, vol. 96, no. 7, pp. 1011–1014 (2007).

Dragseth, Kenneth A., "A Minneapolis Suburb Reaps Early Benefits From a Late Start," *School Administrator*, (March 1999). http://tinyurl.com/cuob4h

Durmer, Jeffrey S., and David F. Dinges, "Neurocognitive Consequences of Sleep Deprivation," *Seminars in Neurology*, vol. 25, no. 1, pp. 117–129 (2005).

Eisenmann, Joey C., Panteleimon Ekkekakis, and Megan Holmes, "Sleep Duration and Overweight Among Australian Children and Adolescents," *Acta Pædiatrica*, vol. 95, no. 8, pp. 956–963 (2006).

Ellenbogen, Jeffrey M., Peter T. Hu, Jessica D. Payne, Debra Titone, and Matthew P. Walker, "Human Relational Memory Requires Time and Sleep," *Proceedings of the National Academy of Sciences*, vol. 104, no. 18, pp. 7723–7728 (2007).

Fallone, Gahan, Christine Acebo, Ronald Seifer, and Mary A. Carskadon, "Experimental Restriction of Sleep Opportunity in Children: Effects on Teacher Ratings," *Sleep*, vol. 28, no. 12, pp. 1561–1567 (2005).

Fredriksen, Katia, Jean Rhodes, Ranjini Reddy, and Niobe Way, "Sleepless in Chicago: Tracking the Effects of Adolescent Sleep Loss During the Middle School Years," *Child Development*, vol. 75, no. 1, pp. 84–95 (2004).

Gavin, Kara, "Link Found Between Kids' Sleep, Behavior Problems" [Press release], University of Michigan, Ann Arbor (2002).

Gibson, Edward S., A. C. Peter Powles, Lehana Thabane, Susan O'Brien, Danielle Sirriani Molnar, Nik Trajanovic, Robert Ogilvie, Colin Shapiro, Mi Yan, and Lisa Chilcott-Tanser, " 'Sleepiness' Is Serious in Adolescence: Two Surveys of 3235 Canadian Students," *BMC Public Health*, vol. 6, no. 116 (2006).

Graham, Mary C. (Ed.), *Sleep Needs, Patterns and Difficulties of Adolescents: Summary of a Workshop*. Washington DC: National Academy of Sciences, National Academy Press (2000).

Gregory, Alice M., Jan Van der Ende, Thomas A. Willis, and Frank C. Verhulst, "Parent-Reported Sleep Problems During Development and Self-reported Anxiety/Depression, Attention Problems, and Aggressive Behavior Later in Life," *Archives of Pediatrics & Adolescent Medicine*, vol. 162, no. 4, pp. 330–335 (2008).

Gupta, Neeraj K., William H. Mueller, Wenyaw Chan, and Janet C. Meininger, "Is Obesity Associated With Poor Sleep Quality in Adolescents?" *American Journal of Human Biology*, vol. 14, no. 6, pp. 762–768 (2002).

Hassan, F., M. M. Davis, and R. Chervin, "Insufficient Nights of Sleep and Childhood Obesity in a Nationally Representative Dataset," *Journal of Sleep and Sleep Disorders Research*, vol. 31, 2008 Abstract Supplement, p. A64 (2008).

Hensley, Timothy K., Centers for Disease Control, Atlanta, e-mails to authors (2007).

"Highlights," National Sleep Foundation, Sleep in America Poll, 2004, Washington DC (2004).

Hofferth, Sandra L., and John F. Sandberg, "How American Children Spend Their Time," *Journal of Marriage and Family*, vol. 63, no. 2, pp. 295–308 (2001).

Horne, James, "Too Weighty a Link Between Short Sleep and Obesity?" *Sleep*, vol. 31, no. 5, pp. 595–596 (2008).

Htwe, Z. W., D. Cuzzone, M. B. O'Malley, and E. B. O'Malley, "Sleep Patterns of High School Students Before and After Delayed School Start

Time," *Journal of Sleep and Sleep Disorders Research*, vol. 31, 2008 Abstract Supplement, pp. A74-A75 (2008).

Huppé, Jean-François, "Children Who Sleep Less Are Three Times More Likely to Be Overweight" [Press release], Université Laval, Quebec City, Canada (2006).

Iglowstein, Ivo, Oskar G. Jenni, Luciano Molinari, and Remo H. Largo, "Sleep Duration From Infancy to Adolescence: Reference Values and Generational Trends," *Pediatrics*, vol. 111, no. 2, pp. 302–307 (2003).

Kiess, W., C. Marcus, and M. Wabitsch (Eds.), *Obesity in Childhood and Adolescence, Pediatric Adolescent Medicine*, vol. 9. Switzerland: Karger, Basel (2004).

Kiess, Wieland, e-mails with authors (2007).

Krebs, Nancy F., John H. Himes, Dawn Jacobson, Theresa A. Nicklas, Patricia Guilday, and Dennis Styne, "Assessment of Child and Adolescent Overweight and Obesity," *Pediatrics*, vol. 120, Supplement, pp. S193–S228 (2007).

Landhuis, Carl Erik, Richie Poulton, David Welch, and Robert John Hancox, "Childhood Sleep Time and Long-Term Risk for Obesity: A 32-Year Prospective Birth Cohort Study," *Pediatrics*, vol. 122, no. 5, pp. 955–960 (2008).

LeBourgeois, Monique K., and John R. Harsh, "Racial Gaps in School Readiness: The Importance of Sleep and Rhythms?" Paper presented at the Associated Professional Sleep Societies' 21st Annual Meeting, Salt Lake City (2007).

Lim, L., S. Su, S. Fook, and P. Lee, "Sleep Deprivation Among Adolescents in Singapore," *Journal of Sleep and Sleep Disorders Research*, vol. 31, 2008 Abstract Supplement, p. A86 (2008).

Liu, Xianchen, Erika E. Forbes, Neal D. Ryan, Dana Rofey, Tamara S. Hannon, and Ronald E. Dahl, "Rapid Eye Movement Sleep in Relation to Overweight in Children and Adolescents," *Archives of General Psychiatry*, vol. 65, no. 8, pp. 924–932 (2008).

Lumeng, Julie C., Deepak Somashekar, Danielle Appugliese, Niko Kaciroti, Robert F. Corwyn, and Robert H. Bradley, "Shorter Sleep Duration Is Associated With Increased Risk for Being Overweight at Ages 9 to 12 Years," *Pediatrics*, vol. 120, no. 5, pp. 1020–1029 (2007).

Martin, Douglas, "Late to Bed, Early to Rise Makes a Teen-Ager...Tired," *New York Times*, p. 4A.24 (Aug. 1, 1999).

McKenna, Ellen, "Sleep Disorders Can Impair Children's IQs as Much as Lead Exposure" [Press release], University of Virginia Health System (2007).

McNamara, J., C. McCrae, and W. Berg, "The Impact of Sleep on Children's Executive Functioning," *Journal of Sleep and Sleep Disorders Research*, vol. 30, 2007 Abstract Supplement, p. A79 (2007).

Mendoza, Martha, e-mails with authors (2007).

Mendoza, Martha, "Review Finds Nutrition Education Failing," Associated Press via Yahoo! News (2007).

Millman, Richard P., and Working Group on Sleepiness in Adolescents/Young Adults and AAP Committee on Adolescence, "Excessive Sleepiness in Adolescents and Young Adults: Causes, Consequences, and Treatment Strategies," Technical report, American Academy of Pediatrics, National Heart, Lung, and Blood Institute, and National Center on Sleep Disorders Research, *Pediatrics*, vol. 115, no. 6, pp. 1774–1786 (2005).

"National Sleep Foundation 2004 Sleep in America Summary of Findings," National Sleep Foundation, Washington DC (2004).

"National Sleep Foundation 2006 Sleep in America Poll Highlights and Key Findings," National Sleep Foundation, Washington DC (2006).

"National Sleep Foundation 2006 Sleep in America Poll Summary of Findings," National Sleep Foundation, Washington DC (2006).

National Sleep Foundation web site: http://tinyurl.com/5b47dq

Nixon, Gillian M., John M. D. Thompson, Dug Yeo Han, David M. Becroft, Phillipa M. Clark, Elizabeth Robinson, Karen E. Waldie, Chris J. Wild, Peter N. Black, and Edwin A. Mitchell, "Short Sleep Duration in Middle Childhood: Risk Factors and Consequences," *Sleep*, vol. 31, no. 1, pp. 71–78 (2008).

"Obesity 'Not Individuals' Fault," BBC News (2007). http://tinyurl.com/ch2nx2

Owens, Judith, Rolanda Maxim, Melissa McGuinn, Chantelle Nobile, Michael Msall, and Anthony Alario, "Television-Viewing Habits and Sleep Disturbance in School Children," *Pediatrics*, vol. 104, no. 3, pp. e27 et seq. (1999).

Park, Madison, "Falling Asleep in Class? Blame Biology," CNN.com (2008). http://tinyurl.com/6q26f8

Prescott, Bonnie, "Study Shows How Sleep Improves Memory" [Press release], Harvard University, Cambridge, MA (2005).

Ramsey, Kathryn Moynihan, Biliana Marcheva, Akira Kohsaka, and Joseph Bass, "The Clockwork of Metabolism," *The Annual Review of Nutrition*, vol. 27, pp. 219–240 (2007).

Redding, Jerry, United States Department of Agriculture, Washington DC, e-mails to authors (2007).

Rogers, Naomi L., Jillian Dorrian, and David F. Dinges, "Sleep, Waking and Neurobehavioural Performance," *Frontiers in Bioscience*, vol. 8, pp. s1056–1067 (2003).

Sadeh, Avi, Reut Gruber, and Amiram Raviv, "The Effects of Sleep Restriction and Extension on School-Age Children: What a Difference an Hour Makes," *Child Development*, vol. 74, no. 2, pp. 444–455 (2003).

Schardt, David, "How Sleep Affects Your Weight," *Nutrition Action Newsletter*, pp. 10–11 (2005).

Schechter, Michael S., and the Section on Pediatric Pulmonology, Subcommittee on Obstructive Sleep Apnea Syndrome, "Technical Report: Diagnosis and Management of Childhood Obstructive Sleep Apnea Syndrome," *Pediatrics*, vol. 109, no. 4, pp. e69 et seq. (2002).

Schoenborn, Charlotte A., and Patricia F. Adams, "Sleep Duration as a Correlate of Smoking, Alcohol Use, Leisure-Time Physical Inactivity, and Obesity Among Adults: United States, 2004–2006," NCHS Health E-Stat, Centers for Disease Control, Atlanta (2008).

Sekine, Michikazu, Takashi Yamagami, Kyoko Handa, Tomohiro Saito, Seiichiro Nanri, Katsuhiko Kawaminami, Noritaka Tokui, Katsumi Yoshida, and Sadanobu Kagamimori, "A Dose-Response Relationship Between Short Sleeping Hours and Childhood Obesity: Results of the Toyama Birth Cohort Study," *Child: Care, Health & Development*, vol. 28, no. 2, pp. 163–170 (2002).

Spiegel, Karine, "Sleep Loss as a Risk Factor for Obesity and Diabetes," *International Journal of Obesity*, vol. 3, no. 1, pp. 27–28 (2008).

Spiegel, Karine, Kristen Knutson, Rachel Leproult, Esra Tasali, and Eve Van Cauter, "Sleep Loss: A Novel Risk Factor for Insulin Resistance and Type 2 Diabetes," *Journal of Applied Physiology*, vol. 99, no. 5, pp. 2008–2019 (2005).

Spiegel, Karine, Esra Tasali, Plamen Penev, and Eve Van Cauter, "Brief Communication: Sleep Curtailment in Healthy Young Men Is Associated With Decreased Leptin Levels, Elevated Ghrelin Levels, and Increased Hunger and Appetite," *Annals of Internal Medicine*, vol. 141, no. 11, pp. 846–850 (2005).

Spruyt, K., O. San Capdevila, S.M. Honaker, J. L. Bennett, and D. Gozal, "Obesity, Snoring, and Physical Activity in School-Aged Children," *Journal of Sleep and Sleep Disorders Research*, vol. 31, 2008 Abstract Supplement, p. A76 (2008).

Stice, Eric, Heather Shaw, and C. Nathan Marti, "A Meta-analytic Review of Obesity Prevention Programs for Children and Adolescents: The Skinny on Interventions that Work," *Psychological Bulletin*, vol. 132, no. 5, pp. 667–691 (2006).

Stickgold, Robert, and Matthew P. Walker, "Memory Consolidation and Reconsolidation: What Is the Role of Sleep?," *Trends in Neuroscience*, vol. 28, no. 8, pp. 408–415 (2005).

Stickgold, Robert, and Matthew P. Walker, "Sleep-Dependent Memory Consolidation and Reconsolidation," *Sleep Medicine*, vol. 8, no. 4, pp. 331–343 (2007).

Taheri, S, "The Link Between Short Sleep Duration and Obesity: We Should Recommend More Sleep to Prevent Obesity," *Archives of Diseases in Childhood*, vol. 91, no. 11, pp. 881–884 (2006).

Tasali, Esra, Rachel Leproult, David A. Ehrmann, and Eve Van Cauter, "Slow-wave Sleep and the Risk of Type 2 Diabetes in Humans," *Proceedings of the National Academy of Sciences* (Early Edition) (2007).

Taveras, Elsie M., Alison E. Field, Catherine S. Berkey, Sheryl L. Rifas-Shiman, A., Lindsay Frazier, Graham A. Colditz, and Matthew W. Gillman, "Longitudinal Relationship Between Television Viewing and Leisure-Time Physical Activity During Adolescence," *Pediatrics*, vol. 119, no. 2, pp. e314–e319 (2007).

Taveras, Elise M., Sheryl L. Rifas-Shiman, Emily Oken, Erica P. Gunderson, and Matthew W. Gillman, "Short Sleep Duration in Infancy and Risk of Childhood Overweight," *Archives of Pediatrics & Adolescent Medicine*, vol. 162, no. 4, pp. 305–311 (2008).

Thomas, H., "Obesity Prevention Programs for Children and Youth: Why Are Their Results So Modest?" McMaster University manuscript (2006).

Touchette, Évelyne, Dominique Petit, Jean R. Séguin, Michel Boivin, Richard E. Tremblay, and Jacques Y. Montplaisir, "Associations Between

Sleep Duration Patterns and Behavioral/Cognitive Functioning at School Entry," *Sleep*, vol. 30, no. 9, pp. 1213–1219 (2007).

Tzischinsky, O., S. Hadar, and D. Lufi, "Delaying School Start Time by One Hour: Effects on Cognitive Performance in Adolescents," *Journal of Sleep and Sleep Disorders Research*, vol. 31, 2008 Abstract Supplement, p. A369 (2008).

Utter, Jennifer, Dianne Neumark-Sztainer, Robert Jeffrey, and Mary Story, "Couch Potatoes or French Fries: Are Sedentary Behaviors Associated With Body Mass Index, Physical Activity, and Dietary Behaviors Among Adolescents?" *Journal of the American Dietetic Association*, vol. 103, no. 10, pp. 1298–1305 (2003).

Van Cauter, Eve, Kristen Knutson, Rachel Leproult, and Karine Spiegel, "The Impact of Sleep Deprivation on Hormones and Metabolism," *Medscape Neurology & Neurosurgery*, vol. 7, no. 1 (2005).

Van Cauter, Eve, Karine Spiegel, Esra Tasali, and Rachel Leproult, "Metabolic Consequences of Sleep and Sleep Loss," *Sleep Medicine*, vol. 9, supp. 1, pp. S23-28 (2008).

Vandewater, Elizabeth A., "Media Use and Children's Health," Paper presented at the Population Association of America Annual Meeting, New York City (2007).

Wahlstrom, Kyla L., e-mails with authors (2007).

Wahlstrom, Kyla L., "The Prickly Politics of School Starting Times," *Phi Delta Kappan*, vol. 80, no. 5, pp. 344–347, Minneapolis (1999).

Wahlstrom, Kyla L., "School Start Time Study: Final Summary [vol. 1]," School Start Time Reports, Center for Applied Research and Educational Improvement (CAREI), University of Minnesota, Minneapolis (Undated).

Wahlstrom, Kyla L., "School Start Time Study: Technical Report Vol. II, Analysis of Student Survey Data," Center for Applied Research and Educational Improvement, University of Minnesota, Minneapolis (Undated).

Wahlstrom, Kyla L., Mark L. Davison, Jiyoung Choi, and Jesse N. Ross, "Minneapolis Public Schools Start Time Study Executive Summary," Center for Applied Research and Educational Improvement, University of Minnesota, Minneapolis (2001).

Wahlstrom, Kyla L., G. Wrobel, and P. Kubow, "Minneapolis Public Schools Start Time Study: Executive Summary," Center for Applied Research and Educational Improvement, University of Minnesota, Minneapolis (1998).

Walker, Matthew P., and Robert Stickgold, "Sleep-Dependent Learning and Memory Consolidation," *Neuron*, vol. 44, no. 1, pp. 121–133 (2004).

Walker, Matthew P., and Robert Stickgold, "Sleep, Memory & Plasticity," *Annual Review of Psychology*, vol. 57, pp. 139–166 (2006).

Warner, Suzanne, Greg Murphy, and Denny Meyer, "Holiday and School-term Sleep Patterns of Australian Adolescents." *Journal of Adolescence*, vol. 31, no. 5, pp. 595–608 (2008).

Werner, Helene, Luciano Molinari, Caroline Guyer, and Oskar G. Jenni, "Agreement Rates Between Actigraphy, Diary, and Questionnaire for Children's Sleep Patterns," *Archives of Pediatrics and Adolescent Medicine*, vol. 162, no. 4, pp. 350–358 (2008).

Wolfson, Amy R., and Mary A. Carskadon, "Sleep Schedules and Daytime Functioning in Adolescents," *Child Development*, vol. 69, no. 4, pp. 875–887 (1998).

Wolfson, Amy R., and Mary A. Carskadon, "A Survey of Factors Influencing High School Start Times," *NASSP Bulletin*, vol. 89, no. 642, pp. 47–66 (2005).

Wong, Maria M., and Tim Roehrs, "Sleep Problems in Early Childhood May Predict Substance Use During Adolescence" [Press release], *Alcoholism: Clinical & Experimental Research* (2004).

Young, Terry, "Increasing Sleep Duration for a Healthier (and Less Obese?) Population Tomorrow," *Sleep*, vol. 31, no. 5, pp. 593–594 (2008).

Chapter 3, Why White Parents Don't Talk About Race

Baron, Andrew Scott, and Mahzarin R. Banaji, "The Development of Implicit Attitudes: Evidence of Race Evaluations From Ages 6 and 10 and Adulthood," *Psychological Science*, vol. 17, no. 1, pp. 53–58 (2006).

Bigler, Rebecca S., "The Use of Multicultural Curricula and Materials to Counter Racism in Children," *Journal of Social Issues*, vol. 55, no. 4, pp. 687–705 (1999).

Bigler, Rebecca S., and Lynn S. Liben, "A Developmental Intergroup Theory of Social Stereotypes and Prejudice," *Advances in Child Development and Behavior*, vol. 34, pp. 39–89 (2006).

Bigler, Rebecca S., and Lynn S. Liben, "Developmental Intergroup Theory: Explaining and Reducing Children's Social Stereotyping and Prejudice,"

Current Directions in Psychological Science, vol. 16, no. 3, pp. 162–166 (2007).

Brief of 553 Social Scientists as Amici Curiae in Support of Respondents, *Meredith v. Jefferson County Board of Education* (Nos. 05-908 and 05-915) (2006).

Brown, Tony N., Emily E. Tanner-Smith, Chase L. Lesane-Brown, and Michael E. Ezell, "Child, Parent, Situational Correlates of Familial Ethnic/Race Socialization," *Journal of Marriage and Family*, vol. 69, no. 1, pp. 14–25 (2007).

Copenhaver-Johnson, Jeane F., e-mails with authors (2007).

Copenhaver-Johnson, Jeane F., Joy T. Bowman, and Angela C. Johnson, "Santa Stories: Children's Inquiry About Race during Picturebook Read-Alouds," *Language Arts*, vol. 84, no. 3, pp. 234–244 (2007).

Crystal, David S., Hirozumi Watanabe, and Ru San Chen, "Preference for Diversity in Competitive and Cooperative Contexts: A Study of American and Japanese Children and Adolescents," *International Journal of Behavioral Development*, vol. 24, no. 3, pp. 348–355 (2000).

Harris-Britt, April, Ndidi A. Okeke, Cleo Samuel, and Beth E. Kurtz-Costes, "Mediational Influences in the Relationship Between Racial Socialization and Achievement Outcomes in Late Childhood," Poster presented at the Biennial Meeting of the Society for Research in Child Development, Boston (2007).

Harris-Britt, April, Cecelia Valrie, Beth Kurtz-Costes, and Stephanie J. Rowley, "Perceived Racial Discrimination and Self-Esteem in African-American Youth," *Journal of Adolescent Research*, vol. 17, no. 4, pp. 669–682 (2007).

Hughes, Julie M., Rebecca S. Bigler, and Sheri R. Levy, "Consequences of Learning About Historical Racism Among European American and African American Children," *Child Development*, vol. 78, no. 6, pp. 1689–1705 (2007).

"The Impact of Racial and Ethnic Diversity on Educational Outcomes: Cambridge, MA School District," The Civil Rights Project, Harvard University, Cambridge, MA (2002).

"The Impact of Racial and Ethnic Diversity on Educational Outcomes: Lynn, MA School District," The Civil Rights Project, Harvard University, Cambridge, MA (2002).

Katz, Phyllis A., "Racists or Tolerant Multiculturalists," *American Psychologist*, vol. 58, no. 11, pp. 897–909 (2003).

Kelly, David J., Paul C. Quinn, Alan M. Slater, Kang Lee, Liezhong Ge, and Olivier Pascalis, "The Other-Race Effect Develops During Infancy: Evidence of Perceptual Narrowing," *Psychological Science*, vol. 18, no. 12, pp. 1084–1089 (2007).

Kurlaendar, Michal, and John T. Yun, "Is Diversity a Compelling Educational Interest? Evidence From Louisville." In: G. Orfield (Ed.), *Diversity Challenged: Evidence in the Impact of Affirmative Action*, pp. 111–141. Cambridge, MA: Harvard Educational Publishing Group (2001).

Meredith v. Jefferson County Board of Education, 551 U.S. ___ (2007).

"Mission Statement," Civil Rights Project web site (2007). http://www.civilrightsproject.ucla.edu/aboutus.php

Moody, James, "Race, School Integration, and Friendship Segregation in America," *American Journal of Sociology*, vol. 107, no. 3, pp. 679–716 (2001).

Oyserman, Daphna, Daniel Brickman, Deborah Bybee, and Aaron Celious, "Fitting in Matters: Markers of In-Group Belonging and Academic Outcomes," *Psychological Science*, vol. 17, no. 10, pp. 854–861 (2006).

Patterson, Meagan M., and Rebecca S. Bigler, "Preschool Children's Attention to Environmental Messages About Groups: Social Categorization and the Origins of Intergroup Bias," *Child Development*, vol. 77, no. 4, pp. 847–860 (2006).

Pettigrew, Thomas F., and Linda R. Tropp, "A Meta-analytic Test of Intergroup Contact Theory," *Journal of Personality and Social Psychology*, vol. 90, no. 5, pp. 751–783 (2006).

Polite, Lillian, and Elizabeth Baird Saenger, "A Pernicious Silence: Confronting Race in the Elementary Classroom," *Phi Delta Kappan*, vol. 85, no. 4, pp. 274–278 (2003).

Rooney-Rebeck, Patricia, and Leonard Jason, "Prevention of Prejudice in Elementary School Students," *Journal of Primary Prevention*, vol. 7, no. 2, pp. 63–73 (1986).

Rosales, Melodye, *Twas the Night B'fore Christmas: An African-American Version*. New York: Scholastic (1996).

Stephan, Walter G., "Improving Intergroup Relations in the Schools." In: C. H. Rossell, D. J. Armor, and H. J. Walberg (Eds.), *School Desegregation in the 21st Century*, pp. 267–290. Westport, CT: Praeger Publishers (2002).

Tynes, Brendesha M., "Role Taking in Online 'Classrooms': What Adolescents Are Learning About Race and Ethnicity," *Developmental Psychology*, vol. 43, no. 6, pp. 1312–1320 (2007).

Vittrup, Birgitte, and George W. Holden, "Why White Parents Don't Talk to Their Children About Race," Poster presented at the Biennial Meeting of the Society for Research in Child Development, Boston (2007).

Vittrup Simpson, Birgitte, *Exploring the Influences of Educational Television and Parent-Child Discussions on Improving Children's Racial Attitudes*, Doctoral Dissertation, University of Texas at Austin Repository, Austin, TX (2007).

Chapter 4, Why Kids Lie

"An Act to Amend the Criminal Code (protection of children and other vulnerable persons) and the Canada Evidence Act," Bill C-2, First Session, 38th Parliament, 53 Elizabeth II, House of Commons, Canada (2004).

Alwin, Duane F., "Changes in Qualities Valued in Children in the United States, 1964 to 1984," *Social Science Research*, vol. 18, no. 3, pp. 195–236 (1989).

Arruda, Cindy M., Megan K. Brunet, Mina E. Poplinger, Ilana Ross, Anjanie McCarthy, Victoria Talwar, and Kang Lee, " 'I Cannot Tell a Lie': Enhancing Truth-Telling in Children Through the Use of Traditional Stories," Poster presented at the Biennial Meeting of the Society for Research in Child Development, Boston (2007).

Berthoud-Papandropoulou, Ioanna, and Helga Kilcher, "Is a False Belief Statement a Lie or a Truthful Statement? Judgments and Explanations of Children Aged 3 to 8," *Developmental Science*, vol. 6, no. 2, pp. 173–177 (2003).

Billings, F. James, Tanya Taylor, James Burns, Deb L. Corey, Sena Garven, and James M. Wood, "Can Reinforcement Induce Children to Falsely Incriminate Themselves?" *Law and Human Behavior*, vol. 31, no. 2, pp. 125–139 (2007).

Bull, Ray, and Aldert Vrji, "People's Insight into Their Own Behaviour and Speech Content While Lying," *British Journal of Psychology*, vol. 92, no. 2, pp. 373–389 (2001).

Bussey, Kay, "Children's Categorization and Evaluation of Different Types of Lies and Truths," *Child Development*, vol. 70, no. 6, pp. 1338–1347 (1999).

Bussey, Kay, "Parental and Interviewer Influences on Children's Lying and Truth Telling," Remarks and paper presented at the Biennial Meeting of the Society for Research in Child Development, Boston (2007).

Crossman, Angela M., and Michael Lewis, "Adults' Ability to Detect Children's Lying," *Behavioral Sciences and the Law*, vol. 24, no. 5, pp. 703–715 (2006).

den Bak, Irene M., and Hildy S. Ross, "I'm Telling! The Content, Context and Consequences of Children's Tattling on Their Siblings," *Social Development*, vol. 5, no. 3, pp. 292–309 (1996).

DePaulo, Bella M., Matthew E. Ansfield, Susan E. Kirkendol, and Joseph M. Boden, "Serious Lies," *Basic and Applied Social Psychology*, vol. 26, nos. 2-3, pp. 147–167 (2004).

DePaulo, Bella M., Deborah A. Kashy, Susan E. Kirkendol, Jennifer A. Epstein, and Melissa M. Wyer, "Lying in Everyday Life," *Journal of Personality and Social Psychology*, vol. 70, no. 5, pp. 979–995 (1996).

Edelstein, Robin S., Tanya L. Luten, Paul Ekman, and Gail S. Goodman, "Detecting Lies in Children and Adults," *Law and Human Behavior*, vol. 30, no. 1, pp. 1–10 (2006).

Ekman, Paul, "Would a Child Lie?" *Psychology Today*, vol. 23, no. 62, pp. 7–8 (1989).

Friman, Patrick C., Douglas W. Woods, Kurt A. Freeman, Rich Gilman, Mary Short, Ann M. McGrath, and Michael L. Handwerk, "Relationships Between Tattling, Likeability, and Social Classification: A Preliminary Investigation of Adolescents in Residential Care," *Behavior Modification*, vol. 28, no. 3, pp. 331–348 (2004).

Fu, Genyue, and Kang Lee, "Social Grooming in the Kindergarten: The Emergence of Flattery Behavior," *Developmental Science*, vol. 10, no. 2, pp. 255–265 (2007).

Gervais, Jean, Richard E. Tremblay, Lyse Desmarais-Gervais, and Frank Vitaro, "Children's Persistent Lying, Gender Differences, and Disruptive Behaviours: A Longitudinal Perspective," *International Journal of Behavioral Development*, vol. 24, no. 2, pp. 213–221 (2000).

Global Deception Research Team, "A World of Lies," *Journal of Cross-Cultural Psychology*, vol. 37, no. 1, pp. 60–74 (2006).

Hancock, Jeffrey T., Jennifer Thom-Santelli, and Thompson Ritchie, "Deception and Design: The Impact of Communication Technology on Lying Behavior," Paper presented at CHI, Vienna, Austria (2004).

Josephson Institute of Ethics, 2006 Report Card on the Ethics of American Youth—Part One—Integrity (2006).

Leach, Amy-May, R.C.L. Lindsay, Rachel Koehler, Jennifer L. Beaudry, Nicholas C. Bala, Kang Lee, and Victoria Talwar, "The Reliability of Lie Detection Performance," *Law and Human Behavior*, vol. 37, no. 1, pp. 96–109 (2009).

Leach, Amy-May, Victoria Talwar, Kang Lee, Nicholas Bala, and R.C.L. Lindsay, "'Intuitive' Lie Detection of Children's Deception by Law Enforcement Officials and University Students," *Law and Human Behavior*, vol. 28, no. 6, pp. 661–685 (2004).

Lee, Kang, "Promoting Honesty in Young Children," Remarks and paper presented at the Biennial Meeting of the Society for Research in Child Development, Boston (2007).

Peterson, Candida C., James L. Peterson, and Diane Seeto, "Developmental Changes in Ideas About Lying," *Child Development*, vol. 54, no. 6, pp. 1529–1535 (1983).

Poplinger, Mina E., Victoria Talwar, Kang Lee, Fen Xu, and Genyue Fu, "The Development of White Lie-Telling Among Children Three to Five Years," Poster presented at the Biennial Meeting of the Society for Research in Child Development, Boston (2007).

Ross, Hildy S., and Irene M. den Bak-Lammers, "Consistency and Change in Children's Tattling on their Siblings: Children's Perspectives on the Moral Rules and Procedures of Family Life," *Social Development*, vol. 7, no. 3, pp. 275–300 (1998).

Strichartz, Abigail F., and Roger V. Burton, "Lies and Truth: A Study of the Development of the Concept," *Child Development*, vol. 61, no. 1, pp. 211–220 (1990).

Strömwall, Leif A., and Pär Anders Granhaget, "Detecting Deceit in Pairs of Children," *Journal of Applied Social Psychology*, vol. 37, no. 6, pp. 1285–1304 (2007).

Talwar, Victoria, e-mails with authors (2007–2009).

Talwar, Victoria, "Sociocognitive Correlates of Children's Lying, Executive Functioning, and False Beliefs," Remarks and paper presented at the Biennial Meeting of the Society for Research in Child Development, Boston (2007).

Talwar, Victoria, Heidi Gordon, and Kang Lee, "Lying in the Elementary School Years: Verbal Deception and Its Relation to Second-Order Belief Understanding," *Developmental Psychology*, vol. 43, no. 3, pp. 804–810 (2007).

Talwar, Victoria, and Kang Lee, "Development of Lying to Conceal a Transgression: Children's Control of Expressive Behavior During Verbal Deception," *International Journal of Behavioral Development*, vol. 26, no. 5, pp. 436–444 (2002).

Talwar, Victoria, and Kang Lee, "Emergence of White Lie-Telling in Children Between 3 and 7 Years of Age," *Merrill-Palmer Quarterly*, vol. 48, no. 2, pp. 160–181 (2002).

Talwar, Victoria, and Kang Lee, "Social and Cognitive Correlates of Children's Lying Behavior," *Child Development*, vol. 79, no. 4., pp. 866–881 (2008).

Talwar, Victoria, Kang Lee, Nicholas Bala, and R. C. L. Lindsay, "Children's Conceptual Knowledge of Lie-Telling and Its Relation to Their Actual Behaviors: Implications for Court Competence Examination," *Law and Human Behavior*, vol. 26, no. 4, pp. 395–415 (2002).

Talwar, Victoria, Kang Lee, Nicholas Bala, and R. C. L. Lindsay, "Children's Lie-Telling to Conceal a Parent's Transgression: Legal Implications," *Law and Human Behavior*, vol. 28, no. 4, pp. 411–435 (2004).

Talwar, Victoria, Kang Lee, Nicholas Bala, and R. C. L. Lindsay, "Adults' Judgments of Children's Coached Reports," *Law and Human Behavior*, vol. 30, no. 5, pp. 561–5701 (2006).

Talwar, Victoria, Susan M. Murphy, and Kang Lee, "White Lie-Telling in Children for Politeness Purposes," *International Journal of Behavioral Development*, vol. 31, no. 1, pp. 1–11 (2007).

Vrij, Aldert, "Why Professionals Fail to Catch Liars and How They Can Improve," *Legal and Criminological Psychology*, vol. 9, no. 2, pp. 159–181 (2004).

Vrij, Aldert, Lucy Akehurst, Stavroula Soukara, and Ray Bull, "Detecting Deceit Via Analyses of Verbal and Nonverbal Behavior in Children and Adults," *Human Communication Research*, vol. 30, no. 1, pp. 8–41 (2004).

Wagland, Paul, and Kay Bussey, "Factors that Facilitate and Undermine

Children's Beliefs About Truth Telling," *Law and Human Behavior*, vol. 29, no. 6, pp. 639–655 (2005).

Wilson, Anne E., Melissa D. Smith, and Hildy S. Ross, "The Nature and Effects of Young Children's Lies," *Social Development*, vol. 12, no. 1, pp. 21–45 (2003).

Wilson, Anne E., Melissa D. Smith, Hildy S. Ross, and Michael Ross, "Young Children's Personal Accounts of Their Sibling Disputes," *Merrill-Palmer Quarterly*, vol. 50, no. 1, pp. 39–60 (2004).

Chapter 5, The Search for Intelligent Life in Kindergarten

Amso, Dima, and B. J., Casey, "Beyond What Develops When: Neuroimaging May Inform How Cognition Changes With Development," *Current Directions in Psychological Science*, vol. 15, no. 1, pp. 24–29 (2006).

"Answers About Elementary School Enrollment, Part 3," City Blog, *New York Times* (2008). http://tinyurl.com/9taksw

Azari, Nina P., Janpeter Nickel, Gilbert Wunderlich, Michael Niedeggen, Harald Hefter, Lutz Tellmann, Hans Herzog, Petra Stoerig, Dieter Birnbacher, and Rüdiger J. Seitz, "Neural Correlates of Religious Recitation," *European Journal of Neuroscience*, vol. 13, no. 8, pp. 1649–1652 (2001).

Barber, Nigel, "Educational and Ecological Correlates of IQ: A Cross-National Investigation," *Intelligence*, vol. 33, no. 3, pp. 273–284 (2005).

Barnea-Goraly, Naama, Vinod Menon, Mark Eckert, Leanne Tamm, Roland Bammer, Asya Karchemskiy, Christopher C. Dant, and Allan L. Reiss, "White Matter Development During Childhood and Adolescence: A Cross-Sectional Diffusion Tensor Imaging Study," *Cerebral Cortex*, vol. 15, no. 12, pp. 1848–1854 (2005).

Bartels, Andreas, and Semir Zeki, "The Neural Basis of Romantic Love," *NeuroReport*, vol. 11, no. 17, pp. 3829–3834 (2000).

Baxter, Betty Carpenter, *The Relationship of Early Tested Intelligence on the WPPSI to Later Tested Aptitude on the SAT*, Doctoral Dissertation, Columbia University, New York City (1988).

Casey, B. J., Sarah Getz, and Adriana Galvan, "The Adolescent Brain," *Developmental Review*, vol. 28, no. 1, pp. 62–77 (2008).

Casey, B. J., Nim Tottenham, Conor Liston, and Sarah Durston, "Imaging the Developing Brain: What Have We Learned about Cognitive Development?," *Trends in Cognitive Science*, vol. 9, no. 3, pp. 104–110 (2005).

"Chancellor Proposes Change to New Citywide Standard for Gifted and Talented Programs" [Press release], New York City Public Schools, New York City (2008). http://tinyurl.com/6vgkz5

Colom, Roberto, "Intelligence Assessment." In: Charles Spielberger (Ed.), *Encyclopedia of Applied Psychology*, vol. 2, pp. 307–314. Oxford: Academic Press (2004).

Colom, Roberto, Rex E. Jung, and Richard J. Haier, "Distributed Brain Sites for the G-Factor of Intelligence," *NeuroImage*, vol. 31, no. 3, pp. 1359–1365 (2006).

Colom, Roberto, Rex E. Jung, and Richard J. Haier, "Finding the G-Factor in Brain Structure Using the Method of Correlated Vectors," *Intelligence*, vol. 34, no. 6, pp. 561–570 (2006).

Demetriou, Andreas, and Smaragda Kazi, "Self-Awareness in *g* (with Processing Efficiency and Reasoning)," *Intelligence*, vol. 34, no. 3, pp. 297–317 (2006).

Demetriou, Andreas, and Athanassios Raftopoulous, "Modeling the Developing Mind: From Structure to Change," *Developmental Review*, vol. 19, no. 3, pp. 319–368 (1999).

Detterman, Douglas K., e-mails with authors (2008).

Detterman, Douglas K., "Validity of IQ: What Does IQ Predict?" PowerPoint presentation (Undated).

Dietz, Greg, "WISC-IV—Wechsler Intelligence Scale for Children—Fourth Edition," PowerPoint presentation (Undated).

Duncan, Greg J., Amy Claessens, Aletha C. Huston, Linda Pagani, Mimi Engel, Holly Sexton, Chantelle J. Dowsett, Katherine Manguson, Pamela Klebanov, Leon Feinstein, Jeanne Brooks-Gunn, Kathryn Duckworth, and Crista Japel, "School Readiness and Later Achievement," *Developmental Psychology*, vol. 43, no. 6, pp. 1428–1446 (2007).

Fischer, Kurt, "Dynamic Cycles of Cognitive and Brain Development: Measuring Growth in Mind, Brain, and Education." In: A. M. Battro, K. W. Fischer, and P. Léna (Eds.), *The Educated Brain*, pp. 127–150. Cambridge, UK: Cambridge University Press (2006).

Fischer, Kurt W., and Samuel P. Rose, "Dynamic Development of

Coordination of Components in Brain and Behavior: A Framework for Theory and Research." In: G. Dawson and K. W. Fisher (Eds.), *Human Behavior and the Developing Brain*, pp. 3–66. New York: Guilford Press (1994).

Giedd, Jay N., "The Teen Brain: Insights from Neuroimaging," Remarks and paper presented at the Biennial Meeting of the Society for Research on Adolescence, Chicago (2008).

Giedd, Jay N., "The Teen Brain: Insights from Neuroimaging," *Journal of Adolescent Health*, vol. 42, no. 4, pp. 335–343 (2008).

"Gifted and Talented Proposal," New York City Public Schools Presentation, New York City (2007).

Gogtay, Nitin, Jay N. Giedd, Leslie Lusk, Kiralee M. Hayashi, Deanna Greenstein, A. Catherine Vaituzis, Tom F. Nugent III, David H. Herman, Liv S. Clasen, Arthur W. Toga, Judith L. Rapoport, and Paul M. Thompson, "Dynamic Mapping of Human Cortical Development During Childhood Through Early Adulthood," *Proceedings of the National Academy of Science*, vol. 101, no. 21, pp. 8174–8179 (2004).

Green, Elizabeth, "City Lowers Gifted, Talented School Standards," *New York Sun* (2008).

Haier, Richard J., "The End of Intelligence Research," *Intelligence*, vol. 14, no. 4, pp. 371–374 (1990).

Hemmati, Toni, Jeremy F. Mills, and Daryl G. Kroner, "The Validity of the Bar-On Emotional Intelligence Quotient in an Offender Population," *Personality and Individual Differences*, vol. 37, no. 4, pp. 695–706 (2004).

Herszenhorn, David M., "In Testing for Gifted Programs, a Few Knots," *New York Times*, p. B.1, (Jan. 10, 2007).

Honzik, M. P, J. W. Macfarlane, and L. Allen, "The Stability of Mental Test Performance Between Two and Eighteen Years," *Journal of Experimental Education*, vol. 17, no. 2, pp. 309–324 (1948).

Horowitz, Frances D., Remarks as discussant/chair for paper symposium, "Development of Giftedness and Talent Across the Life Span," American Psychological Association Annual Convention, Boston (2008).

Izard, Carroll, Sarah Fine, David Schultz, Allison Mostow, Brian Ackerman, and Eric Youngstrom, "Emotion Knowledge as a Predictor of Social Behavior and Academic Competence in Children at Risk," *Psychological Science*, vol. 12, no. 1, pp. 18–23 (2001).

Kaplan, Charles, "Predictive Validity of the WPPSI-R: A Four Year Follow-Up Study," *Psychology in the Schools*, vol. 33, no. 3, pp. 211–220 (1996).

Kim, Juhn, and Hoi K. Suen, "Predicting Children's Academic Achievement from Early Assessment Scores: A Validity Generalization Study," *Early Childhood Research Quarterly*, vol. 18, no. 4, pp. 547–566 (2003).

Johnson, Wendy, Rex E. Jung, Roberto Colom, and Richard J. Haier, "Cognitive Abilities Independent of IQ Correlate with Regional Brain Structure," *Intelligence*, vol. 36, no. 1, pp. 18–28 (2008).

June, Rex E., and Richard J. Haier, "The Parieto-Frontal Integration Theory (P-FIT) of Intelligence: Converging Neuroimaging Evidence," *Behavioral and Brain Sciences*, vol. 30, no. 2, pp. 135–187 (2007).

Laidra, Kaia, Helle Pullmann, and Jüri Allik, "Personality and Intelligence as Predictors of Academic Achievement: A Cross-sectional Study From Elementary to Secondary School," *Personality and Individual Differences*, vol. 42, no. 3, pp. 441–451 (2007).

Lee, Kun Ho, Yu Yong Choi, Jeremy R. Gray, Sun Hee Cho, Jeong-Ho Chae, Seungheun Lee, and Kyungjin Kim, "Neural Correlates of Superior Intelligence: Stronger Recruitment of Posterior Parietal Cortex," *NeuroImage*, vol. 29, no. 2, pp. 578–586 (2006).

"Legislative Update," *It Takes...*, Newsletter from Curriculum and Instruction Division of Advanced Academic Programs, Miami-Dade County Public Schools, Miami-Dade County, FL (2008).

Lenroot, Rhoshel K., and Jay N. Giedd, "Brain Development in Children and Adolescents: Insights from Anatomical Magnetic Resonance Imaging," *Neuroscience and Biobehavioral Reviews*, vol. 30, no. 6, pp. 718–729 (2006).

Lerch, Jason P., Keith Worsley, W. Philip Shaw, Deanna K. Greenstein, Rhoshel K. Lenroot, Jay Giedd, and Alan C. Evans, "Mapping Anatomical Correlations Across Cerebral Cortex (MACACC) Using Cortical Thickness from MRI," *NeuroImage*, vol. 31, no. 3, pp. 993–1003 (2006).

Lohman, David F., "Tables of Prediction Efficiencies" (2003).

Lohman, David F., "Understanding and Predicting Regression Effects in the Identification of Academically Gifted Children," Paper presented at American Educational Research Association Annual Meeting, San Francisco (2006).

Lohman, David F., e-mails with authors (2008).

Lohman, David F., and Katrina A. Korb, "Gifted Today But Not Tomorrow?

Longitudinal Changes in ITBS and CogAT Scores During Elementary School," *Journal for the Education of the Gifted*, 29, no. 4, pp. 451–484 (2006).

Lohman, David F., and Joni Lakin, "Nonverbal Test Scores as One Component of an Identification System: Integrating Ability, Achievement, and Teacher Ratings," Paper presented at 8th Biennial Henry B. and Jocelyn Wallace National Research Symposium on Talent Development, University of Iowa, Iowa City (2006).

Mathews, Dona J., "Developmental Transitions in Giftedness and Talent: Childhood to Adolescence," Remarks and paper presented at the American Psychological Association Annual Convention, Boston (2008).

Mayer, John D., Richard D. Roberts, and Sigal G. Barsade, "Human Abilities: Emotional Intelligence," *Annual Review of Psychology*, vol. 59, pp. 507–536 (2008).

Mayer, John D., Peter Salovey, and David R. Caruso, "Emotional Intelligence: New Ability or Eclectic Traits?," *American Psychologist*, vol. 63, no. 6, pp. 503–517 (2008).

McCall, Robert B., Mark I. Appelbaum, and Pamela S. Hogarty, "Developmental Changes in Mental Performance," *Monographs of the Society for Research in Child Development*, vol. 38, no. 3, pp. 1–84 (1973).

Mervielde, Ivan, Veerle Buystt, and Filip De Fruyt, "The Validity of the Big-Five as a Model for Teachers' Ratings of Individual Differences Among Children Aged 4–12 Years," *Personality and Individual Differences*, vol. 18, no. 4, pp. 525–534 (1995).

Mostow, Allison J., Carroll E. Izard, Sarah Fine, and Christopher J. Trentacosta, "Modeling Emotional, Cognitive, and Behavioral Predictors of Peer Acceptance," *Child Development*, vol. 73, no. 6, pp. 1775–1787 (2002).

Nagy, Zoltan, Helena Westerberg, and Torkel Klingberg, "Maturation of White Matter Is Associated With the Development of Cognitive Functions During Childhood," *Journal of Cognitive Neuroscience*, vol. 16, no. 7, pp. 1227–1233 (2004).

Newsome, Shaun, Arla L. Day, and Victor M. Catano, "Assessing the Predictive Validity of Emotional Intelligence," *Personality and Individual Differences*, vol. 29, no. 6, pp. 1005–1016 (2000).

Noble, Kimberly G., Nim Tottenham, and B. J. Casey, "Neuroscience Perspectives on Disparities in School Readiness and Cognitive Achievement," *Future of Children*, vol. 15, no. 1, pp. 71–89 (2005).

Novak, Patricia A., William T. Tsushima, and Matthew M. Tsushima, "Predictive Validity of Two Short-Forms of the WPPSI: A 3-year Follow-Up Study," *Journal of Clinical Psychology*, vol. 47, no. 5, pp. 698–702 (1991).

O'Connor, Raymond M., and Ian S. Little, "Revisiting the Predictive Validity of Emotional Intelligence: Self-Report Versus Ability-Based Measures," *Personality and Individual Differences*, vol. 35, no. 8, pp. 1893–1902 (2003).

Passingham, Richard, "Brain Development and IQ," *Nature*, vol. 440, no. 7084, pp. 619–620 (2006).

Paus, Tomáš, "Mapping Brain Maturation and Cognitive Development During Adolescence," *Trends in Cognitive Science*, vol. 9, no. 2, pp. 60–68 (2005).

Paus, Tomáš, Alex Zijdenbos, Keith Worsley, D. Louis Collins, Jonathan Blumenthal, Jay N. Giedd, Judith L. Rapoport, and Alan C. Evans, "Structural Maturation of Neural Pathways," *Science*, vol. 283, no. 5409, pp. 1908–1911 (1999).

Pfeiffer, Steven I., e-mails with authors (2008).

Pfeiffer, Steven I., and Yaacov Petscher, "Identifying Young Gifted Children Using the Gifted Rating Scales—Preschool/ Kindergarten Form," *Gifted Child Quarterly*, vol. 52, no. 1, pp. 19–29 (2008).

Phelps, Elizabeth A., Kevin J. O'Connor, J. Christopher Gatenby, John C. Gore, Christian Grillon, and Michael Davis, "Activation of the Left Amygdala to a Cognitive Representation of Fear," *Nature Neuroscience*, vol. 4, no. 4, pp. 437–441 (2001).

Qin, Yulin, Cameron S. Carter, Eli M. Silk, V. Andrew Stenger, Kate Fissell, Adam Goode, and John R. Anderson, "The Change of the Brain Activation Patterns as Children Learn Algebra Equation Solving," *Proceedings of the National Academy of Science*, vol. 101, no. 15, pp. 5686–5691 (2004).

"Removal of Students from the Gifted and Talented Program," State Department of Education Criteria, Office of Curriculum and Standards, Division of Curriculum Services and Assessment, South Carolina (2004). http://tinyurl.com/bpftog

Rivera, S. M., A. L. Reiss, M. A. Eckert, and V. Menon, "Developmental Changes in Mental Arithmetic: Evidence for Increased Functional Specialization in the Left Inferior Parietal Cortex," *Cerebral Cortex*, vol. 15, no. 11, pp. 1779–1790 (2005).

Robinson, Ann, and Pamela R. Clinkenbeard, "Giftedness: An Exceptionality Examined," *Annual Review of Psychology*, vol. 49, pp. 117–139 (1998).

Robinson, N., and L. Weimer, "Selection of Candidates for Early Admission to Kindergarten and First Grade." In: W. T. Southern and E. Jones (Eds.), *The Academic Acceleration of Gifted Children*, pp. 29–50. New York: Teachers College Press (1991).

Rock, Donald A., and A. Jackson Stenner, "Assessment Issues in the Testing of Children at School Entry," *Future of Children*, vol. 15, no. 1, pp. 15–34 (2005).

Rubia, Katya, Anna B. Smith, James Woolley, Chiara Nosarti, Isobel Heyman, Eric Taylor, and Mick Brammer, "Progressive Increase of Frontostriatal Brain Activation From Childhood to Adulthood During Event-Related Tasks of Cognitive Control," *Human Brain Mapping*, vol. 27, no. 12, pp. 973–993 (2006).

Salovey, Peter, "Emotional Intelligence: Is There Anything to It?" Remarks presented for the G. Stanley Hall Lecture, American Psychological Association Annual Convention, Boston (2008).

Saulny, Susan, "Gifted Classes Will Soon Use Uniform Test, Klein Decides," *New York Times*, p. B.1 (Nov. 16, 2005).

Scherf, K. Suzanne, John A. Sweeney, and Beatriz Luna, "Brain Basis of Developmental Change in Visuospatial Working Memory," *Journal of Cognitive Neuroscience*, vol. 18, no. 7, pp. 1045–1058 (2006).

Schlaggar, Bradley L., Timothy T. Brown, Heather M. Lugar, Kristina M. Visscher, Francis M. Miezin, and Stevan E. Petersen, "Functional Neuroanatomical Differences Between Adults and School-Age Children in the Processing of Single Words," *Science*, vol. 296, no. 5572, pp. 1476–1479 (2002).

Schmithorst, Vincent J., and Scott K. Holland, "Sex Differences in the Development of Neuroanatomical Functional Connectivity Underlying Intelligence Found Using Bayesian Connectivity Analysis," *NeuroImage*, vol. 35, no. 1, pp. 406–419 (2007).

Schmithorst, Vincent J., Scott K. Holland, and Elena Plante, "Cognitive Modules Utilized for Narrative Comprehension in Children: A Functional Magnetic Resonance Imaging Study," *NeuroImage*, vol. 29, no. 1, pp. 254–266 (2006).

Schmithorst, Vincent J., Marko Wilke, Bernard J. Dardzinski, and Scott K. Holland, "Correlation of White Matter Diffusivity and Anisotropy With

Age during Childhood and Adolescence: A Cross-sectional Diffusion-Tensor MR Imaging Study," *Radiology*, vol. 222, pp. 212–218 (2002).

Schwartz, David M., "WISC-IV—Wechsler Intelligence Scale for Children—Fourth Edition, WISC-IV Comprehensive PowerPoint Presentation" (Undated).

Schwartz, Edward M., and Anna S. Elonen, "IQ and the Myth of Stability: A 16-Year Longitudinal Study of Variations in Intelligence Test Performance," *Journal of Clinical Psychology*, vol. 31, no. 4, pp. 687–694 (1975).

Shaw, Philip, "Intelligence and the Developing Human Brain," *BioEssays*, vol. 29, no. 10, pp. 962–973 (2007).

Shaw, P., D. Greenstein, J. Lerch, L. Clasen, R. Lenroot, N. Gogtay, A. Evans, J. Rapoport, and J. Giedd, "Intellectual Ability and Cortical Development in Children and Adolescents," *Nature*, vol. 440, no. 7084, pp. 676–679 (2006).

Sontag, L. W., C. T. Baker, and V. L. Nelson, "Mental Growth and Personality Development: A Longitudinal Study," *Monographs of the Society for Research in Child Development*, vol. 23, no. 2 (Serial No. 68) (1958).

Sowell, Elizabeth R., Paul M. Thompson, Christiana M. Leonard, Suzanne E. Welcome, Eric Kan, and Arthur W. Toga, "Longitudinal Mapping of Cortical Thickness and Brain Growth in Normal Children," *Journal of Neuroscience*, vol. 24, no. 38, pp. 8223–8231 (2004).

Sparrow, Sara S., and Suzanne T. Gurland, "Assessment of Gifted Children with the WISC-III." In: A. Prifitera and D. Saklofske (Eds.), *WISC-III Clinical Use and Interpretation: Scientist-Practitioner Perspectives*, pp. 59–72. San Diego: Academic Press (1998).

Sparrow, Sara S., Stephen I. Pfeiffer, and Tina M. Newman, "Assessment of Children who are Gifted with the WISC-IV." In: A. Prifitera, D. Saklofske, and L. Weiss (Eds.), *WISC-IV Clinical Use and Interpretation: Scientist-Practitioner Perspectives*, pp. 281–297. Burlington, VT: Elsevier Academic Press (2005).

Spinelli, Lydia, "Assessing Young Children for Admissions," Remarks at NYSAIS Admissions Directors Conference (2006). http://tinyurl.com/br2vwt

Sternberg, Robert J., Elena L. Grigorenko, and Donald A. Bundy, "The Predictive Value of IQ," *Merrill-Palmer Quarterly*, vol. 47, no. 1, pp. 1–41 (2001).

Thomas, Kathleen M., Ruskin H. Hunt, Nathalie Vizueta, Tobias Sommer, Sarah Durston, Yihong Yang, and Michael S. Worden, "Evidence of Developmental Differences in Implicit Sequence Learning: An fMRI Study of Children and Adults," *Journal of Cognitive Neuroscience*, vol. 16, no. 8, pp. 1339–1351 (2004).

Tsushima, William T., Vincent A. Onorato, Frederick T. Okumura, and Dalton Sue, "Predictive Validity of the Star: A Need for Local Validation," *Educational and Psychological Measurement*, vol. 43, no. 2, pp. 663–665 (1983).

Tsushima, William T., and Victoria M. Stoddard, "Predictive Validity of a Short-Form WPPSI With Prekindergarten Children: A 3-Year Follow-Up Study," *Journal of Clinical Psychology*, vol. 42, no. 3, pp. 526–527 (1986).

Van Rooy, David L., and Chockalingam Viswesvaran, "Emotional Intelligence: A Meta-analytic Investigation of Predictive Validity and Nomological Net," *Journal of Vocational Behavior*, vol. 65, no. 1, pp. 71–95 (2004).

VanTassel-Baska, Joyce, Annie Xuemei Feng, and Brandy L. Evans, "Patterns of Identifications and Performance Among Gifted Students Identified Through Performance Tasks: A Three-Year Analysis," *Gifted Child Quarterly*, vol. 51, no. 3, pp. 218–231 (2007).

VanTassel-Baska, Joyce, Dana Johnson, and Linda D. Avery, "Using Performance Tasks in the Identification of Economically Disadvantaged and Minority Gifted Learners: Findings From Project STAR," *Gifted Schools Quarterly*, vol. 46, no. 2, pp. 110–123 (2002).

Weiss, Lawrence, Donald Saklofske, Aurelio Prifitera, and James Holdnack, *WISC-IV Advanced Clinical Interpretation*. London: Academic Press (2006).

Williams, Leanne M., Mary L. Phillips, Michael J. Brammer, David Skerrett, Jim Lagopoulos, Chris Rennie, Homayoun Bahramali, Gloria Olivieri, Anthony S. David, Anthony Peduto, and Evian Gordon, "Arousal Dissociates Amygdala and Hippocampal Fear Responses: Evidence from Simultaneous fMRI and Skin Conductance Recording," *NeuroImage*, vol. 14, no. 5, pp. 1070–1079 (2001).

"Windows and Classrooms: A Study of Student Performance and the Indoor Environment," Technical report, California Energy Commission (2003).

Worrell, Frank C., "What Does Gifted Mean? Personal and Social Identity Perspectives on Giftedness in Adolescence," Remarks and paper presented at the American Psychological Association Annual Convention, Boston (2008).

Chapter 6, The Sibling Effect

Bagley, Sarah, Jo Salmon, and David Crawford, "Family Structure and Children's Television Viewing and Physical Activity," *Medicine & Science in Sports & Exercise*, vol. 38, no. 5, pp. 910–918 (2006).

Brody, Gene H., "Sibling Relationship Quality: Its Causes and Consequences," *Annual Review of Psychology*, vol. 49, pp. 1–24 (1998).

Camodeca, Marina, and Ersilia Menesini, "Is Bullying Just a School Problem: Similarities Between Siblings and Peers?" Poster presented at the Biennial Meeting of the Society for Research in Child Development, Boston (2007).

Campione-Barr, Nicole, and Judith G. Smetana, "But It's My Turn in the Front Seat! Adolescent Siblings' Conflicts, Relationships, and Adjustment," Remarks and paper presented at the Biennial Meeting of the Society for Research on Adolescence, Chicago (2008).

Chen, X., Z. Wang, J. Gao, and W. Hu, "College Students' Social Anxiety Associated with Stress and Mental Health," *Wei Sheng Yan Jiu*, vol. 36, no. 2, pp. 197–209 (2007).

Day, Lincoln H., "Is There Any Socially Significant Psychological Difference in Being an Only Child?: The Evidence from Some Adult Behavior," *Journal of Applied Social Psychology*, vol. 21, no. 9, pp. 754–773 (1991).

DeHart, Ganie B., Bobette Buchanan, Carjah Dawkins, and Jill Rabinowitz, "Preschoolers' Use of Assertive and Affiliative Language with Siblings and Friends," Poster presented at the Biennial Meeting of the Society for Research in Child Development, Boston (2007).

Ding, Qu Jian, and Therese Hesketh, "Family Size, Fertility Preferences, and Sex Ratio in China in the Era of the One Child Family Policy: Results from National Family Planning and Reproductive Health Survey," *BMJ*, vol. 333, pp. 371–373 (2006).

Downey, Douglas B., and Dennis J. Condron, "Playing Well With Others in Kindergarten: The Benefit of Siblings at Home," *Journal of Marriage and Family*, vol. 66, no. 2, pp. 333–350 (2004).

Dunn, Judy, and Shirley McGuire, "Sibling and Peer Relationships in Childhood," *Journal of Child Psychology and Psychiatry*, vol. 33, no. 1, pp. 67–105 (1992).

Fields, Jason, "Living Arrangements of Children: 1996," Current Population Report, p70-74, US Census Bureau, Washington DC (1996).

Goldberg, Shmuel, Eran Israeli, Shepard Schwartz, Tzippora Shochat, Gabriel Izbicki, Ori Toker-Maimon, Eyal Klement, and Elie Picard, "Asthma Prevalence, Family Size, and Birth Order," *Chest*, vol. 131, no. 6, pp. 1747–1752 (2007).

Hesketh, T., J. D. Qu, and A. Tomkins, "Health Effects of Family Size: Cross Sectional Survey in Chinese Adolescents," *Archives of the Diseases of Childhood*, vol. 88, no. 6, pp. 467–471 (2003).

Hesketh, Therese, Li Lu, and Zhu Wei Xing, "The Effect of China's One-Child Family Policy after 25 Years," *New England Journal of Medicine*, vol. 353, no. 11, pp. 1171–1176 (2005).

Kennedy, Denise, and Laurie Kramer, "Building Emotion Regulation in Sibling Relationships," Poster presented at the Biennial Meeting of the Society for Research in Child Development, Boston (2007).

Kennedy, Denise E., and Laurie Kramer, "Improving Emotional Regulation and Sibling Relationship Quality: The More Fun With Sisters and Brothers Program," *Family Relations*, vol. 57, no. 5, pp. 567–578 (2008).

Kennedy Kubose, Denise, "Mothers and Fathers Regulation of Siblings' Emotionality," Paper presented at the National Council on Family Relations Conference, Pittsburgh (2007).

Kennedy Kubose, Denise, e-mails with authors (2007–2008).

Kinra, S., G. Davey Smith, M. Jeffreys, D. Gunnell, B. Galobardes, and P. McCarron, "Association Between Sibship Size and Allergic Diseases in the Glasgow Alumni Study," *Thorax*, vol. 61, no. 1, pp. 48–53 (2006).

Kowal, Amanda K., Jennifer L. Krull, and Laurie Kramer, "Shared Understanding of a Parental Differential Treatment in Families," *Social Development*, vol. 15, no. 2, pp. 276–295 (2006).

Kramer, Laurie, e-mails with authors (2007–2008).

Kramer, Laurie, "The Essential Ingredients of Successful Sibling Relationships: An Emerging Framework for Advancing Theory and Practice," Manuscript under review (2009).

Kramer, Laurie, and Lisa A. Baron, "Intergenerational Linkages: How Experiences With Siblings Relate to the Parenting of Siblings," *Journal of Social and Personal Relationships*, vol. 12, no. 1, pp. 67–87 (1995).

Kramer, Laurie, and John Gottman, "Becoming a Sibling: With a Little Help from My Friends," *Developmental Psychology*, vol. 28, no. 4, pp. 685–699 (1992).

Kramer, Laurie, and Amanda K. Kowal, "Sibling Relationship Quality from Birth to Adolescence: The Enduring Contribution of Friends," *Journal of Family Psychology*, vol. 19. no. 4, pp. 503–511 (2005).

Kramer, Laurie, Sonia Noorman, and Renee Brockman, "Representations of Sibling Relationships in Young Children's Literature," *Early Childhood Research Quarterly*, vol. 14, no. 4, pp. 555–574 (1999).

Kramer, Laurie, Lisa A. Perozynski, and Tsai-Yen Chung, "Parental Responses to Sibling Conflict: The Effects of Development and Parent Gender," *Child Development*, vol. 70, no. 6, pp. 1401–1414 (1999).

Kramer, Laurie, and Chad Radey, "Improving Sibling Relationships among Young Children: A Social Skills Training Model," *Family Relations*, vol. 46, no. 3, pp. 237–246 (1997).

Kramer, Laurie, and Dawn Ramsburg, "Advice Given to Parents on Welcoming a Second Child: A Critical Review," *Family Relations*, vol. 51, no. 1, pp. 2–14 (2002).

Kreider, Rose M., "Living Arrangements of Children: 2004," Current Population Report, p 70–114, US Census Bureau, Washington DC (2008).

Krombhholz, Heinz, "Physical Performance in Relation to Age, Sex, Birth Order, Social Class, and Sports Activities of Preschool Children," *Perceptual Motor Skills*, vol. 102, no. 2, pp. 477–484 (2006).

Liu, Chenying, Tsunetsugti Munakata, and Francis N. Onuoha, "Mental Health Condition of the Only Child," *Adolescence*, vol. 40, no. 160, pp. 831–845 (2005).

Mancillas, Adriean, "Challenging the Stereotypes About Only Children: A Review of the Literature and Implications for Practice," *Journal of Counseling & Development*, vol. 84, no. 3, pp. 268–275 (2006).

McGuire, Shirley, Beth Manke, Afsoon Eftekhari, and Judy Dunn, "Children's Perceptions of Sibling Conflict During Middle Childhood: Issues and Sibling (Dis)similarity," *Social Development*, vol. 9, no. 2, pp. 173–190 (2000).

Mosier, Christine E., and Barbara Rogoff, "Privileged Treatment of Toddlers: Cultural Aspects of Individual Choice and Responsibility," *Developmental Psychology*, vol. 39, no. 6, pp. 1047–1060 (2003).

Perlman, Michal, Daniel A. Garfinkel, and Sheri L. Turrell, "Parent and Sibling Influences on the Quality of Children's Conflict Behaviours across the Preschool Period," *Social Development*, vol. 16, no. 4, pp. 1–23 (2007).

Punch, Samantha, " 'You Can Do Nasty Things to Your Brothers and Sisters Without a Reason': Siblings' Backstage Behaviors," *Children & Society*, vol. 22, no. 5, pp. 333–344 (2007).

Ram, Avigail, and Hildy S. Ross, "Problem Solving, Contention, and Struggle: How Siblings Resolve a Conflict of Interests," *Child Development*, vol. 72, no. 6, pp. 1710–1722 (2001).

Riggio, Heidi, "Personality and Social Skill Differences Between Adults With and Without Siblings," *Journal of Psychology*, vol. 133, no. 5, pp. 514–522 (1999).

Ross, Hildy S., "Negotiating Principles of Entitlement in Sibling Property Disputes," *Developmental Psychology*, vol. 32, no. 1, pp. 90–101 (1996).

Ross, Hildy, Michael Ross, Nancy Stein, and Tom Trabasso, "How Siblings Resolve Their Conflicts," *Child Development*, vol. 77, no. 6, pp. 1730–1745 (2006).

Saporetti, G., S. Sancini, L. Bassoli, B. Castelli, and A. Pellai, "Analisi del Rischio per i Disturbi del Comportamento Alimentare in una Scuola Media Superiore: Una Ricerca Basata sull'Eating Attitudes Test 26" ["Risk Assessment for Eating Disorders in a High School: A Study Based on the Eating Attitudes Test 26"], *Minerva Pediatrica*, vol. 56, no. 1, pp. 83–90 (2004).

Smith, Julie, and Hildy Ross, "Training Parents to Mediate Sibling Disputes Affects Children's Negotiation and Conflict Understanding," *Child Development*, vol. 78, no. 3, pp. 790–805 (2007).

"Table F2. Family Households, by Type, Age of Own Children, and Educational Attainment of Householder: 2007," 2007 Annual Social and Economic Supplement, Current Population Survey, U.S. Census Bureau, Washington DC (2008).

T-Ping, Cheng, Cassimiro Afonso Nunes, Gabriel Rabelo Guimarães, João Penna Martins Vieira, Luc Louis Maurice Weckx, and Tanner José Arantes Borges, "Accidental Ingestion of Coins by Children: Management at the ENT Department of the João XXIII Hospital," *Revista Brasileira de Otorrinolaringologia* (English edition), vol. 72, no. 4, pp. 470–474 (2006).

Williams, H. C., A. Pottier, and D. Strachan, "The Descriptive Epidemiology of Warts in British Schoolchildren," *British Journal of Dermatology*, vol. 128, no. 5, pp. 504–511 (1993).

Wilson, Anne E., and Melissa Smith, "Young Children's Personal Accounts of Their Sibling Disputes," *Merrill-Palmer Quarterly*, vol. 50, no. 1, pp. 39–60 (2004).

Wolke, Dieter, and Muthanna M. Samara, "Bullied by Siblings: Association With Peer Victimisation and Behaviour Problems in Israeli Lower Secondary School Children," *Journal of Child Psychology and Psychiatry*, vol. 45, no. 5, pp. 1015–1029 (2004).

Chapter 7, The Science of Teen Rebellion

Adelman, Clifford, "Principal Indicators of Student Academic Histories in Postsecondary Education, 1972–2000," U.S. Department of Education, Institute of Education Sciences, Washington DC (2004).

"The American Freshman: Forty-Year Trends: 1966–2006," HERI Research Brief, Higher Education Research Institute, University of California, Los Angeles (2007).

"The American Freshman: National Norms for Fall 2006," HERI Research Brief, Higher Education Research Institute, University of California, Los Angeles (2007).

"The American Freshman: National Norms for Fall 2008," HERI Research Brief, Higher Education Research Institute, University of California, Los Angeles (2009).

"Analysis of the 2003–04 Budget Bill: California State University (6610)," Legislative Analyst's Office, California State Government, Sacramento, CA (2003). http://tinyurl.com/a74blb

Baird, Abigail A., "Real Effects of the Imaginary Audience: Peers Influence Neural Activity During Decision Making Among Adolescents," Paper presented at the Biennial Meeting of the Society for Research on Adolescence, Chicago (2008).

Baird, Abigail A., and Jonathan A. Fugelsang, "The Emergence of Consequential Thought: Evidence from Neuroscience," *Philosophical Transactions of the Royal Society B*, vol. 359, no. 1451, pp. 1797–1804 (2004).

Barnes, Tom, "Debate Rages Over Requiring Students to Pass Tests to Graduate," *Pittsburgh Post-Gazette* (2007).

Bramlett, Matthew D., and William D. Mosher, *Cohabitation, Marriage, Divorce, and Remarriage in the United States*, Vital and Health Statistics,

National Center for Health Statistics, Hyattsville, MD, vol. 23, no. 22 (2002).

Byrne, Ciara, Tabitha R. Holmes, and Lynne A. Bond, "Parent-Adolescent Conflict: Distinguishing Constructive from Destructive Experiences," Poster presented at the Biennial Meeting of the Society for Research in Child Development, Boston (2007).

Caldwell, Linda, TimeWise Focus Group Interview Results, Unpublished (Undated).

Caldwell, Linda, "TimeWise Taking Charge of Leisure Time," Fact Sheet, ETR Associates, Santa Cruz, CA (Undated).

Caldwell, Linda L., "TimeWise: Taking Charge of Leisure Time: Final Report to NIDA," Pennsylvania State University, University Park, PA (2004).

Caldwell, Linda L., "Educating For, About, and Through Leisure." In: P. A. Witt. and L. L. Caldwell (Eds.), *Recreation and Youth Development*, pp. 193–218. State College, PA: Venture Publishing (2005).

Caldwell, Linda L., "Leisure and Health: Why Is Leisure Therapeutic?" *British Journal of Guidance & Counselling*, vol. 33, no. 1, pp. 7–26 (2005).

Caldwell, Linda L., "TimeWise Description," Caldwell web site, Pennsylvania State University. http://www.personal.psu.edu/llc7/TimeWise.htm

Caldwell, Linda L., e-mails with authors (2007–2008).

Caldwell, Linda L., Cheryl K. Baldwin, Theodore Walls, and Ed Smith, "Preliminary Effects of a Leisure Education Program to Promote Healthy Use of Free Time among Middle School Adolescents," *Journal of Leisure Research*, vol. 36, no. 3, pp. 310–335 (2004).

Caldwell, Linda L., and Nancy Darling, "Testing A Leisure-based, Ecological Model of Substance Use: Suggestions for Prevention," Paper presented at the Biennial Meeting of the Society for Research on Adolescence, Chicago (2000).

Caldwell, Linda L., Nancy Darling, Laura L. Payne, and Bonnie Dowdy, " 'Why Are You Bored?' ": An Examination of Psychological and Social Control Causes of Boredom Among Adolescents," *Journal of Leisure Research*, vol. 31, no. 2, pp. 103–121 (1999).

Caldwell, Linda L., and Edward A. Smith, "Leisure as a Context for Youth Development and Delinquency Prevention," *Australian and New Zealand Journal of Criminology*, vol. 39, no. 3, pp. 398–418 (2006).

Caldwell, Linda, Edward Smith, Lisa Wegner, Tania Vergnani, Elias Mpofu, Alan J. Flisher, and Catherine Mathews, "Health Wise South Africa: Development of a Life Skills Curriculum for Young Adults," *World Leisure*, no. 3, pp. 4–17 (2004).

Chao, Ruth K., and Christine Aque, "Adolescents' Feelings About Parental Control: Cultural Explanations for Ethnic Group Differences in Effects of Parental Control," Paper presented at the Biennial Meeting of the Society for Research in Child Development, Boston (2007).

Chyung, Yun-Joo, Nancy Darling, and Linda Caldwell, "Parental Monitoring and Legitimacy of Parental Authority: Flip Sides of the Same Coin?" Poster presented at the Biennial Meeting of the Society for Research on Adolescence, San Diego (1998).

Cumsille, Patricio, and Nancy Darling, "Parental Attempts to Know and Actual Knowledge of Adolescent Behavior and Adolescent Adjustment in a Chilean Sample," Poster presented at the Society for Prevention Research Annual Meeting, Seattle (2002).

Cumsille, Patricio, Nancy Darling, Brian P. Flaherty, and M. Loreto Martínez, "Chilean Adolescents' Beliefs about the Legitimacy of Parental Authority: Individual and Age-Related Differences," *International Journal of Behavioral Development*, vol. 30, no. 2, pp. 97–106 (2006).

Cumsille, Patricio, Nancy Darling, and Liane Peña-Alampay, "Rules, Legitimacy Beliefs, Obligation to Obey, and Parent-Adolescent Conflict: A Chilean and Filipino Comparison," Poster presented at the Biennial Meeting of the Society for Research on Adolescence, New Orleans (2002).

Darling, Nancy, e-mails with authors (2007–2008).

Darling, Nancy, Remarks as discussant for paper symposium, "The Social Construction of Adolescent Autonomy: The Role of Social Relationships," Biennial Meeting of the Society for Research on Adolescence, Chicago (2008).

Darling, Nancy, Patricio Cumsille, Linda L. Caldwell, and Bonnie Dowdy, "Predictors of Adolescents' Disclosure to Parents and Perceived Parental Knowledge: Between- and Within-Person Differences," *Journal of Youth and Adolescence*, vol. 35, no. 4, pp. 667–678 (2006).

Darling, Nancy, Patricio Cumsillo, and Bonnie Dowdy, "Parenting Style, Legitimacy of Parental Authority, and Adolescents' Willingness to Share Information With their Parents: Why Do Adolescents Lie?" Paper presented at the Meeting of the International Society for the Study of Personal Relationships, Saratoga, NY (1998).

Darling, Nancy, Patricio Cumsille, and M. Loreto Martínez, "Individual Differences in Adolescents' Beliefs About the Legitimacy of Parental Authority and Their Own Obligation to Obey: A Longitudinal Investigation," *Child Development*, vol. 79, no. 4, pp. 1103–1118 (2008).

Darling, Nancy, Patricio Cumsille, and M. Loreto Martínez, "Adolescents as Active Agents in the Socialization Process: Legitimacy of Parental Authority and Obligation to Obey as Predictors of Obedience," *Journal of Adolescence*, vol. 30, no. 2, pp. 297–311 (2007).

Darling, Nancy, Patricio Cumsille, and Liane Peña-Alampay, "Rules, Obligation to Obey, and Obedience: Age-Related Differences in Three Cultures," Paper presented at the Society for Research in Adolescence, Tampa (2003).

Darling, Nancy, Patricio Cumsille, and Liane Peña-Alampay, "Rules, Legitimacy of Parental Authority, and Obligation to Obey in Chile, the Philippines, and the United States," *New Directions in Child and Adolescent Development*, vol. 108, pp. 47–60 (2005).

Darling, Nancy, Patricio Cumsille, Liane Peña-Alampay, and Erin Hiley Sharp, "To Feel Trusted: Correlates of Adolescents' Beliefs that They Are Trusted by Parents in Two Cultural Contexts," Poster presented at the Society for Research in Adolescence, Tampa (2003).

Darling, Nancy, Patricio Cumsille Eltit, and M. Loreto Martínez, "Adolescent Disclosure of Information Across Domains: A Person Centered Analysis of Chilean Youth," Paper presented at the Society for Research in Child Development Biannual Meeting, Atlanta (2005).

Darling, Nancy, Katherine Hames, and Patricio Cumsille, "When Parents and Adolescents Disagree: Disclosure Strategies and Motivations," Poster presented at the Biennial Meeting of the Society for Research on Adolescence, Chicago (2000).

"Early Assessment Program," Office of the Chancellor, California State University, Long Beach, CA (2008). http://www.calstate.edu/eap/

Galvan, Adriana, Todd A. Hare, Matthew Davidson, Julie Spicer, Gary Glover, and B. J. Casey, "The Role of Ventral Frontostriatal Circuitry in Reward-Based Learning in Humans," *Journal of Neuroscience*, vol. 25, no. 38, pp. 8650–8656 (2005).

Galvan, Adriana, Todd A. Hare, Cindy E. Parra, Jackie Penn, Henning Voss, Gary Glover, and B. J. Casey, "Earlier Development of the Accumbens Relative to Orbitofrontal Cortex Might Underlie Risk-Taking Behavior in Adolescents," *Journal of Neuroscience*, vol. 26, no. 25, pp. 6885–6892 (2006).

Galvan, Adriana, Todd A. Hare, Henning Voss, Gary Glover, and B. J. Casey, "Risk-Taking and The Adolescent Brain: Who Is at Risk?" *Developmental Science*, vol. 10, no. 2, pp. F8–F14 (2007).

Hancock, Jeffrey T., Jennifer Thom-Santelli, and Thompson Ritchie, "Deception and Design: The Impact of Communication Technology on Lying Behavior," Paper presented at CHI, Vienna (2004).

Holmes, Tabitha R., Lynne A. Bond, and Ciara Byrne, "Mothers' Beliefs about Knowledge and Mother-Adolescent Conflict," *Journal of Social and Personal Relationships*, vol. 25, no. 4, pp. 561–586 (2008).

Hutchinson, Susan L., Cheryl K. Baldwin, and Linda L. Caldwell, "Differentiating Parent Practices Related to Adolescent Behavior in the Free Time Context," *Journal of Leisure Research*, vol. 35, no. 4, pp. 396–422 (2003).

Kuhnen, Camelia M., and Brian Knutson, "Neural Basis of Financial Risk Taking," *Neuron*, vol. 47, no. 5, pp. 763–770 (2005).

Laird, Robert D., Michael M. Criss, Gregory S. Pettit, Kenneth A. Dodge, and John E. Bates, "Parents' Monitoring Knowledge Attenuates the Link Between Antisocial Friends and Adolescent Delinquent Behavior," *Journal of Abnormal Child Psychology*, vol. 74, no. 3, pp. 752–768 (2007).

Laird, Robert D., Gregory S. Pettit, John E. Bates, and Kenneth A. Dodge, "Parents' Monitoring-Relevant Knowledge and Adolescents' Delinquent Behavior: Evidence of Correlated Developmental Changes and Reciprocal Influences," *Child Development*, vol. 74, no. 3, pp. 752–768 (2003).

"Life Expectancy," Fastats, National Center for Health Statistics, Hyattville, MD (2008). http://www.cdc.gov/nchs/fastats/lifexpec.htm

McAlary, John J., Press release, The New York State Board of Law Examiners, Albany, NY (2008).

Morisi, Teresa L., "Youth Enrollment and Employment During the School Year," *Monthly Labor Review*, vol. 131, no. 2, pp. 51–63 (2008).

Parsad, Basmat, and Laurie Lewis, "Remedial Education at Degree-Granting Postsecondary Institutions in Fall 2000," NCES 2004–010, Project

Officer: Bernard Greene, U.S. Department of Education, National Center for Education Statistics, Washington DC (2003).

Perkins, Serena A., and Elliot Turiel, "To Lie or Not to Lie: To Whom and Under What Circumstances," *Child Development*, vol. 78, no. 2, pp. 609–621 (2007).

Pesavento, Lisa C. (Ed.), "Leisure Education in the Schools," Position statement submitted to the American Association for Leisure and Recreation (AALR) (2003).

Pinch, Katherine, "Surely You Don't Mean Me? Leisure Education and the Park and Recreation Professional," *California Parks & Recreation*, vol. 59, no. 3, p. 3 (2003).

"Proficiency Reports of Students Entering the CSU System, California State University," Office of the Chancellor, California State University, Long Beach, CA (2008). http://www.asd.calstate.edu/performance/proficiency.shtml

Rearick, Jacki, and Linda L. Caldwell, "Evaluation of an After-School Program Affiliated with the Central Blair County Recreation and Park Commission," NRPA Report (2001).

"A Record Pool Leads to a Record-low Admissions Rate," Harvard University Gazette (On-line), Harvard University, Cambridge, MA (2008). http://www.news.harvard.edu/gazette/2008/04.03/99-admissions.html

Shanahan, Lilly, Susan M. McHale, D. Wayne Osgood, and Ann C. Crouter, "Conflict Frequency With Mothers and Fathers from Middle Childhood to Late Adolescence: Within- and Between-Families Comparisons," *Developmental Psychology*, vol. 43, no. 3, pp. 539–550 (2007).

Sharp, Erin Hiley, Linda L. Caldwell, John W. Graham, and Ty A. Ridenour, "Individual Motivation and Parental Influence on Adolescents' Experiences of Interest in Free Time: A Longitudinal Examination," *Journal of Youth and Adolescence*, vol. 35, no. 3, pp. 359–372 (2006).

Smetana, Judith G., "Adolescent Disclosure and Secrecy—The Who, What, Where and Why," Paper presented at the Biennial Meetings of the European Association for Research on Adolescence, Antalya, Turkey (2006).

Smetana, Judith G. "Daily Variations in Latino, African American, and European American Teens' Disclosure and Secrecy With Parents and Best Friends," Remarks presenting paper by Judith G. Smetana, Denise C. Gettman, Myriam Villalobos, and Marina A. Tasopoulos, to the Biennial Meeting of the Society for Research in Child Development, Boston (2007).

Smetana, Judith G., e-mails with authors (2007–2008).

Smetana, Judith G., "'It's 10 O'Clock: Do You Know Where Your Children Are?' Monitoring and Adolescents' Information Management," *Child Development Perspectives*, vol. 2, no. 1, pp. 19–25 (2008).

Smetana, Judith G., Nicole Campione-Barr, and Aaron Metzger, "Adolescent Development in Interpersonal and Societal Contexts," *Annual Review of Psychology*, vol. 57, pp. 255–284 (2006).

Smetana, Judith G., Denise C. Gettman, Myriam Villalobos, and Marina A. Tasopoulos, "Daily Variations in African American, Latino, and European American Teens' Disclosure with Parents and Best Friends," Paper presented at the Biennial Meeting of the Society for Research in Child Development, Boston (2007).

Smetana, Judith G., Aaron Metzger, Denise C. Gettman, and Nicole Campione-Barr, "Disclosure and Secrecy in Adolescent-Parent Relationships," *Child Development*, vol. 77, no. 1, pp. 201–217 (2006).

Spear, L. P., "The Adolescent Brain and Age-Related Behavioral Manifestations," *Neuroscience and Behavioral Reviews*, vol. 24, no. 4, pp. 417–463 (2000).

Steinberg, Laurence, "'We Know Some Things': Parent-Adolescent Relationships in Retrospect and Prospect," *Journal of Research on Adolescence*, vol. 11, no. 1, pp. 1–19 (2001).

Steinberg, Laurence, "Risk Taking in Adolescence: What Changes, and Why?" *Annals of the New York Academy of Science*, vol. 1021, pp. 51–58 (2004).

Steinberg, Laurence, "Risk Taking in Adolescence: New Perspectives From Brain and Behavioral Science," *Current Directions in Psychological Science*, vol. 16, no. 2, pp. 55–59 (2007).

Steinberg, Laurence, "A Social Neuroscience Perspective on Adolescent Risk-Taking," *Developmental Review*, vol. 28, no. 1, pp. 78–106 (2008).

"Table 24-1, Percentage of High School Completers who Were Enrolled in College the October Immediately Following High School Completion, By Race/Ethnicity and Family Income: 1972–2006," National Center for Education Statistics, US Department of Education, Washington DC (2008).

Tasopoulos, Marina A., Jenny Yau, and Judith G. Smetana, "Mexican American, Chinese American and European American Teens' Disclosure to Parents about Their Activities," Poster presented at the Biennial Meeting of the Society for Research in Child Development, Boston (2007).

Tibbits, Melissa K., Linda L. Caldwell, Edward A. Smith, and Laura Ferrer-Wreder, "Boredom As a Risk Factor for Academic Failure and Substance Use in Adolescence," Poster presented at the Biennial Meeting of the Society for Research in Child Development, Boston (2007).

Turiel, Elliot, "Honesty, Deception, and Social Resistance in Adolescents and Adults," Remarks and paper presented at at the Biennial Meeting of the Society for Research in Child Development, Boston (2007).

"Wake Up Moms and Dads!..." [Press release], WE TV, New York (2008).

Wang, Qian, and Eva Pomerantz, "The Role of Parents' Autonomy Support and Control in American and Chinese Adolescents' Psychological Functioning," Paper presented at the Biennial Meeting of the Society for Research in Child Development, Boston (2007).

Warr, Mark, "The Tangled Web: Delinquency, Deception, and Parental Attachment," *Journal of Youth and Adolescence*, vol. 36, no. 5, pp. 607–622 (2007).

Watts, Clifton E., Jr., and Linda L. Caldwell, "Exploring the Effects of Adolescent Perceptions of Parenting in Free Time and Gender on Adolescent Motivation in Free Time," Proceedings of the 2006 Northeastern Recreation Research Symposium, pp. 326–334 (2006).

Watts, Clifton E., and Linda L. Caldwell, "Self-Determination and Free Time Activity Participation as Predictors of Initiative," *Journal of Leisure Research*, vol. 40, no. 1, pp. 156–181 (2008).

Chapter 8, Can Self-Control Be Taught?

Ammerman, Alice S., Christine H. Lindquist, Kathleen N. Lohr, and James Hersey, "The Efficacy of Behavioral Interventions to Modify Dietary Fat and Fruit and Vegetable Intake: A Review of the Evidence," *Preventive Medicine*, vol. 35, no. 1, pp. 25–41 (2002).

Barnett, W. Steven, Donald J. Yarosz, Jessica Thomas, and Amy Hornbeck, "Educational Effectiveness of a Vygotskian Approach to Preschool

Education: A Randomized Trial," National Institute of Early Education Research, Rutgers University, New Brunswick, NJ (2006).

Baumeister, Roy F., Kathleen D. Vohs, and Dianne M. Tice, "The Strength Model of Self-Control," *Current Directions in Psychological Science*, vol. 16, no. 6, pp. 351–355 (2007).

Blair, Clancy, "School Readiness Integrating Cognition and Emotion in a Neurobiological Conceptualization of Children's Functioning at School Entry," *American Psychologist*, vol. 57, no. 2, pp. 111–127 (2002).

Blair, Clancy, and Adele Diamond, "Biological Processes in Prevention and Intervention: The Promotion of Self-Regulation as a Means of Preventing School Failure," *Development and Psychopathology*, vol. 20, pp. 899–911 (2008).

Bodrova, Elena, and Deborah J. Leong, *Tools of the Mind: The Vygotskian Approach to Early Childhood Education*. New York: Merrill/Prentice Hall (1996).

Bodrova, Elena, and Deborah J. Leong, "Tools of the Mind: A Case Study of Implementing the Vygotskian Approach in American Early Childhood and Primary Classrooms," International Bureau of Education / UNESCO (2001). http://www.ibe.unesco.org/publications/Monograph/inno07.pdf.25

"D.A.R.E. Works...And We Can Prove It!," D.A.R.E. web site, (2008). http://www.dare.com/home/tertiary/Default3ade.asp?N=Tertiary-&S=5

Daugherty, Martha, and C. Stephen White, "Relationships Among Private Speech and Creativity Measurements of Young Children," *Gifted Child Quarterly*, vol. 52, no. 1, pp. 30–39 (2008).

Diamond, Adele, and Dima Amso, "Contributions of Neuroscience to Our Understanding of Cognitive Development," *Current Directions in Psychological Science*, vol. 17, no. 2, pp. 136–141 (2008).

Diamond, Adele, Steven Barnett, Jessica Thomas, and Sarah Munro, "Preschool Program Improves Cognitive Control," *Science*, vol. 318, no. 5855, pp. 1387–1388 (2007).

Dignath, Charlotte, Gerhard Buettner, and Hans-Peter Langfeldt, "How Can Primary School Students Learn Self-Regulated Learning Strategies Most Effectively? A Meta-analysis on Self-Regulation Training Programmes," *Educational Research Review*, vol. 3, no. 2, pp. 101–129 (2008).

Garon, Nancy, Susan E. Bryson, and Isabel M. Smith, "Executive Function in Preschoolers: A Review Using an Integrative Framework," *Psychological Bulletin*, vol. 134, no. 1, pp. 31–60 (2008).

Graziano, Paulo A., Rachael D. Reavis, Susan P. Keane, and Susan D. Calkins, "The Role of Emotion Regulation in Children's Early Academic Success," *Journal of School Psychology*, vol. 45, no. 1, pp. 3–19 (2007).

Hamilton, Denise, "The Truth about DARE: The Big-Bucks Antidrug Program for Kids Doesn't Work," *New Times* (Mar. 20, 1997).

Johnson, Glen, "Revamped Teen Driving Law Appears to Make Impact in First Year," AP via Boston.com (2008).

Kanof, Marjorie E., "Youth Illicit Drug Use Prevention: DARE Long-Term Evaluations and Federal Efforts to Identify Effective Programs," United States General Accounting Office, Washington DC, GAO-03-172R (2003).

Lynam, Donald R., Richard Milich, Rick Zimmerman, Scott P. Novak, T. K. Logan, Catherine Martin, Carl Leukefeld, and Richard Clayton, "Project DARE: No Effects at 10-Year Follow-up," *Journal of Counseling and Clinical Psychology*, vol. 67, no. 4, pp. 590–593 (1999).

Mayhew, Daniel R., Herbert M. Simpson, Allan F. Williams, and Susan A. Ferguson, "Effectiveness and Role of Driver Education and Training in a Graduated Licensing System," *Journal of Public Health Policy*, vol. 19, no. 1, pp. 51–67 (1998).

Masicampo, E. J., and Roy F. Baumeister, "Toward a Physiology of Dual-Process Reasoning and Judgment: Lemonade, Willpower, and Expensive Rule-Based Analysis," *Psychological Science*, vol. 19, no. 3, pp. 255–260 (2008).

National Institute of Early Education Research, Rutgers University, "Preschool Program Shown to Improve Key Cognitive Functions (Including Working Memory and Control of Attention and Action)" [Press release] (2007).

Notaa, Laura, Salvatore Soresia, and Barry J. Zimmerman, "Self-Regulation and Academic Achievement and Resilience: A Longitudinal Study," *International Journal of Educational Research*, vol. 41, no. 3, pp. 198–215 (2004).

Rittle-Johnson, Bethany, Megan Saylor, and Kathryn E. Swygert, "Learning from Explaining: Does It Matter if Mom Is Listening?" *Journal of Experimental Child Psychology*, vol. 100, no. 3, pp. 215–224 (2008).

Shamosh, Noah A., and Jeremy R. Gray, "The Relation Between Fluid Intelligence and Self-Regulatory Depletion," *Cognition and Emotion*, vol. 21, no. 8, pp. 1833–1843 (2007).

Shepard, Edward W. III, "The Economic Costs of DARE," Research Paper No. 22, Institute of Industrial Relations, Le Moyne College, Syracuse, NY (2001).

Sherman, Lawrence W., Denise Gottfredson, Doris MacKenzie, John Eck, Peter Reuter, and Shawn Bushway, "Preventing Crime: What Works, What Doesn't, What's Promising," National Institute of Justice Report to the United States Congress, University Park, MD (1998).

Snyder, Leslie B., Mark A. Hamilton, and Elizabeth W. Mitchell, "A Meta-analysis of the Effect of Mediated Health Communication Campaigns on Behavior Change in the United States," *Journal of Health Communication*, vol. 9, supp. 1, pp. 71–96 (2004).

Stice, Eric, Heather Shaw, Emily Burton, and Emily Wade, "Dissonance and Healthy Weight Eating Disorder Prevention Programs: A Randomized Efficacy Trial," *Journal of Consulting and Clinical Psychology*, vol. 74, no. 2, pp. 263–275 (2006).

Vernick, Jon S., Guohua Li, Susanne Ogaitis, Ellen J. MacKenzie, Susan P. Baker, and Andrea C. Gielen, "Effects of High School Driver Education on Motor Vehicle Crashes, Violations, and Licensure," *American Journal of Preventive Medicine*, vol. 16, no. 1S, pp. 40–46 (1999).

Welsh, Brandon C., and David P. Farrington, "Effects of Closed-Circuit Television on Crime," *Annals of the American Academy of Political and Social Science*, vol. 587, no. 1, pp. 110–135 (2003).

Wilfley, Denise E., Tiffany L. Tibbs, Dorothy J. Van Buren, Kelle P. Reach, Mark S. Walker, and Leonard H. Epstein, "Lifestyle Interventions in the Treatment of Childhood Overweight: A Meta-analytic Review of Randomized Controlled Trials," *Health Psychology*, vol. 26, no. 5, pp. 521–532 (2007).

Williams, A. F., "Young Driver Risk Factors: Successful and Unsuccessful Approaches for Dealing With Them and an Agenda for the Future," *Injury Prevention*, vol. 12, supp. 1, pp. 4–8 (2006).

Chapter 9, Plays Well With Others

Allen, Joseph P., Remarks as discussant for paper symposium, "How and Why Does Peer Influence Occur? Socialization Mechanisms From a

Developmental Perspective," Biennial Meeting of the Society for Research on Adolescence, Chicago (2008).

Allen, Joseph P., and F. Christy McFarland, "Leaders and Followers: Sex, Drug Use, and Friendship Quality Predict Observed Susceptibility to Peer Influence," Paper presented at the Biennial Meeting of the Society for Research on Adolescence, Chicago (2008).

Allen, Joseph P., Maryfrances R. Porter, and F. Christy McFarland, "Leaders and Followers in Adolescent Close Friendships: Susceptibility to Peer Influence as a Predictor of Risky Behavior, Friendship Instability, and Depression," *Development and Psychopathology*, vol. 18, pp. 155–172 (2006).

Baird, Abigail A., "Real Effects of the Imaginary Audience: Peers Influence Neural Activity During Decision Making Among Adolescents," Paper presented at the Biennial Meeting of the Society for Research on Adolescence, Chicago (2008).

Balch, Christan, Caitlin Bango, Meagan Howell, and Research Team 07, "Losers, Jerks, and Idiots: A Longitudinal Study of Put-Downs, Name-Calling, and Relational Aggression on Television Shows for Children and Teens (1983–2006)," Paper presented at the Eastern Colleges Science Conference, College of Mount Saint Vincent, Riverdale, NY (2007).

Bowker, Julie C. Wojslawowicz, "Stability of and Behaviors Associated with Perceived Popular Status Across the Middle School Transition," Remarks presenting paper by Allison A. Buskirk, Kenneth H. Rubin, Julie C. Wojslawowicz Bowker, Cathryn Booth-LaForce, and Linda Rose-Krasnor, at the Biennial Meeting of the Society for Research in Child Development, Boston (2007).

Buckley, Catherine K., and Sarah J. Schoppe-Sullivan, "Relations Between Paternal Involvement and Coparenting: The Moderating Roles of Parental Beliefs and Family Earner Status," Paper presented at the 2006 National Council on Family Relations Conference, Minneapolis (2006).

Buckley, Catherine K., and Sarah J. Schoppe-Sullivan, "Father Involvement, Coparenting, and Child and Family Functioning," Paper presented at the Biennial Meeting of the Society for Research in Child Development, Boston (2007).

Burr, Jean E., Jamie M. Ostrov, Elizabeth A. Jansen, Crystal Cullerton-Sen, and Nicki R. Crick, "Relational Aggression and Friendship During Early

Childhood: 'I Won't Be Your Friend!' " *Early Education & Development*, vol. 16, no. 2, pp. 161–183 (2005).

Bylaw 04/05V41, Town of Rocky Mountain House, Canada (2004).

California Department of Education, "Zero Tolerance: Information Regarding Zero Tolerance Policies for Firearms in Schools." http://www.cde.ca.gov/ls/ss/se/zerotolerance.asp

Card, Noel, "Introduction," Remarks at the Peer Relations Conference, Biennial Meeting of the Society for Research on Adolescence, Chicago (2008).

Card, Noel A., Remarks as discussant for paper symposium, "Distinguishing Forms and Functions of Relational Aggression to Understand Sex Differences, Social Interaction, and Mental Health," Biennial Meeting of the Society for Research on Adolescence, Chicago (2008).

Card, Noel A., Brian D. Stucky, Gita M. Sawalani, and Todd D. Little, "Direct and Indirect Aggression during Childhood and Adolescence: A Meta-analytic Review of Gender Differences, Intercorrelations, and Relations to Maladjustment," *Child Development*, vol. 79, no. 5, pp. 1185–1229 (2008).

Cillessen, Antonius H. N., and Casey Borch, "Developmental Trajectories of Adolescent Popularity: A Growth Curve Modeling Analysis," *Journal of Adolescence*, vol. 29, no. 6, pp. 935–959 (2006).

Cillessen, Antonius H. N., and Lara Mayeux, "From Censure to Reinforcement: Developmental Changes in the Association Between Aggression and Social Status," *Child Development*, vol. 75, no. 1, pp. 147–163 (2004).

Cillessen, Antonius H. N., and Lara Mayeux, "Variations in the Association Between Aggression and Social Status: Theoretical and Empirical Perspectives." In: P. H. Hawley, T. D. Little, and P. C. Rodkin (Eds.), *Aggression and Adaptation: The Bright Side to Bad Behavior*, pp. 135–156. New York: Lawrence Erlbaum Associates, Inc. (2007).

Cillessen, Antonius H. N., and Amanda J. Rose, "Understanding Popularity in the Peer System," *Current Directions in Psychological Science*, vol. 14, no. 2, pp. 102–105 (2005).

Cohn, Andrea, and Andrea Canter, "Bullying: Facts for Schools and Parents," National Association of School Psychologists, NASP Resources, NASP web site. http://www.nasponline.org/resources/factsheets/bullying_fs.aspx

Crick, Nikki R., Jamie M. Ostrov, Karen Appleyard, Elizabeth A. Jansen, and Juan F. Casas, "Relational Aggression in Early Childhood: 'You Can't

Come to My Birthday Unless....'" In: M. Putallaz and K. L. Bierman (Eds.), *Aggression, Antisocial Behavior, and Violence Among Girls: A Developmental Perspective*, Duke Series in Child Development and Public Policy, pp. 71–89. New York: Guilford Press (2005).

Cummings, E. Mark, "Coping With Background Anger in Early Childhood," *Child Development*, vol. 58, no. 4, pp. 976–984 (1987).

Cummings, E. Mark, "Marital Conflict and Children's Functioning," *Social Development*, vol. 3, no. 1, pp. 16–36 (1994).

Cummings, E. Mark, Marcie C. Goeke-Morey, and Lauren M. Papp, "Children's Responses to Everyday Marital Conflict Tactics in the Home," *Child Development*, vol. 74, no. 6, pp. 1918–1929 (2003).

Cummings, E. Mark, Marcie C. Goeke-Morey, and Lauren M. Papp, "A Family-Wide Model for the Role of Emotion in Family Functioning," *Marriage & Family Review*, vol. 34, no. 1–2, pp. 13–34 (2003).

Cummings, E. Mark, Marcie C. Goeke-Morey, and Lauren M. Papp, "Everyday Marital Conflict and Child Aggression," *Journal of Abnormal Child Psychology*, vol. 32, no. 2, pp. 191–202 (2004).

Cummings, E. Mark, Carolyn Zahn-Waxler, and Marian Radke-Yarrow, "Developmental Changes in Children's Reactions to Anger in the Home," *Journal of Child Psychology and Psychiatry*, vol. 25, no. 1, pp. 63–74 (1984).

Davies, Patrick T., Melissa L. Sturge-Apple, Dante Cicchetti, and E. Mark Cummings, "The Role of Child Adrenocortical Functioning in Pathways Between Interparental Conflict and Child Maladjustment," *Developmental Psychology*, vol. 43, no. 4, pp. 918–930 (2007).

Davies, Patrick T., Melissa L. Sturge-Apple, Marcia A. Winter, E. Mark Cummings, and Deirdre Farrell, "Child Adaptation Development in Contexts of Interparental Conflict Over Time," *Child Development*, vol. 77, no. 1, pp. 218–233 (2006).

deBruyn, Eddy H., and Antonius H. N. Cillessen, "Popularity in Early Adolescence: Prosocial and Antisocial Subtypes," *Journal of Adolescent Research*, vol. 21, no. 6, pp. 1–21 (2006).

deBruyn, Eddy H., and Antonius H. N. ("Toon") Cillessen, "Associations Between Sociometric and Perceived Popularity, Bullying & Victimization in a Dutch Normative Early Adolescent Sample (N=1207)," Paper presented at the Biennial Meeting of the Society for Research in Child Development, Boston (2007).

Dodge, Kenneth A., and Jennifer E. Lansford, "The Relation Between Cultural Norms for Corporal Punishment and Societal Rates of Violent Behavior," Remarks and paper presented at the Biennial Meeting of the Society for Research in Child Development, Boston (2007).

El-Sheihk, Mona, and E. Mark Cummings, "Children's Responses to Angry Adult Behavior as a Function of Experimentally Manipulated Exposure to Resolved and Unresolved Conflicts," *Social Development*, vol. 4, no. 1, pp. 75–91 (1995).

Faircloth, W. Brad, E. Mark Cummings, Jennifer Cummings, Patricia M. Mitchell, Nakya Reeves, and Carolyn Shivers, "Launch Models of Change: The Effect of Baseline Levels of Marital Conflict Knowledge on Marital Outcomes," Poster presented at the Biennial Meeting of the Society for Research in Child Development, Boston (2007).

Farmer, Thomas W., and Hongling Xie, "Aggression and School Social Dynamics: The Good, The Bad and the Ordinary," *Journal of School Psychology*, vol. 45, no. 5, pp. 461–478 (2007).

George, Melissa R. W., Peggy Sue Keller, Kalsea J. Koss, Caroline Connelly Rycyna, Patrick T. Davies, and E. Mark Cummings, "Links Between Mother and Child Emotional Responses to Marital Conflict," Poster presented at the Biennial Meeting of the Society for Research in Child Development, Boston (2007).

Gershoff, Elizabeth T., "The Relation Between Cultural Norms for Corporal Punishment and Societal Rates of Violent Behavior," Remarks presenting paper by Elizabeth T. Gershoff, Andrew Grogan-Kaylor, Jennifer E. Lansford, Lei Chang, Kenneth A. Dodge, Arnaldo Zelli, and Kirby Deater-Deckard, at the Biennial Meeting of the Society for Research in Child Development, Boston (2007).

Gershoff, Elizabeth Thompson, "Corporal Punishment by Parents and Associated Child Behaviors and Experiences: A Meta-analytic and Theoretical Review," *Psychological Bulletin*, vol. 128, no. 4, pp. 539–579 (2002).

Gershoff, Elizabeth Thompson, Pamela C. Miller, and George W. Holden, "Parenting Influences from the Pulpit: Religious Affiliation as a Determinant of Parental Corporal Punishment," *Journal of Family Psychology*, vol. 13, no. 3, pp. 307–320 (1999).

Hawley, Patricia, "Behaving Within Peer Relations," Remarks at the Peer

Relations Conference, Biennial Meeting of the Society for Research on Adolescence, Chicago (2008).

Hawley, Patricia H., "Social Dominance and Prosocial and Coercive Strategies of Resource Control in Preschoolers," *International Journal of Behavioral Development*, vol. 26, no. 2, pp. 167–176 (2002).

Hawley, Patricia H., "Prosocial and Coercive Configurations of Resource Control in Early Adolescence: A Case for the Well-Adapted Machiavellian," *Merrill-Palmer Quarterly*, vol. 49, no. 3, pp. 279–309 (2003).

Hawley, Patricia H., "Strategies of Control, Aggression, and Morality in Preschoolers: An Evolutionary Perspective," *Journal of Experimental Child Psychology*, vol. 85, no. 3, pp. 213–235 (2003).

Hawley, Patricia H., "Social Dominance in Childhood and Aggression: Why Social Competence and Aggression May Go Hand in Hand." In: P. H. Hawley, T. D. Little, and P. C. Rodkin (Eds.), *Aggression and Adaptation: The Bright Side to Bad Behavior*, pp. 1–29. New York: Lawrence Erlbaum Associates, Inc. (2007).

Hawley, Patricia H., Todd D. Little, and Noel A. Card, "The Allure of a Mean Friend: Relationship Quality and Processes of Aggressive Adolescents with Prosocial Skills," *International Journal of Behavioral Development*, vol. 31, no. 2, pp. 170–180 (2007).

House of Commons Education and Skills Committee, Bullying: Government Response to the Committee's Third Report of Session 2006–07, Third Special Report of Session 2006–07 (2007).

Jacobs, Lorna, Rosie A. Ensor, and Claire H. Hughes, "Preschoolers' Spontaneous and Responsive Prosocial Behaviors With Peers," Poster presented at the Biennial Meeting of the Society for Research in Child Development, Boston (2007).

Kochakian, Mary Jo, "Children Need to See Parents' Fights Resolved," *Hartford Courant*, p. C1 (Jul. 12, 1994).

LaFontana, Kathryn M., and Antonius H. N. Cillessen, "Children's Perceptions of Popular and Unpopular Peers: A Multimethod Assessment," *Developmental Psychology*, vol. 38, no. 5, pp. 635–647 (2002).

Lansford, Jennifer E., Kirby Deater-Deckard, Kenneth A. Dodge, John E. Bates, and Gregory S. Pettit, "Ethnic Differences in the Link Between Physical Discipline and Later Adolescent Externalizing Behaviors," *Journal of Child Psychology and Psychiatry*, vol. 45, no. 4, pp. 801–812 (2004).

Lansford, Jennifer E., Kenneth A. Dodge, Patrick S. Malone, Dario Bacchini, Arnaldo Zelli, Nandita Chaudhary, Beth Manke, Lei Chang, Paul Oburu, Kerstin Palmérus, Concetta Pastorelli, Anna Silvia Bombi, Sombat Tapanya, Kirby Deater-Deckard, and Naomi Quinn, "Physical Discipline and Children's Adjustment: Cultural Normativeness as a Moderator," *Child Development*, vol. 76, no. 6, pp. 1234–1246 (2005).

Lansford, Jennifer E., Patrick S. Malone, Kenneth A. Dodge, and Lei Chang, "Perceptions of Parental Rejection and Hostility as Mediators of the Link between Discipline and Adjustment in Five Countries," Paper presented at the Biennial Meeting of the Society for Research on Adolescence, Chicago (2008).

Little, Todd D., Christopher C. Henrich, Stephanie M. Jones, and Patricia H. Hawley, "Disentangling the 'Whys' from the 'Whats' of Aggressive Behaviour," *International Journal of Behavioral Development*, vol. 27, no. 2, pp. 122–133 (2003).

Lowery, Steven, Russell Michaud, James Aucoin, and Joshua Skellet, "Sticks and Stones: Put-Downs in Television Programs Aimed at Children and Teens, Their Potential Effects, and Whether Media Literacy Education Can Make a Difference," Paper presented at the Eastern Colleges Science Conference, Niagara University, Niagara, NY (2008).

Luckner, Amy E., "Relational Aggression and 'Rough and Tumble' Social Interactions," Remarks presenting paper by Amy E. Luckner, Peter E. L. Marks, and Nicki R. Crick at Biennial Meeting of the Society for Research on Adolescence, Chicago (2008).

Maurer, Megan, Steven Lowery, George Figueroa, and James Aucoin, " 'You Weasley Wimps!' Put-Downs in TV Shows for Children and Teens," Paper presented at the Eastern Colleges Science Conference, College of Mount Saint Vincent, Riverdale, NY (2007).

Mayeux, Lara, and Antonius H. N. Cillessen, "The Role of Status Awareness in the Association Between Status and Aggression," Paper presented at the Biennial Meeting of the Society for Research in Child Development, Boston (2007).

Mayeux, Lara, and Antonius H. N. Cillessen, "Self-Perceptions Matter: The Role of Status Awareness in the Association between Status and Aggression," Paper presented at the Biennial Meeting of the Society for Research in Child Development, Boston (2007).

Mayeux, Lara, Marlene J. Sandstrom, and Antonius H. N. Cillessen, "Is Being Popular a Risky Proposition?" *Journal of Research on Adolescence*, vol. 18, no. 1, pp. 49–74 (2008).

Mitchell, Patricia M., Kathleen P. McCoy, Laura C. Froyen, Christine E. Merrilees, and E. Mark Cummings, "Prevention of the Negative Effects of Marital Conflict: An Education Program for Children," Poster presented at the Biennial Meeting of the Society for Research in Child Development, Boston (2007).

Mullins, Adam D., and Jamie M. Ostrov, "Educational Media Exposure in Early Childhood: Effects on Displayed and Received Aggressive and Prosocial Behavior," Poster presented at the Biennial Meeting of the Society for Research in Child Development, Boston (2007).

National Council of State Legislatures, "Select School Safety Enactments (1994–2003): Bullying and Student Harassment." http://www.ncsl.org/programs/cyf/bullyingenac.htm40.

Ostrov, Jamie M., "Forms and Functions of Aggression and Social-Psychological Adjustment," Remarks presenting paper by Jamie M. Ostrov and Rebecca J. Houston at Biennial Meeting of the Society for Research on Adolescence, Chicago (2008).

Ostrov, Jamie M., and Nikki R. Crick, "Current Directions in the Study of Relational Aggression During Early Childhood," *Early Education & Development*, vol. 16, no. 2, pp. 109–113 (2005).

Ostrov, Jamie M., Douglas A. Gentile, and Nicki R. Crick, "Media Exposure, Aggression and Prosocial Behavior During Early Childhood: A Longitudinal Study," *Social Development*, vol. 15, no. 4, pp. 612–627 (2006).

Ostrov, Jamie M., and Caroline F. Keating, "Gender Differences in Preschool Aggression During Free Play and Structured Interactions: An Observational Study," *Social Development*, vol. 13, no. 2, pp. 255–277 (2004).

Pepler, Debra J., and Wendy M. Craig, "A Peek Behind the Fence: Naturalistic Observations of Aggressive Children With Remote Audiovisual Recording," *Developmental Psychology*, vol. 31, no. 4, pp. 548–553 (1995).

Pepler, Debra J., Wendy M. Craig, and William L. Roberts, "Observations of Aggressive and Nonaggressive Children on the School Playground," *Merrill-Palmer Quarterly*, vol. 44, no. 1, pp. 55–76 (1998).

Pronk, Rhiane E., "Forms and Functions of Aggression and Social-Psychological Adjustment," Remarks presenting paper by Rhiane E. Pronk and Melanie J. Zimmer-Gembeck at Biennial Meeting of the Society for Research on Adolescence, Chicago (2008).

Puckett, Marissa, and Antonius H. N. Cillessen, "Moderation by Prosocial Behavior of the Effect of Relational Aggression on Perceived Popularity," Poster presented at the Biennial Meeting of the Society for Research in Child Development, Boston (2007).

Regnerus, Mark, Christian Smith, and Melissa Fritsch, "Religion in the Lives of American Adolescents: A Review of the Literature," Research Report no. 3, National Study of Youth and Religion, The University of North Carolina at Chapel Hill (2003).

Rodkin, Philip C., Thomas W. Farmer, Ruth Pearl, and Richard Van Acker, "They're Cool: Social Status and Peer Group Supports for Aggressive Boys and Girls," *Social Development*, vol. 15, no. 2, pp. 175–204 (2006).

Rosenzweig, Paul, and Trent England, "Zero Tolerance for Common Sense," Heritage Foundation (2004). http://www.heritage.org/Press/Commentary/ed080504a.cfm

Russell, Stephen T., "Behaving Within Peer Relations," Remarks at the Peer Relations Conference, Biennial Meeting of the Society for Research on Adolescence, Chicago (2008).

Sandstrom, Marlene J., and Antonius H. N. Cillessen, "Likeable Versus Popular: Distinct Implications for Adolescent Adjustment," *International Journal of Behavioral Development*, vol. 30, no. 4, pp. 305–314 (2006).

Sandstrom, Marlene Jacobs, and Lydia J. Romano, "Stability of and Behaviors Associated with Perceived Popular Status Across the Middle School Transition," Remarks presenting paper by Marlene Jacobs Sandstrom and Lydia J. Romano at the Biennial Meeting of the Society for Research in Child Development, Boston (2007).

Scheibe, Cynthia, and George Figueroa, "Sticks and Stones: Teasing, Put-Downs and Derogatory Language on TV Shows for Children and Adolescents," Poster presented at the Biennial Meeting of the Society for Research in Child Development, Boston (2007).

Skiba, Russell J., "Zero Tolerance, Zero Evidence, An Analysis of School Disciplinary Practice," Indiana Education Policy Center, Policy Research Report #SRS2 (2000).

Skiba, Russell, Cecil R. Reynolds, Sandra Graham, Peter Sheras, Jane Close Conoley, and Enedina Garcia-Vazquez, "Are Zero Tolerance Policies

Effective in Schools?" Zero Tolerance Task Force Report, American Psychological Association (2006).

Chapter 10, Why Hannah Talks and Alyssa Doesn't

Bahrick, Lorraine E., and Robert Lickliter, "Intersensory Redundancy Guides Attentional Selectivity and Perceptual Learning in Infancy," *Developmental Psychology*, vol. 36, no. 1, pp. 190–201 (2000).

Bahrick, Lorraine E., and Robert Lickliter, "Intersensory Redundancy Guides Perceptual and Cognitive Development," *Advances in Child Behavior and Development*, vol. 30, pp. 153–187 (2002).

Bornstein, Marc H., Linda R. Cote, Sharone Maital, Kathleen Painter, Sung-Yun Park, Liliana Pascual, Marie-Germaine Pêcheux, Josette Ruel, Paola Venuti, and Andre Vyt, "Cross-Linguistic Analysis of Vocabulary in Young Children: Spanish, Dutch, French, Hebrew, Italian, Korean, and American English," *Child Development*, vol. 75, no. 4, pp. 1115–1139 (2004).

Bornstein, Marc H., Catherine S. Tamis-LeMonda, Chun-Shin Hahn, and O. Maurice Haynes, "Maternal Responsiveness to Young Children at Three Ages: Longitudinal Analysis of a Multidimensional, Modular, and Specific Parenting Construct," *Developmental Psychology*, vol. 44, no. 3, pp. 867–874 (2008).

Bornstein, Marc H., Catherine S. Tamis-LeMonda, and O. Maurice Haynes, "First Words in the Second Year: Continuity, Stability and Models of Concurrent and Predictive Correspondence in Vocabulary and Verbal Responsiveness Across Age and Context," *Infant Behavior and Development*, vol. 22, no. 1, pp. 65–85 (1999).

Briesch, Jacqueline M., Jennifer A. Schwade, and Michael H. Goldstein, "Responses to Prelinguistic Object-Directed Vocalizations Facilitate Word Learning in 11-Month-Olds," Poster presented at the Biennial International Conference in Infant Studies, Vancouver, Canada (2008).

Brink, Ryan N. S., Larissa K. Samuelson, Emily R. Fassbinder, and Peter Gierut, "The Lasting Lessons of Early Adolescent Friendships: The Benefits of Autonomy and the Mixed Blessings of Early Intensity," Paper presented at the Biennial Meeting of the Society for Research in Child Development, Boston (2007).

Brooks, Rechele, and Andrew N. Meltzoff, "Infant Gaze Following and Pointing Predict Accelerated Vocabulary Growth Through Two Years of Age: A Longitudinal, Growth Curve Modeling Study," *Journal of Child Language*, vol. 35, no. 1, pp. 207–220 (2008).

Burr, Kathy, "Baby Einstein, Unique Multilingual Developmental Video for Infants, Released at Atlanta Maternity Fest Intelligence" [Press release], The Baby Einstein Company, Atlanta (1997).

Cameron-Faulkner, Thea, Elena Lieven, and Michael Tomasello, "A Construction Based Analysis of Child Directed Speech," *Cognitive Science*, vol. 27, no. 6, pp. 843–873 (2003).

Dale, Philip, Remarks as discussant for paper symposium, "Predictors, Prevalence and Natural History of Language Outcomes in a Community Cohort of Australian Children: The Early Language in Victoria Study," The XI Congress of the International Association for the Study of Child Language, Edinburgh, Scotland (2008).

Engle, Mary Koelbel, Federal Trade Commission Letter to Timothy Muris, O'Melveny & Myers, LLP, regarding end of investigation into Baby Einstein marketing practices, Washington DC (2007).

Evans, Gary W., "Child Development and the Physical Environment," *Annual Review of Psychology*, vol. 57, pp. 423–451 (2006).

Fenson, Larry, Steve Pethick, Connie Renda, Jeffrey L. Cox, Philip S. Dale, and J. Steven Reznick, "Short-Form Versions of the MacArthur Communicative Development Inventories," *Applied Psycholinguistics*, vol. 21, no. 1, pp. 95–116 (2000).

Fernald, Anne, and Nereyda Hurtado, "Names in Frames: Infants Interpret Words in Sentence Frames Faster Than Words in Isolation," *Developmental Science*, vol. 9, no. 3, pp. F33–F40 (2006).

Fitch, W. Tecumseh, Marc D. Hauser, and Noam Chomsky, "The Evolution of the Language Faculty: Clarifications and Implications," *Cognition*, vol. 97, no. 2, pp. 179–210 (2005).

Gogate, Lakshmi J., and Lorraine E. Bahrick, "Intersensory Redundancy Facilitates Learning of Arbitrary Relations between Vowel Sounds and Objects in Seven-Month-Old Infants," *Journal of Experimental Child Psychology*, vol. 69, no. 2, pp. 133–149 (1998).

Goldin-Meadow, Susan, e-mails with authors (2007–2008).

Goldstein, Michael H., e-mails with authors (2008–2009).

Goldstein, Michael H., Marc H. Bornstein, Jennifer A. Schwade, Fern Baldwin, and Rachel Brandstadter, "Five-Month-Old Infants Have Learned the Value of Babbling," Poster presented at the Biennial Meeting of the Society for Research in Child Development, Boston (2007).

Goldstein, Michael H., Andrew P. King, and Meredith J. West, "Social Interaction Shapes Babbling: Testing Parallels Between Birdsong and Speech," *Proceedings of the National Academy of Sciences*, vol. 100, no. 13, pp. 8030–8035 (2003).

Goldstein, Michael H., and Jennifer A. Schwade, "Social Feedback to Infants' Babbling Facilitates Rapid Phonological Learning," *Psychological Science*, vol. 19, no. 5, pp. 515–523 (2008).

Goldstein, Michael H., Jennifer A. Schwade, and Supriya Syal, "Prelinguistic Infants Learn Novel Phonological Patterns from Mothers' Contingent Speech," Poster presented at the XI Congress of the International Association for the Study of Child Language, Edinburgh, Scotland (2008).

Goldstein, Michael H., and Meredith J. West, "Consistent Responses of Human Mothers to Prelinguistic Infants: The Effect of Prelinguistic Repertoire Size," *Journal of Comparative Psychology*, vol. 113, no. 1, pp. 52–58 (1999).

Goodman, Judith C., Philip S. Dale, and Ping Li, "Does Frequency Count? Parental Input and the Acquisition of Vocabulary," *Journal of Child Language*, vol. 35, no. 3, pp. 515–531 (2008).

Gopnik, Alison, "The Theory Theory as an Alternative to the Innateness Hypothesis." In: L. Antony and N. Hornstein (Eds.), *Chomsky and His Critics*, pp. 238–254. New York: Basil Blackwell (2003).

Gros-Louis, Julie, Meredith J. West, Michael H. Goldstein, and Andrew P. King, "Mothers Provide Differential Feedback to Infants' Prelinguistic Sounds," *International Journal of Behavioral Development*, vol. 30, no. 6, pp. 509–516 (2006).

Hart, Betty, and Todd R. Risley, *Meaningful Differences in the Everyday Experience of Young American Children*. Baltimore: Paul H. Brookes Publishing Co., Inc. (1995/2007).

Hauser, Marc D., Noam Chomsky, and W. Tecumseh Fitch, "The Faculty of Language: What Is It, Who Has It, and How Did It Evolve?" *Science*, vol. 298, no. 5598, pp. 1569–1579 (2002).

Hollich, George, Rochelle S. Newman, and Peter W. Jusczyk, "Infants' Use of Synchronized Visual Information to Separate Streams of Speech," *Child Development*, vol. 76, no. 3, pp. 598–613 (2005).

Iger, Robert, Letter to Mark A. Emmert regarding press release concerning study on children's language development and media viewing, *Seattle Post-Intelligencer* (Aug. 14, 2007). http://seattlepi.nwsource.com/local/327427_letter14ww.html

Jackendoff, Ray, and Steven Pinker, "The Nature of the Language Faculty and Its Implications for Evolution of Language (Reply to Fitch, Hauser, and Chomsky)," *Cognition*, vol. 97, no. 2, pp. 211–225 (2005).

Jusczyk, Peter W., "How Infants Begin to Extract Words from Speech," *Trends in Cognitive Sciences*, vol. 3, no. 9, pp. 323–328 (1999).

Kaplan, Peter S., Michael H. Goldstein, Elizabeth R. Huckeby, and Robin Panneton Cooper, "Habituation, Sensitization, and Infants' Responses to Motherese Speech," *Developmental Psychobiology*, vol. 28, no. 1, pp. 4S–57 (1995).

King, Andrew P., Meredith J. West, and Michael H. Goldstein, "Non-Vocal Shaping of Avian Song Development: Parallels to Human Speech Development," *Ethology*, vol. 111, no. 1, pp. 101–117 (2005).

Klimkiewicz, Joann, "Imprinting Infants," *Hartford Courant* (Jul. 24, 2006).

Kuhl, Patricia K., "A New View of Language," *Proceedings of the National Academy of Sciences*, vol. 97, no. 22, pp. 11850–11857 (2000).

Kuhl, Patricia K., "Early Language Acquisition: Cracking the Speech Code," *Nature Reviews: Neuroscience*, vol. 5, no. 11, pp. 831–843 (2004).

Kuhl, Patricia K., "Is Speech Learning 'Gated' by the Social Brain?" *Developmental Science*, vol. 10, no. 1, pp. 110–120 (2007).

Kuhl, Patricia K., "Language and the Baby Brain," Remarks at the American Association for the Advancement of Science Annual Meeting, Boston (2008).

Kuhl, Patricia K., Barbara T. Conboy, Sharon Coffey-Corina, Denise Padden, Maritza Rivera-Gaxiola, and Tobey Nelson, "Phonetic Learning as a Pathway to Language: New Data and Native Language Magnet Theory Expanded (NLM-e)," *Philosophical Transactions of the Royal Society B*, vol. 363, no. 1493, pp. 979–1000 (2008).

Kuhl, Patricia K., Feng-Ming Tsao, and Huei-Mei Liu, "Foreign-Language Experience in Infancy: Effects of Short-Term Exposure and Social

Interaction on Phonetic Learning," *Proceedings of the National Academy of Sciences*, vol. 100, no. 15, pp. 9096–9101 (2003).

"Lena: Every Word Counts," Infoture, Inc., Boulder, CO (2008). http://www.lenababy.com

Linebarger, Deborah L., and Dale Walker, "Infants' and Toddlers' Television Viewing and Language Outcomes," *American Behavioral Scientist*, vol. 48, no. 5, pp. 624–645 (2005).

Linn, Susan, e-mails with authors (2008).

McMurray, Bob, "Defusing the Childhood Vocabulary Explosion," *Science*, vol. 317, no. 5838, p. 631 (2007).

Meltzoff, Andrew, "Social Cognition and Early Language Development in Infancy," Remarks at the XI Congress of the International Association for the Study of Child Language, Edinburgh, Scotland (2008).

Meltzoff, Andrew N., and Jean Decenty, "What Imitation Tells Us About Social Cognition: A Rapprochement Between Developmental Psychology and Cognitive Neuroscience," *Philosophical Transactions of the Royal Society B*, vol. 358, no. 1431, pp. 491–500 (2003).

Mendelsohn, Alan L., Samantha B. Berkule, Suzy Tomopoulos, Catherine S. Tamis-LeMonda, Harris S. Huberman, Jose Alvir, and Benard P. Dreyer, "Infant Television and Video Exposure Associated With Limited Parent-Child Verbal Interactions in Low Socioeconomic Status Households," *Archives of Pediatric and Adolescent Medicine*, vol. 162, no. 5, pp. 411–417 (2008).

Morris, Casie, "Baby Einstein Receives Parent's Choice Award," *Expectations Monthly*, vol. 3, no. 2, p. 2 (1997).

Newman, Rochelle, Nan Bernstein Ratner, Ann Marie Jusczyk, Peter W. Jusczyk, and Kathy Ayala Dow, "Infants' Early Ability to Segment the Conversational Speech Signal Predicts Later Language Development: A Retrospective Analysis," *Developmental Psychology*, vol. 42, no. 4, pp. 643–655 (2006).

Newman, Rochelle, Jane Tsay, and Peter Jusczyk, "The Development of Speech Segmentation Abilities." In D. Houston, A. Seidl, G. Hollich, E. Johnson, and A. Jusczyk (Eds.), Jusczyk Lab Final Report (2003). http://hincapie.psych.purdue.edu/Jusczyk

Nicely, Pamela, Catherine S. Tamis-LeMonda, and Marc. H. Bornstein, "Mothers' Attuned Responses to Infant Affect Expressivity," *Infant Behavior and Development*, vol. 22, no. 4, pp. 557–568 (2000).

Oller, D. Kimbrough, "The Creation of Phonological Categories and the Negotiation of Word Meanings in Early Lexical Development," Remarks and paper by D. Kimbrough Oller and Heather Ramsdell, presented at the XI Congress of the International Association for the Study of Child Language, Edinburgh, Scotland (2008).

Onnia, Luca, Heidi R. Waterfall, and Shimon Edelman, "Learn Locally, Act Globally: Learning Language from Variation Set Cues," *Cognition*, vol. 109, no. 3, pp. 423–430 (2008).

Özçaliskan, Seyda, and Susan Goldin-Meadow, "Do Parents Lead Their Children by the Hand?," *Journal of Child Language*, vol. 32, no. 3, pp. 481–505 (2005).

Pinker, Steven, *The Language Instinct: How the Mind Creates Language*. New York: HarperPerennial (2000).

Ratner, Nan, "Perceptual and Productive Sensitivities to Native Phonology That Facilitate Language Acquisition," Remarks and paper presented at the XI Congress of the International Association for the Study of Child Language, Edinburgh, Scotland (2008).

Rivera-Gaxiola, Maritza, CA Lindsay Klarman, Adrian Garcia-Sierra, and Patricia K. Kuhl, "Neural Patterns to Speech and Vocabulary Growth in American Infants," *NeuroReport*, vol. 16, no. 5, pp. 498–498 (2005).

Rost, Gwyneth, and Bob McMurray, "Phonological Variability and Word Learning: Infants Can Learn Lexical Neighbors," Paper presented at the XI Congress of the International Association for the Study of Child Language, Edinburgh, Scotland (2008).

Samuelson, Larissa, "Input Variability and the Shape Bias: It Matters What Statistics You Get and When You Get Them," Remarks and paper presented at the XI Congress of the International Association for the Study of Child Language, Edinburgh, Scotland (2008).

Samuelson, Larissa K., "Attentional Biases in Artificial Noun Learning Tasks: Generalizations Across the Structure of Already-Learned Nouns." In: L. R. Gleitman and A. K. Joshi (Eds.), *Proceedings of the Twenty-Second Annual Conference of the Cognitive Science Society*, pp. 423–428. Philadelphia: Lawrence Erlbaum Associates, Inc. (2000).

Samuelson, Larissa K., "Statistical Regularities in Vocabulary Guide Language Acquisition in Connectionist Models and 15–20 Month Olds," *Developmental Psychology*, vol. 38, no. 6, pp. 1016–1037 (2002).

Samuelson, Larissa K., e-mails with authors (2008).

Samuelson, Larissa K., and Jessica S. Horst, "Are Word Learning Biases Created in the Moment? Task and Stimulus Factors Affect the Shape and Material Biases," Paper presented at the Biennial International Conference in Infant Studies, Chicago (2004).

Schwade, Jennifer A., e-mails with authors (2008–2009).

Schwade, Jennifer A., Michael H. Goldstein, Jennifer S. Stone, and Anya V. Z. Wachterhauser, "Children's Use of Speech and Motion Cues When Learning Novel Words," Poster presented at the Biennial International Conference in Infant Studies, Chicago (2004).

Schwarz, Joel, "Baby DVDs, Videos, May Hinder, Not Help, Infants' Language Development" [Press release], University of Washington (2007).

Shin, Annys, "Diaper Demographic; TV, Video Programming for the Under-2 Market Grows Despite Lack of Clear Educational Benefit," *Washington Post*, p. D.1 (Feb. 24, 2007).

Smith, Linda B., "Weird Loops: From Object Recognition to Symbolic Play to Learning Nouns and Back," Remarks and paper presented at the American Psychological Association Annual Convention, Boston (2008).

Smith, Linda B., Susan S. Jones, Barbara Landau, Lisa Gershkoff-Stowe, and Larissa Samuelson, "Object Name Learning Provides On-the-Job Training for Attention," *Psychological Science*, vol. 13, no. 1, pp. 13–19 (2002).

Snedeker, Jesse, Joy Geren, and Carissa L. Shafto, "Starting Over: International Adoption as a Natural Experiment in Language Development," *Psychological Science*, vol. 18, no. 1, pp. 79–87 (2007).

Stoel-Gammon, Carol, "Lexical Acquisition: Effects of Phonology," Remarks on paper by Carol Stoel-Gammon and Anna Vogel Sosa presented at the XI Congress of the International Association for the Study of Child Language, Edinburgh, Scotland (2008).

Syal, Supriya, Michael H. Goldstein, Jennifer A. Schwade, and Mu Young Kim, "Learning While Babbling: Prelinguistic Object-Directed Vocalizations Facilitate Learning in Real Time and Developmental Time," Poster presented at the Biennial Meeting of the Society for Research in Child Development, Boston (2007).

Tamis-LeMonda, Catherine S., "Introduction: Maternal Sensitivity: Individual, Contextual and Cultural Factors in Recent Conceptualizations," *Early Development and Parenting*, vol. 5, no. 4, pp. 167–171 (1996).

Tamis-LeMonda, Catherine S., e-mails with authors (2008).

Tamis-LeMonda, Catherine S., and Marc H. Bornstein, "Maternal Responsiveness and Early Language Acquisition," *Advances in Child Development and Behavior*, vol. 29, pp. 89–127 (2002).

Tamis-LeMonda, Catherine S., Marc H. Bornstein, and Lisa Baumwell, "Maternal Responsiveness and Children's Achievement of Language Milestones," *Child Development*, vol. 72, no. 3, pp. 748–767 (2001).

Tomblin, Bruce, Remarks as discussant for paper symposium, "Predictors, Prevalence and Natural History of Language Outcomes in a Community Cohort of Australian Children: The Early Language in Victoria Study," XI Congress of the International Association for the Study of Child Language, Edinburgh, Scotland (2008).

Walker, Dale, e-mails with authors (2008).

Walker, Dale, Charles Greenwood, Betty Hart, and Judith Carta, "Prediction of School Outcomes Based on Early Language Production and Socioeconomic Factors," *Child Development*, vol. 65, no. 3, pp. 606–621 (1994).

Walker-Andrews, Arlene S., "Infants' Perception of Expressive Behaviors: Differentiation of Multimodal Information," *Psychological Bulletin*, vol. 121, no. 3, pp. 437–456 (1997).

Waterfall, Heidi, *A Little Change Is a Good Thing: Feature Theory, Language Acquisition and Variation Sets*, University of Chicago, Doctoral Dissertation. Chicago (2006).

Waterfall, Heidi R., e-mails with authors (2008–2009).

Waterfall, Heidi R., "A Little Change Is a Good Thing: The Relation of Variation Sets to Children's Noun, Verb and Verb-Frame Development," Manuscript in preparation (2009).

West, Meredith J., Andrew P. King, and Michael H. Goldstein, "Singing, Socializing, and the Music Effect." In: P. Marler and H. Slabbekoom (Eds.), *Nature's Music*, pp. 374–387. London: Academic Press (2004).

Wightman, Frederic, Doris Kistler, and Douglas Brungart, "Informational Masking of Speech in Children: Auditory-Visual Integration," *Journal of Acoustical Society of America*, vol. 119, no. 6, pp. 3940–3949 (2006).

Zimmerman, Frederick J., Dimitri A. Christakis, and Andrew N. Meltzoff, "Associations Between Media Viewing and Language Development in Children Under Age 2 Years," *Journal of Pediatrics*, vol. 151, no. 4, pp. 364–368 (2007).

Zimmerman, Frederick J., Dimitri A. Christakis, and Andrew N. Meltzoff, "Television and DVD/Video Viewing in Children Younger than 2 Years," *Archives of Pediatric and Adolescent Medicine*, vol. 161, no. 5, pp. 473–479 (2007).

Conclusion

Bono, Giacomo, and Jeffrey J. Froh, "Gratitude in School: Benefits to Students and Schools." In: R. Gilman, E. S. Huebner, and M. Furlong (Eds.), *Handbook of Positive Psychology in the Schools: Promoting Wellness in Children and Youth*. Mahwah, NJ: Lawrence Erlbaum Associates, Inc. (2009).

Diener, Ed, Richard E. Lucas, and Christie Napa Scollon, "Beyond the Hedonic Treadmill: Revisiting the Adaptation Theory of Well-Being," *American Psychologist*, vol. 61, no. 4, pp. 305–314 (2006).

Earley, P. Christopher, "Trust, Perceived Importance of Praise and Criticism, and Work Performance: An Examination of Feedback in the United States and England," *Journal of Management*, vol. 12, no. 4, 457–473 (1986).

Emmons, Robert A., *Thanks! How the New Science of Gratitude Can Make You Happier*. Boston: Houghton Mifflin Co. (2007).

Emmons, Robert A., and Michael E. McCullough, "Counting Blessings Versus Burdens: An Empirical Investigation of Gratitude and Subjective Well-Being in Daily Life," *Journal of Personality and Social Psychology*, vol. 84, no. 2, pp. 377–389 (2003).

Froh, Jeffrey J., Gratitude Questionnaire, Author's Manuscript (Undated).

Froh, Jeffrey J. (Ed.), Student Gratitude Essays (Undated).

Froh, Jeffrey J., Research Agenda, Froh Lab web site (2007). http://tinyurl.com/5v9nda

Froh, Jeffrey J., "A Lesson in Thanks," *Greater Good*, vol. 4, no. 1, p. 23 (2007).

Froh, Jeffrey J., and Giacomo Bono, "The Gratitude of Youth." In: S. J. Lopez (Ed.), *Positive Psychology: Exploring the Best in People*. Westport, CT: Greenwood (2008).

Froh, Jeffrey J., Todd B. Kashdan, Kathleen M. Ozimkowski, and Norman Miller, "Who Benefits the Most from a Gratitude Intervention in Children and Adolescents? Examining Trait Positive Affect as Moderator," *Journal of Positive Psychology* (under review) (2008).

Froh, Jeffrey J., David N. Miller, and Stephanie F. Snyder, "Gratitude in Children and Adolescents: Development, Assessment, and School-Based Intervention," *School Psychology Forum: Research in Practice*, vol. 2, no. 1, pp. 1–13 (2007).

Froh, Jeffrey J., William J. Sefnick, and Robert A. Emmons, "Counting Blessings in Early Adolescents: An Experimental Study of Gratitude and Subjective Well-Being," *Journal of School Psychology*, vol. 46, no. 2, pp. 213–233 (2008).

Froh, Jeffrey J., Charles Yurkewicz, and Todd B. Kashdan, "Gratitude and Subjective Well-Being in Early Adolescence: Examining Gender Differences," *Journal of Adolescence*, doi:10.1016/j.adolescence.2008.06.006 (in press) (2008).

Kashdan, Todd B., Anjali Mishra, William E. Breen, and Jeffrey J. Froh, "Gender Differences in Gratitude: Examining Appraisals, Narratives, and the Willingness to Express Emotions, and Changes in Psychological Needs," *Journal of Personality*, vol. 77, no. 3 (Early view) (2009).

McCausland, W. D., K. Pouliakas, and I. Theodossiou, "Some Are Punished and Some Are Rewarded: A Study of the Impact of Performance Pay on Job Satisfaction," University of Aberdeen Business School Working Paper No. 2007–06 (2007).

Padilla-Walker, Laura, "Characteristics of Mother-Child Interactions Related to Adolescents' Positive Values and Behaviors," *Journal of Marriage and Family*, vol. 69, pp. 675–686 (2007).

Padilla-Walker, Laura M., and Gustavo Carlo, "Personal Values as a Mediator Between Parent and Peer Expectations and Adolescent Behaviors," *Journal of Family Psychology*, vol. 21, no. 3, pp. 538–541 (2007).

Prelip, Mike, Wendy Slusser, Rebecca Davids, Linda Lange, Sumiko Takayanagi, Stephanie Vecchiarelli, and Charlotte Neumann, "Los Angeles Unified School District Nutrition Network Impact Evaluation Project: 2005–2006 Final Report," UCLA Nutrition Friendly Schools and Communities Group, UCLA School of Public Health, Los Angeles (2006).

ABOUT THE AUTHORS

Po Bronson and Ashley Merryman's articles on the science of children for *New York Magazine* won the magazine journalism award from the American Association for the Advancement of Science, as well as the Clarion Award from the Association for Women in Communications. Their articles for *Time Magazine* won the award for outstanding journalism from the Council on Contemporary Families.

Prior to collaborating with Merryman, Bronson authored five books, including the #1 *New York Times* bestseller *What Should I Do With My Life?* Merryman's journalism has appeared in *The Washington Post* and *The National Catholic Reporter*.

Bronson lives in San Francisco with his wife and their two children. Merryman lives in Los Angeles, where she runs a church-based tutoring program for inner-city children.

INDEX

actigraphs, 32
"acting white," 65–66
ADHD, and sleep deprivation, 31, 248*n*
age spacing, and sibling effect, 128–29
aggression (aggressive behavior), 179–96
   bullying and, 187–89
   educational television and, 179–82
   parental conflicts and, 183–85
   parenting styles and, 194–96
   physical punishment and, 183–85
   popularity and, 189–93
   self-esteem and, 18–19, 246–47*n*
Aigner-Clark, Julie, 201–2
alcohol use, 19, 138, 143, 159, 190, 258*n*, 261*n*
Allen, Joseph, 187–88, 190
amygdala, 35, 256*n*
antisocial behavior, 192–93, 263*n*
Arruda, Cindy, 77–79
Atkinson, Richard, 40, 42
attention switching, 169

Baby Einstein, 199–204
baby videos (DVDs), and language acquisition, 199–204
Baird, Abigail, 146–47
Banaji, Mahzarin, 18
Bar-On, Reuven, 107
Baumeister, Roy, 18–19, 246–47*n*
Berenstain Bears, 126
biases, 53–55, 59, 63–64, 98
Bigler, Rebecca, 47, 48, 50, 52–53, 58–59, 62–63
bistrategic controllers, 193
Black Santa and White Santa, 66–69
Blackwell, Lisa, 17

Blair, Clancy, 174
Blos, Peter, 151
Bodrova, Elena, 162–63, 164, 166, 170, 172
boredom, and teen rebellion, 136, 141–47, 258*n*
Bornstein, Marc, 207–8
Bowman, Joy, 66–69
Boy Who Cried Wolf, 83–84
brain anatomy
   developmental shifts in, 112, 257*n*
   intelligence tests and, 109–13, 255–56*n*
   love, religion, and danger and, 112, 256–57*n*
   parenting and, 6, 245*n*
   persistence and, 24, 247*n*
   self-control and, 169–73
   sleep deprivation and, 33–35
   teen rebellion and, 143–47, 258–59*n*
Branden, Nathaniel, 18
Brickman, Philip, 228–29
Brook, Judith, 20
buddy reading, 162, 168, 175
bullying, and aggressive behavior, 187–89
Bunge, Silvia, 171–73

Caldwell, Linda, 136–43
Campbell, Donald, 228–29
canonical syllables, 213–14
Carskadon, Mary, 32, 33, 35–36, 38
cartoons, and aggressive behavior, 179–82
categorization, 52–53, 56–57, 62
cerebral cortex, and intelligence, 110–11
children's books, sibling relationships in, 126–27
Chomsky, Noam, 222–23

Cicero, 228
Cillessen, Antonius, 191–92, 238
circadian clock, 35–36
Civil Rights Project, 57–58, 59
Cloninger, Robert, 24, 247n
Cognitive Abilities Test, 97, 102
cognitive control, 171–73
College Board, 36
color-blindness, and race, 49, 53, 54–55
Comprehensive Testing Battery III, 100
conflict between parents, and aggressive behavior, 183–85
conflict prevention, and siblings, 119–20, 122–27, 257n
control. *See* self-control
Copenhaver-Johnson, Jeane, 66–69
corporal punishment, and aggressive behavior, 185–87, 261n
cortisol, 40, 184
Crick, Nikki, 190–91
Crocker, Jennifer, 22
cross-cultural differences in use of corporal punishment, 185–87, 261n
Crossman, Angela M., 252n
Csikszentmihalyi, Mihaly, 142
Cummings, E. Mark, 183–85, 187

Dahl, Ronald, 38
Dale, Philip, 223
danger, and brain anatomy, 112, 256–57n
Danner, Frederick, 30, 36–37
D.A.R.E. (Drug Abuse Resistance Education), 159, 260n
Darling, Nancy, 136–41, 147–48, 150–51, 233, 238
DeHart, Ganie, 120–21
DePaulo, Bella, 90–91
depression, and sleep deprivation, 36–37
developmental shifts in brain, 112, 257n
diabetes, 40
Diamond, Adele, 170
Dignath, Charlotte, 174
Dinges, David, 44
discrimination, 57, 63–64
Disengaged Dads, 195–96
Disney, 199, 203
distractions, 168–69, 170–71, 173–74
Diverse Environment Theory, 55–62
Dobson, James, 187
Dodge, Kenneth, 185–87, 260–61n
"Don't Tell" rule, 88–89

dopamine, 143–44, 145, 173
Downey, Geraldine, 18
driver education (Driver's Ed), 157–58, 173
drug-prevention and dropout programs, 159, 260n
Duncan, Greg, 108–9
Dweck, Carol, 13–25, 246n

educational television, and aggressive behavior, 179–82
effortful control. *See* self-control
effort vs. praise, 15, 17–18, 22–24
Ekman, Paul, 81
Emmons, Robert, 227–32
emotional intelligence, 106–8, 254–55n
Emotional Intelligence (Goleman), 106–7
empathy, 82, 238
EQ-i (Emotional Quotient Inventory), 107
Erikson, Erik, 151
essentialism, 53
ethnic/cross-cultural differences in use of corporal punishment, 185–87, 261n
ethnic pride, 64–65
Evans, Gary, 210
excessive praise, 20–22, 24
executive functioning, 34, 169–70, 252n
extroversion, and academic achievement, 108–9

Fallacy of Similar Effect, 237–38
Fallacy of the Good/Bad Dichotomy, 238
fantasy play, shared, 129–30
fat children. *See* obesity
Fels Longitudinal Study, 256n
Fletcher, Mary Lynn, 120
flow, 142
Frede, Ellen, 163–64
Freud, Anna, 151
Freud, Sigmund, 127–28
Froh, Jeffrey, 229–36

Galvan, Adriana, 143–45, 258–59n
gaze aversion, and lie-detection, 251n
Gentile, Douglas, 179–81
George Washington and the Cherry Tree, 83–84, 86
ghrelin, 40
Giedd, Jay, 110
gifted students. *See also* intelligence tests
underestimating of abilities, 12, 246n

Index

glucose, 34, 41
Golding, William, 182
Goldstein, Michael, 210–16, 220–21, 223
Goleman, Daniel, 106–7, 254–55n
Gottman, John, 121, 129
Grant, Cary, ix–x, 245n
gratitude, 227–36
gratitude journals, 227–28, 230–32
Gurland, Suzanne, 256n

Haier, Richard, 111–13
Hall, G. Stanley, 118
Harris-Britt, April, 63–64
Hart, Betty, 205–6, 209–10, 224
Hawley, Patricia, 192–93, 238
hedonic treadmill, 228–29, 235
high school start times, and sleep deprivation, 36–38, 249n
hippocampus, 34, 35, 256n
Holmes, Tabitha, 149–50, 152
Hornbeck, Amy, 163–64
human growth hormone, 40

identity crisis, 151
Iger, Robert A., 199, 203
impulsivity, 109, 171–72, 174
individualism, 65
in-group preferences, 52–55
insulin, 41
intelligence, and ability to lie, 82–83, 252n
intelligence tests (IQ tests), 95–114
    age for initial screening, 100–102, 104–5
    brain anatomy and, 109–13, 255–56n
    lack of reassessment, 104–6
    other assessments, 106–9
    predictive validity of, 98–102, 173–74, 253–54n
    variance in, 256n

Japanese schools, subgroupism in, 65, 251n
Johnson, Angela, 66–69
journals, gratitude, 227–28, 230–32

Katz, Phyllis, 54–55, 62
Kirsch, Lauri, 104
Kramer, Laurie, 119–30, 238, 257n
Kuhl, Patricia, 201–3

Laird, Robert, 150
Lake Wobegon Effect, 183
language development, 199–224
    baby DVDs and, 199–204
    hearing multiple speakers, 217
    motionese, 217, 219, 221–22
    object labeling, 215–16, 221–22
    parent responsiveness and, 207–16, 220–22
    shape bias, 219–20
    variation sets, 218–19
    word count and, 204–7
    word frames, 217–18
Lansford, Jennifer, 186
Lawton, Joan, ix–x
League of Women Voters, 38
leakage in lies, 79, 82, 85
LeBourgeois, Monique, 33
Lee, Kun Ho, 112–13
Leisure Studies, 136–37, 141
Leong, Deborah, 162–63, 168, 172
leptin, 40
Lewis, Michael, 252n
lie-detection systems, 75, 251n
lies. *See* lying
life expectancy, 136, 258n
Lohman, David, 102, 105
Lord of the Flies (Golding), 182
love, and brain anatomy, 112, 256–57n
lying, 73–92
    age progression of, 80–81, 84
    frequency of, 90–91, 253n
    holding information back (white lies), 86–89
    as more advanced skill, 82–83, 252n
    parents' inability to detect, 75–76, 80, 252n
    Peeking Game, 77–80, 83–86, 252n
    punishment as primary catalyst for, 82, 84–85, 252–53n
    teaching worth of honesty, 83–86
    teen rebellion and, 147–52

MacArthur Communicative Development Inventory, 200–201
McCall, Robert, 256n
McCarthy, Karen, 37
Magic Castle, ix–x
Mahowald, Mark, 37
marital conflict, and aggressive behavior, 183–85
Martin Luther King Jr. Day, 56
materialism, 229, 230
Mayer-Salovey-Caruso Emotional Intelligence Test (MSCEIT), 107

melatonin, 36
Meltzoff, Andrew, 200, 203
memory, and sleep deprivation, 35
Meyer, Wulf-Uwe, 20
Millaway, Sally, 164–65, 175–76
Minnesota Regional Sleep Disorders Center, 37
Mod Squad study, 136–41
Moody, James, 60–61
motionese, 217, 219, 221–22
MSCEIT (Mayer-Salovey-Caruso Emotional Intelligence Test), 107
Muir, Simone, 73–76
multicultural curriculums, 47–51
myelination, 255–56n

National Sleep Foundation, 30, 248n
Ng, Florrie, 22–23
nucleus accumbens, 143–44
Nurture Paradox, 187
Nurture shock, use of term, 6
Nutrition Network, 263n

Obama, Barack, 51
obesity
  sleep deprivation and, 31, 39–42, 249n, 250n
  television connection to, 39–40, 250n
object labeling, 215–16, 221–22
one-child families (onlies), 117–19, 257n
O'Reilly, Brian, 36, 249n
Orfield, Gary, 57–58
Ostrov, Jamie, 179–81, 193
Otis-Lennon School Ability Test, 97
Owens, Judith, 42–43

Padilla-Walker, Laura, 263n
paint-by-numbers kits, 3–4
Palmer Paint Company, 3–4
parent responsiveness, and language acquisition, 207–16, 220–22
parents (parenting styles). *See also* praise
  aggressive behavior and, 183–85, 194–96
  lying and, 75–76, 80, 84–85, 252–53n
  racial attitudes and, 47–69
  teen rebellion and, 139–40, 150–51, 259n
Pearson/Harcourt Assessment, 98
Peeking Game, 77–80, 83–86, 252n
peer pressure, 142, 143, 238
Pepler, Debra, 191

permissive parents, and teen rebellion, 139–40, 150–51
persistence, 24, 247n
personality traits, and academic achievement, 108–9
Peterson, Candida, 81
Pettigrew, Thomas, 59
Pfeiffer, Steven, 102
phase shifts, 36
physical aggression, 179–81
physical punishment, and aggressive behavior, 185–87, 261n
play plans, in Tools of the Mind, 161–62, 165–68
popie-jopie, 190
popularity (popular kids) and aggressive behavior, 189–93
praise (praising), 12–26
  brain anatomy and, 24, 247n
  "early and often," 12–13
  effects of, 14–17
  effort vs., 15, 17–18, 22–24
  excessive, 20–22, 24
  Fallacy of Similar Effect, 237–38
  self-esteem and, 18–19
  specificity of, 19–20, 24–25
praise junkies, 24, 25
prefrontal cortex
  persistence and, 24, 247n
  self-control and, 169–70
  sleep deprivation and, 34
  teen rebellion and, 144–45
private speech, 167, 172–73, 175, 260n
Progressive Dads, 195–96
prosocial behavior, 192–93, 263n
psychodynamic paradigm, 127–28
Psychology of Self-Esteem (Branden), 18
Punch, Samantha, 121, 130
punishment
  aggressive behavior and, 183–87, 261n
  as primary catalyst for lying, 82, 84–85, 252–53n

Racial Attitude Measure, 47–48
racial attitudes, 47–69
  about use of corporal punishment, 185–87, 261n
  conversations about race, 62–69
  Diverse Environment Theory, 55–62
  in-group preferences, 52–55
rebellion. *See* teen rebellion

Index

relational aggression, 179–81, 191
religion, and brain anatomy, 112, 256–57n
remedial programs, 153, 259n
REM sleep, 34
Renaud, Sarah-Jane, 73–76
Reynolds, Cecil, 102, 254n
RIAS (Reynolds Intellectual Assessment Scales), 102
risk-taking, 145–47
Risley, Todd, 205–6, 209–10, 224
Robinson, Jackie, 63
Rock, Donald, 101
Rosales, Melodye, 66–69
Ross, Hildy, 120
rostral lateral prefrontal cortex (RLPFC), 171
Rutter, Michael, 151

Sadeh, Avi, 31–32
Salovey, Peter, 107, 254–55n
Samuelson, Larissa, 219–20
SAT (Scholastic Assessment Test), 36, 249n, 254n
Scheibe, Cynthia, 181–82
Schlaggar, Bradley, 112
schools
   aggressive behavior and, 187–93
   desegregation and Diverse Environment Theory, 57–62
   driving classes, 157–58, 173
   IQ tests. *See* intelligence tests
   racial attitudes. *See* racial attitudes
   start times and sleep deprivation, 36–38, 249n
   Tools of the Mind, 160–70, 172–76
Schoppe-Sullivan, Sarah, 194–96
Schwade, Jennifer, 215–16, 219, 220, 221
segregation, 52–55, 57–62
self-confidence, 5, 11–26, 64–65
self-control, 157–76
   brain anatomy and, 169–73
   interventions and effect sizes, 160, 260n
   Tools of the Mind, 160–70, 172–73, 174–76
self-discipline. *See* self-control
self-esteem, 18–19, 21, 246–47n
Shakespeare, William, 127, 228
shame, and lying, 251n
shape bias, 219–20, 262n
shared fantasy play, 129–30
Shaw, Philip, 110

short-form CDI, 261–62n
sibling effect, 117–30
   best predictors of relationship, 127–30
   conflict prevention and, 119–20, 122–27, 257n
   one-child families (onlies), 117–19, 257n
   parental role, 127–30, 257n
Simon Says (game), 162, 168
Skinner, B. F., 214
sleep (sleep deprivation), 29–44
   brain anatomy and, 33–35
   causes of lost hour, 31, 247–48n
   high school start times and, 36–38, 249n
   obesity and, 31, 39–42, 249n, 250n
   for teenagers, 31, 33, 35–38
sleep shifting, 33
slow-wave sleep, 34, 35, 41
slush hour, 43
Smetana, Judith, 149, 258n
Smith, Linda, 219–20
Snedeker, Jesse, 224
Social Praisers, 24
social skills, and academic achievement, 108–9
Sontag, L. W., 256n
spanking, and aggressive behavior, 185–87, 261n
Sparrow, Sara, 256n
Steinberg, Laurence, 151–52
Stephan, Walter, 59–60
Strand, Steven, 101–2
subgroupism, 65, 251n
Suen, Hoi, 99–100, 108
Sullivan, Kevin, 38
supertraits, 227–39
Suratt, Paul, 33
symbolic thought, 166–67, 237

Talwar, Victoria, 73–80, 82–87, 91–92, 238, 252n
Tamis-LeMonda, Catherine, 207–10, 215, 223–24
tattling, 88–89, 253n
teen rebellion, 133–54
   arguing vs. lying to parents, 147–52, 259n
   boredom and, 136, 141–47, 258n
   brain anatomy and, 143–47, 258–59n
   Mod Squad study, 136–41
   myth of, 151–52, 259n

teen rebellion (*cont.*)
    need for autonomy, 140–41, 258*n*
    permissive parents and, 139–40, 150–51
    popular media and dual narratives of, 152–54
television
    aggressive behavior and, 179–82
    obesity and, 39–40, 250*n*
temptation paradigm, 77–80
tests. *See* intelligence tests
Teti, Douglas, 32
thank-you letters, 234–35
TimeWise, 141–46
Tomblin, Bruce, 223
Tools of the Mind, 160–70, 172–76, 237
Traditional Dads, 195–96
truth bias, 73–76. *See also* lying
Tsushima, William, 100
Turek, Frederick, 42
TV. *See* television
Twas the Night B'fore Christmas (Rosales), 66–69
Tynes, Brendesha, 61

Universal Grammar, 222–23

Van Cauter, Eve, 40–41
Vandewater, Elizabeth, 39–40
variation sets, 218–19, 262*n*

ventral striatum, and persistence, 24
verbal aggression, 179–81
verbal leakage, 79, 82, 85
verbal pedometers, 205–6
violent television, and aggressive behavior, 179–82
Vittrup, Birgitte, 47–51
Vrij, Aldert, 251*n*

Wahlstrom, Kyla, 33, 249*n*
Walker, Dale, 224
Walker, Matthew, 34, 35
Waterfall, Heidi, 219
Wechsler Preschool and Primary Scale of Intelligence (WPPSI), 97, 98–99, 100
Weiss, Lawrence, 98–99
white lies, 86–89
Willingham, Daniel T., 20
word count, and language acquisition, 204–7
word frames, 217–18
WPPSI (Wechsler Preschool and Primary Scale of Intelligence), 97, 98–99, 100

Young-Kleinfeld, Carole, 38

zero tolerance policies in schools, 188–89, 261*n*

ABOUT TWELVE

TWELVE was established in August 2005 with the objective of publishing no more than one book per month. We strive to publish the singular book, by authors who have a unique perspective and compelling authority. Works that explain our culture; that illuminate, inspire, provoke, and entertain. We seek to establish communities of conversation surrounding our books. Talented authors deserve attention not only from publishers, but from readers as well. To sell the book is only the beginning of our mission. To build avid audiences of readers who are enriched by these works—that is our ultimate purpose.

For more information about forthcoming TWELVE books, please go to www.twelvebooks.com.